The White Book

The Beatles, the Bands, the Biz: An Insider's Look at an Era

Ken Mansfield

With
Contributing Editor
Brent Stoker

THOMAS NELSON
Since 1798

NASHVILLE   DALLAS   MEXICO CITY   RIO DE JANEIRO   BEIJING

Playlist

Fourwords
and More

Word One

I first met Ken Mansfield when Apple Records was originally being formed and contracts were being signed for Capitol Records to represent Apple in the USA. Ken was to be "our man" in LA, the U.S. manager of Apple Records.

Ken was different, from another culture, Californian, bronzed, handsome, laid-back, and very cool. We were crazed, English, rock 'n' roll people. I visited LA many times, and, of course, he had the house in the Hollywood Hills, a sparkling pool, and a gigantic convertible Cadillac with a *stereo* radio, unheard of in England in those days; we were very impressed. A real California guy—he worked in our offices in London, and we crashed at his pad in Hollywood.

We all hit it off immediately, and he became an instant member of the team. Even the Beatles took to him straight away, as he was a no-nonsense person and very easy to be around. He did a magnificent job of handling the record label in the good old USA, not an easy task in those days, as the Fab Four were very demanding. Seemingly impossible tasks were always met with a laid-back "No problem."

Many books have been written about those heady days of Apple in the swinging '60s, and Ken's point of view is more astute and accurate than most. His writing reflects his laid-back vision of life back then, and his stories are not only uniquely interesting but also very factual.

Ken has remained a very good friend over the years, and we reminisce often. He is one of the few insiders left that bore witness to the highs and lows of those insane days when we ruled the world.

—**Jack Oliver**
Former General Manager of Apple Records

Word Two

Ken Mansfield brings us a new and closely personal perspective not only on the Beatles but on a whole cast of musical characters from Brian Wilson to Don Ho. He is an observant and perceptive man in the center of the storm; a contradictory man, both ambitious and spiritual, but was at the heart of the record industry during its most exciting years and enjoying every minute of it. I lived through those years with Ken, and we became friends. It is a pleasure to experience so much of it all again through the accuracy of his storytelling and the clarity of his memory.

—Peter Asher
Peter and Gordon, A&R Chief Apple Records, Producer/Manager James Taylor, Linda Ronstadt

Word Three

Ken has a unique gift. He can take you in the room and have you sit with the folks he knows and make you one of the gang, part of the plan. And considering these folks include the Beatles, Dolly Parton, Waylon Jennings, the Beach Boys, Roy Orbison, David Cassidy, and a whole host more, that is some doing. I really enjoyed sitting in on his world, and I respect the affection he has for our game, and what he brought to it will get you.

—Andrew Loog Oldham
Former Rolling Stones Manager and Producer

Word Four

Journalism is normally a very inexact science. Many of the countless books about the Beatles have been written by researchers—not by people who were actually there. Everyone has experienced reading a book or article where one's own inside knowledge about a particular person or event shows up inaccuracies on the part of the writer that totally distort the truth. This book is an exception. I know because I was there for some of it myself. Ken Mansfield and I unknowingly shared the experience of the famous Apple rooftop session where I was nervously adjusting mikes and cables for the sound recording of that unforgettable day. Ken was not only working for the Beatles through their heyday; he was also their trusted friend. There is no one better equipped to tell the Beatles' story truthfully—and more importantly—factually, from the inside.

—Alan Parsons
Engineer to the Beatles and Pink Floyd, Multi-Platinum Producer, Alan Parsons Project

. . . and More

Ken Mansfield was the genius Hollywood recording executive who worked with dozens of musical stars for more than thirty years, helping take them to the very top and then keeping them there. He knows all the secrets, the good and the bad, the happiness and the heartbreaks. He did indeed hold the key to the lifestyles of many of the rich and famous pop superstars.

In his *White Book,* he salutes the Beatles as only a true insider can. He reflects on a period of pop culture and music that set today's stage of the phenomenal megastar side of showbiz. Be you a fan of the "oldies" or a rocker shouting for today's hits, this piece of modern history is a must for anybody who appreciates music. Informative, fun, and warm, it will make you want to have been in the "heat and heart" of it all back then. Ken's book is the time machine that can travel back to that age of innocence that truly changed the world.

In the *White Book*, Ken proves the perfect memory of a charismatic time and place that will never be repeated.

—**Robin Leach**
Producer/Host, Lifestyles of the Rich & Famous
Founder, Editor, and Publisher, Go *magazine*

To Ken, something groovey love from
George Harrison.

The BEATLES

31st July 1969.

Ken Mansfield Esq.,
Capitol Records Inc.,
1750 North Vine,
Hollywood and Vine,
Hollywood,
California 90028.
U.S.A.

Dear Ken,

Just a little note to congratulate you on your well
deserved promotion, which could not have gone to a
better man ... or a shorter one.

Thank you for looking after Apple Records.   Hope to
see you when you're here or I'm there.   Love to
Stan (Gortikov).

Yours, eventually,

FAMOUS
A Show-Bizz Personality
(Tricks on the High Wire a Speciality).

Welcome to the world of Trans World Airlines*

To Kenneth

Dear Kenneth,

Thanks Ken, you're a pal, Kenny, love from Paul, Ron, Ive and Tony

'NO COMMENT' — GEORGE MARTIN
UNFINISHED MUSIC NO. 2: LIFE WITH THE LIONS
JOHN LENNON/YOKO ONO   APPLE RECORDS
MADE IN MERRIE ENGLAND. NOV. '68

Dear Ken   re. Life with the Lions

     We'd like the Zapple. label
to be SILVER not white — it's
more subtle! o.k?

     also it <u>must be out</u> sooner
than June 2nd. Yoko and I
hope to be there (N.Y.) MAY 20th.
— don't spread it round (too much)
until you hear from Derek Taylor.

ζ. MAY 15.th — U. CAN DO iT!

     love

       John + Yoko xx.

Apple Corps Ltd., 3 Savile Row, London, W.1. 01-734 8232. Cables Apcore London, W.1.   Director, N. S. Aspinall.

Introduction

Fading in to White

Without intention I became one of a handful of people who landed in the midst of a mind-boggling occurrence, a fantastic place of rarified air. For the most part, my cohorts were a pretty scruffy crew, a select gaggle of extraordinary participants who had the guts and the gifts to give it a go and make it to the molten center of the rock-and-roll universe. Sadly, almost half of these incredible souls are gone at this point of harmonic history, and they are dearly missed. When it comes to Apple Records and the Beatles, I may have been the one to come the longest distance to join in the fray. To get there I had to hard scramble out of the farthest and deepest realms of our incredibly beautiful northwestern backwoods and swim upstream into a glorious and glamorous society. In recounting these magical times, I want to make it clear that I claim no authority on the phenomenon—only a sense of wonder every time I start remembering things. What amazes me the most is that I was even there.

Most of us who worked our way into the hot heart of the music scene write about our experiences either out of pain or exultation, many times hardly being able to tell the difference between the two. I know for sure that the mad hatters of the music industry, the greatest of the great, would have never been able to be that creative if everything was normal inside.

I see these famous people a little differently than most. I grew up with a cowboy mentality and was taught that when I came across an incorrigible, wild, and cantankerous horse, down inside that brazen exterior was an incredible beast of beauty.

The entertainment industry is likewise loaded with derelict demons, but underneath it all are these incredibly inspired saints of melody and presentation who take us all on a raucous ride to new levels of vision and enjoyment. God love us all—we are a different sort. We know that deep down we are a mess—the famous and the fumbling alike living side by side with the haunting reality that we were never really sure of ourselves. We did know that the only thing we could be sure of was that nothing is ever for sure in the entertainment business. As crazy as that all seems, I have a feeling that certain thrill of uncertainty was probably a great part of what the attraction was all about in the first place.

The White Book is a simple look at a complex happening. To me, when the Beatles took on the *White Album* project, it became more than a record. It became something all-encompassing. It was a bit of everything. Parts of it were about things we will never understand, and there were even bits about things in their lives purposely left to be deciphered, including the sweet, mysterious mixture that comprised their uniqueness and togetherness. I was there during the course of this magic time, and I got the feeling that the *White Album* project had a lot to do with the things that were shaking the complicated world they were living in. I think if you look at the project closely, you will find out that it conceptually had a lot to do with nothing in particular and a whole lot to do with just about everything in their lives at that time. It was a bunch of pieces looking for a whole, while the whole was falling to pieces.

By the time John, Paul, George, and Ringo had reached this point in the life of their band, they were starting to sum total their geniuses, and their personal histories were squirming to individually extricate and explode out of what had gone before into what was left to become. They were four young, principled men who had started their run to the finish line by crossing the sonic stripe that marked the midpoint of the century—the end of the '50s and the beginning of the '60s. The '70s lay ahead, and as that decade beckoned, they were ready to leave "home" one more time—alone.

It would be disingenuous of me to look back and call those times and events the "good old days"—it would be an unfair comparison to the entertainment business as it was known then. I'll just say that those were the "great old days." Those of us who are still alive are still friends and remember the good things about one another because we cared and took care of each other. We came off the streets, down from the hills, out of the woods, and from behind the bushes, with big dreams and even greater expectations. It was simple, it was fun, and it was what we did. Instead of a high-powered and heavily financed consortium putting a bunch of strangers

The mad hatters of the music industry, never been able to be that creative if

together and then creating a professional persona "by the books," we invested in ourselves through years of hard work. We wrote our own story, paid our own way, and picked our own bandmates and associates.

In my case, now that it is all over, I find I need to talk about it and get it off my chest—because that's where my heart is. This is my *White Book*; simple stuff about my life with the Beatles and a few others a bit like them. Although my remembrances herein are primarily about the Fabs, there was a broader tapestry that we were all a part of, and so like their *White Album*, I find I have composed a larger score than what I set out to do. These are personal stories about the real people who occupied this world of faded fantasies and rugged realities. This is not a history book, though the facts are straight. My *White Book* is also a bit like the *White Album* in another way in that it evolved into a project I may have never started if I had known how hard it was going to be getting to the final mix. Let's just call it the "Seinfeld" book about the Beatles. I was told that

the greatest of the great, would have everything was normal inside.

when asked why his TV show was so successful, Jerry Seinfeld would reply that it was because it was the show about nothing. So if you look at this as the Beatles book about nothing, it will take a little pressure off of us all, and you may actually find it all rather interesting, something to enjoy because of its simplicity.

For whatever reason, I have waited a long time.

—Ken Mansfield
Author
Hopeless Romantic
Three Chords and an Attitude
Former U.S. Manager, Apple Records

The Beatles' *Help!* press conference
Hollywood, California, 1965

"Standing there with them that day—I didn't have a clue."

—Ken Mansfield, 2007

Track 1

Eight Arms to Hold You

» *Hollywood, California, August 1965*

Here is how it all began with me and the "lads."

As recently appointed West Coast district promotion manager for Capitol Records, part of my job description included handling all artist relations, activities, concerts, and record promotional matters in the Los Angeles area. The Beatles press conference functionally and geographically clearly fell into that category. Instead of doing computerized cost, budget, and program analysis for the Saturn and Surveyor space programs (my job a few months earlier in San Diego), I was now playing host to the four most famous entertainers in the world. Although the transition was sudden, my own youthful sense of self-importance was so developed that I felt very at ease with the whole assignment. I think if I had any concept of how historical this all was, and how incredibly talented and innovative these guys truly were, I would have probably freaked out!

As it turned out, I was one of the first young American executives the Beatles had worked with since their ascension to stratospheric stardom. Up until then, everyone they met in the executive world outside their isolated and insulated realm was a Lord of E.M.I. (the parent company that owned Capitol Records), a corporate chairman, or something equally as thick and elderly. I was a relatively youthful twenty-seven years old, three years younger than the Beatles' manager, Brian Epstein. Talk about being in the right place at the right time. I think that fact, combined with my unique "head in the sand" approach to awareness, kept me from being numbed by fanhood. This must have made me appear more accessible to them.

The Beatles had come to LA for two consecutive nights' concerts at the Hollywood Bowl as part of their 1965 record-breaking tour. The press conference was purposed to promote this fact, to further our (Capitol's) relationship with the media, and to present the band with their gold records for the *Help!* album. You can only imagine the security measures that had to be taken. We held the press conference on our ground floor and in our biggest recording studio—Studio A. This afforded us one incredible advantage—there was a "load in" door that opened into the back of the main room that was used for carting in instruments and equipment for the recording sessions.

By bringing the Beatles to the press conference in an armored car, we were able to back the rig flush to the back of the building and let the lads disembark directly into the closed studio. We had set a small riser with a long table and four chairs a few feet from the load in door. Brian Epstein was stationed to their left down off the riser (facing the audience), and I

George exuded such a casual, boyish, and natural charm that it virtually shined out loud through the din of the star-worship madness that filled the room of "insiders."

was in the same position on the right. We were then flanked by security police. "Roving security" was handled, of course, by Beatles roadie Mal Evans, who was everywhere at the same time. He had the incredible ability to completely take care of the business of watching out for the lads and to quietly gather a rather respectable social life for himself while he was at it. Once they were in place on the podium, the select and elite of the radio/television/print media, along with those with industry clout, were allowed into the room. They were carefully controlled and guided in a disguised order of importance to specific seating locations in the rows of chairs that had been set up for the occasion.

George Harrison was positioned at my end of the podium and soon began losing interest in the same old questions from the attendees. Because I was stationed next to the makeshift platform, he turned away from the proceedings and began asking me about California in general and Hollywood in specific. He exuded such a casual, boyish, and natural charm that it virtually shined out loud through the din of the star-worship madness that filled the room of "insiders." Eventually, one by one, the other three entered into the conversation when one of the other Beatles was fielding a question. The unabashed innocence in their manner of questioning me about LA further confirmed the existence of this delightful childlike aspect of their basic nature: "Have you ever been to Grauman's Chinese Theater?" "Are James Dean's prints there?" (John) "How far is Mullholland Drive from here?" (George) "Do you know Buck Owens, because I would like to meet him while we are here?" (Ringo) "Gene Vincent was on Capitol—can you get me some of his old records?" (Paul).

Finally they were asked to return their attention to the matter at hand. Paul discreetly called Mal over and told him to get my name so that I could come up to the house the next day and continue the conversation. They had a much-deserved week off from the tour and were spending it secluded in a Beverly Hills gated hillside semi-mansion. They needed a "local," and because I was an associate of sorts, it all fit for me to spend the day with them.

Little did I know at that time that this invitation would be the first of two. This one brought me to 2850 Benedict Canyon Road, their rented house in LA, and I had to change my plans in order to go for the day. The next one, a few short years later, would bring me to 3 Savile Row, their office building in London, and would change my life—forever.

Track 2

The Fool
on the Hill

>> *Benedict Canyon, California, August 1965*

Monday, August 30, 1965, the day after the Beatles' Hollywood press
conference and the first of their two consecutive nights at the Hollywood
Bowl, was absolute madness. Happily following up on Paul's invitation and
then receiving permission from road manager and general assistant, Mal
Evans, to bring a guest, I invited someone I shall call "Bruce" to
accompany me to an afternoon at the house in Benedict Canyon, which
had served as a refuge for the group since the previous Monday.

Bruce was the young music director at KBLA, the fourth rated rock-
and-roll station in LA. I figured if I took him along with me that Capitol
would virtually own airplay at that station, and I did have the recording
careers of other label artists besides the Beatles to consider. The fact
that KBLA was new and on the bottom of the rock-ratings war in LA
would probably endear me to Bruce forever because only one guest could
accompany me to the absolute center of the rock-and-roll universe that
day. Bruce was well aware that I had chosen him over the heavy hitters at
the powerhouse stations, KHJ, KRLA, and KFWB. The politics of the
situation was even more intense, as Bruce's rival, KRLA, was the official
host radio station for the Beatles' shows at the Hollywood Bowl.

Actually I was taking a giant risk by inviting Bruce, because if Dick Moreland, my friend and music director at KRLA, the sponsoring station, found out I had asked Bruce instead of him, I could be losing a lot in order to gain a little. (In all honesty I felt that KBLA was going to move ahead of the other stations in fast order, and so my decision wasn't totally based on Bruce's personality or pure ethics.)

I was no fool, so I didn't come home empty-handed from the day "on the hill." This is the first personalized item I received from the Beatles. Possession, like so many things, is transient, and this album now occupies a treasured spot in someone else's collection!

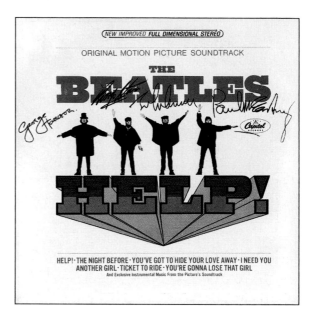

The house on the hill was a point of semi-calm engulfed in a residential traffic jam that was surrounded by a frenzied throng. Getting to the gate was an event in itself. By the time we were within twenty-five yards of the entrance and being ushered on ahead, it became clear to the fans that we were *going in*! That fact alone attracted a misspent form of adoration that led to us giving numerous autographs and receiving many "just let me

Because they seemed unaffected sight of what the attraction was or years, working for them and being

touch someone who is going to touch a Beatle" prods. (You can imagine what it was like when we left with perceived Beatle touches all over us.)

Once inside, it was like being in the eye of a storm. There were quite a few people there: a bongo player was either jamming with or giving Ringo lessons in a pool-side bedroom; some fellow was demonstrating a "Fender Bender" guitar strap to George; John was on the edge of the pool, head down, intently listening to someone who was obviously pouring forth earth-shaking philosophical truisms; Paul was energized and entertaining a small group of industry insiders. A quiet, slender, tanned girl was swimming most of the time without really talking much to anyone. Later on I was introduced to her—Joan Baez.

Most of my attention was drawn to Mal Evans, who was dealing with the onslaught around the edges. Mal and head road manager, Neil Aspinall, both were amazingly adept at organizing and protecting the four lads. They were both confidants and privy to just about everything that went down, somewhat even more so than manager Brian Epstein in the day-to-day Beatle activities. Years later, after Brian died and Apple Records came to fruition, they, along with the label's General Manager, Jack Oliver, were virtually the ones who opened the "apple stand" in the morning and shut out the lights at night, long after everyone else had gone home. That day was the beginning of an incredible friendship between Mal and me that took us right up to the night of his death a little over ten years later.

As the pool was on the hillside of the estate, it was perched on the edge of a forty-foot-high, slightly slanted stone wall that ran up from the canyon below. Mal was running around the edge of the wall, garden-hosing back young people who were trying to scale the abutment. Security guards lined the other ten-foot-high fences that surrounded the property where there was a small but steady stream of crashers being picked up from the ground the minute they made it over. Each one was sternly but

by their fame, I sometimes lost
what it was all about, and in later
with them seemed pretty normal.

courteously escorted back outside. Some individual fans had the pleasure of being escorted several times that day. Every now and then, Paul would look over at one of them and smile and wave like they were old friends. This had an effect comparable to shooting them with a tranquilizer gun. They would bliss out with the recognition and become limp and quiet as they were dragged away and banished to the other side of the fence.

By this time in their careers, the Beatles seemed to have developed an unawareness of anything going on around them except that which was immediately before them. In all honesty, I still didn't get it. They were such nice guys and so courteous during it all—so normal. Because they seemed unaffected by their fame, I sometimes lost sight of what the attraction was or what it was all about, and in later years, working for them and being with them seemed pretty normal.

Back to KBLA and Bruce—I was wrong about my imminently powerful guest. First, KBLA became an even more distant fourth as time rolled on. Second, Bruce wouldn't give me the time of day, let alone airplay, after he got to meet the Beatles. Third, he became a star-glazed fan, hovering and drooling over each Beatle in repeated succession. He then capped the whole thing off by hauling out a pile of KBLA t-shirts for them to autograph!

I drove my guest, who had made a fool of himself on the hill, home. At that time, you could have fooled me as to the effect the band we had just left behind was going to have on my life.

Track 3

Like Peggy Lee Said, "Is That All There Is?"

» *San Diego—Los Angeles, California, 1964–1968*

I will never forget the first time I heard a Beatles record. I was driving down Mission Boulevard in San Diego, California, listening to a local Top 40 station on my way to my consulting job with a firm that specialized in computerized program evaluation and research technique planning for the space industry. It was Winter 1964, and I had heard so much about this new group that I was anxious to hear them. Then the disc jockey front-announced the next record. It was "I Want to Hold Your Hand." When the record ended, I remember being singularly nonplussed to say the least. I couldn't figure what the big deal was all about. I remember thinking after I heard the record—*Is that it? Is that all there is?*

I think later on, when ironically I ended up working with and for the Beatles, that this initial blasé reaction to it all was still my basic operative impression, and that is why it was always so relaxed and natural for me to be involved with them.

I will admit, though, that I have not always been able to maintain such a cool, casual demeanor when working with superstars. Right around the same time that my involvement with the Beatles began, I was called upstairs to the E floor by Capitol Industries president Stanley Gortikov. ("E" stood for executive, and that floor was the ivory portion of the Capitol Tower. It was also the thirteenth floor, but no one called it that!) I was given the assignment to spend the day with Judy Garland in her San Francisco penthouse suite in order to coordinate promotional matters surrounding the launch of the famous "live" duet album (*Judy Garland: Live at the London Palladium*) that was recorded at the London Palladium with her daughter, Liza Minnelli. I could not believe I was going to spend the day with Judy Garland. I have zero memory of leaving Stanley Gortikov's office, finishing my work day, going home for the night, packing, driving to LAX, flying to San Francisco, catching a cab, or anything else until I was let into her penthouse digs at the Fairmount Hotel by some stuffy butler/protector type. I was with Judy Garland, and boy did she treat me like used dirt. She ordered me around, ignored me, yelled at me, didn't acknowledge my presence, acted like she could not stand me, and yet all I cared about was that I was with Judy Garland—no, I was with Dorothy from Oz (or was that from Kansas?). That was, up to that point, one of my most exciting days in the music business. I had spent the day with Judy Garland. Afterward, back in LA, people would ask me how it was working with Judy Garland. I would smile importantly and answer, "Great!"

It does seem funny to me now, as I look back, but I was not really excited when I got to work with the Beatles. I was already working with famous acts every day—many of whom I was a big fan when I was growing up: Stan Kenton, Peggy Lee, George Shearing, Frankie Laine and the Four Freshmen, plus contemporary acts like the Beach Boys, Lou Rawls, Nancy Wilson, Bobby Darin, Bobby Rydell, and Al Martino, who were all big stars in those days. Also the English onslaught had begun at Capitol— the Seekers (actually Australian), Peter and Gordon, Cilla Black, and others. Working with famous acts was just added responsibility and part of the job. As the years passed, I would also be working simultaneously with other Capitol acts like The Band, Quicksilver Messenger Service, Bob Seger, Bobbie Gentry, the Steve Miller Band, and Glen Campbell, to name a few. I grew into my awareness of the Beatles' genius over a period of time, and because of this, I ended up with possibly a deeper reverence than most. (I was never infatuated with them—I slowly fell in love with them and their artistry over the years.)

Part of this unawareness may have developed out of my promotion man mentality at the time. You didn't promote a Beatles record—you just hung on when one came out. While I was busy living in the trenches with my other

It seemed that when a Beatles record was released, all other artists' records and airplay "revolved" around what little time was left aside from the Beatles' airplay. *REVOLVER* was especially well received by the radio stations, and I felt like I had a gun to my head by suffering stations when unauthorized "exclusive" advance airplay started on this classic work. I would then walk out of the offended station, after trying to make amends, and into the waiting arms of the screaming managers and agents of my other unfortunate, unplayed artists that were also on Capitol. I received this autographed copy unsolicited from Apple.

artists, trying to get their records played, I was also spending half my time trying to keep stations from playing advanced copies of new Beatles releases until all the stations could get their own copy. I remember the August 1966 release of the *Revolver* album, in particular, as being one of my roughest releases. I would spend weeks trying to get a new Glen Campbell record on a major station only to have it taken off the air and thrown out the door at me just because the "other" station across town got the Beatles first.

I doubt that anyone outside the very heart of the record business could even imagine what it was like at that time for promotion men at all labels when a new Beatles record was released. First, it immediately knocked competing records out of the coveted No. 1 spot. Every artist, producer, songwriter, and manager, lives to get a No. 1 record. Climbing all the way into the top five or even the No. 2 slot on the national Billboard chart is an incredible feat. But it is like an Olympic medal: only the gold medal really counts in the long run. Having a No. 1 record is the whole deal!

Second, and most important, once a new Beatles record was released and took over the No. 1 slot, no other record could get into the spot. The sad part of this scenario is that a lot of artists during those years had legitimate No. 1 records but had to settle for the No. 2 or lower position because of the Beatles' domination of the top chart positions. This not only affected our competition, but our own (Capitol) artists suffered the same fate. You can imagine the artist relations problems I had at Capitol with some pretty important stars who were on our roster.

Third, the problem for our other artists went even deeper than that because, as in the unisolated case of Glen Campbell mentioned above, Capitol artists were constantly being punished for sins they didn't commit. Listener ratings are everything to the financial health of a radio station, and when one station would get an advance copy of a Beatles record in those days, they immediately garnered approximately 99.99999 percent of the listening audience until their competitors could get their own copy.

Some of you may remember that when a station got an exclusive on a Beatles record they would keep announcing their call letters over the song while they were playing it so that the other stations couldn't copy it off the air and then turn around and play it on their stations. Sometimes this gap between stations having or not having a new Beatles release could be a couple of hours or just a few minutes. That was not the point—even if a station got the record only thirty seconds before its rival, they would scream their exclusive success, proclaim their dominance over their competitors, and announce themselves as "the station where you hear the Beatles first." This would assure them listener loyalty and high ratings for quite some time. The losing stations in these battles would always, of course, have these very calm, intellectual staff meetings to decide what to do when they were beaten by their competitors. Oddly enough, every station nationwide

You didn't promote a **Beatles** record—you just hung on when one came out.

always came up with one of two sophisticated solutions: (a) take all other Capitol artists' records off the play list and throw them out of the window into the street or (b) call the local promotion man over to the station and have him stand in the music director's office and watch his artists' records being thrown out the window into the street.

This was when my job as both national promotion manager and head of the Artist Relations Department would take an abrupt turn into a living nightmare. The artists, publicists, managers, agents, publishers, and even family members would all descend upon me (or my helpless secretary) demanding an explanation. *Of course* I didn't have time to respond because upper management needed to see me so I could explain how this could keep happening. *Of course* I didn't have time to make these explanations because, in addition to losing across-the-board airplay on all my artists, I had to deal with irate music directors and station managers. In the midst of this, I was trying to get my helpless local promotion man a copy of the pirated Beatles record so he could salvage a little of the years of credibility and relationship building that was his lifeblood.

It was almost impossible to maintain complete security over the release of a Beatles record. There are just too many links in the chain of events that any record goes through before it is released. It took only one minimum-wage worker at one of the mechanical levels of production, reproduction, manufacturing, storage, packaging, shipping, or any other phase to accept a bribe equal to a few months' wages, and the whole nightmare was off and running. I couldn't coordinate simultaneous delivery times to the stations because copies of the records would always leak out, and a station would get it before I could get it to everyone at the same time. We tried everything, but nothing worked until I came up with something that was logical and amazingly simple. Best of all, this plan provided me with a great long-term plan for all Beatles releases.

Here is how it worked—the idea was to eliminate the one crucial element in this whole dilemma, and that was the importance of getting the record first. I informed the stations that in the future we would set a specific time and date for airplay on all new Beatles releases so that every radio station in the nation would start on the record at exactly the same second regardless of the size of the station, the market it was in, or the time zone. We would supply the record to all stations simultaneously, well in advance of this target time. Therefore stations wouldn't have to worry about their competitor playing it first. If the "other" station did jump the gun, then the cooperating station would be able to recover immediately, because Capitol (now the good guy) had supplied them with a copy for their protection. If this sounds too simplistic and idealistic, let me explain why this plan did have teeth and did indeed work. If a station did choose to ignore our designated air time and decided to play the copy of the record that we supplied to them ahead of time, or if they had managed to get a pirated copy, then not only would their advantage be lost by the other stations having the copy for immediate response, but in the future the non-complying station would not receive the advance copy of the next new Beatles record. This meant that, in order for a radio station to be the first one to play a Beatles record just one time, they would have to risk the possibility of being the last radio station to get every record after that. That would be their eternal fate in a very competitive industry unless they could figure out a way to obtain and pay for a pirated copy on every succeeding release (which, by the way, happened to be illegal and actually opened them up to other problems).

It only took one minimum-wage worker at one of the mechanical levels of production, reproduction, manufacturing, storage, packaging, shipping, or any other phase to accept a bribe equal to a few months' wages, and the whole nightmare was off and running.

The playing field had definitely been leveled, and this procedure did work—I only wish I had thought of it a lot earlier.

The first day that we put the plan into effect, I found myself once again driving down the freeway, listening to a new Beatles record being played on the car radio. The rock-and-roll irony of this scenario is that this was

In order for a radio station to be the first one to play a Beatles record just one time, they would have to risk the possibility of being the last radio station to get every record after that. That would be their eternal fate in a very competitive industry.

where I first heard a Beatles record, and I was now the one deciding when a Beatles record would be played on the radio.

As I listened, I still wondered what it was all about. This time, however, there was a lot more to it on my mind than *Is that all there is?*

Barbara Ann and the Brian Ban

Los Angeles, California, November 1965

There is one thing that is a given in the record business, and that is you can never separate the artist from the artistry. Probably the single most sensitive issue that a record company executive must not only deal with but had better get a good feel for is understanding and relating to artists and never trying to separate them from their creations once their "masterpiece" is put into the sales, promotion, and merchandising mill.

Let's take a look at the following as an example of how the artist relations aspect of my job played out in everyday life ("everyday life" is a contradiction in terms in the music business). One day Brian Wilson walked into my office to play for me the acetate of his latest offering for a new Beach Boys single. At the time of Brian's visit, I was in charge of single records releases for Capitol, and he wanted to give me an advance private preview.

A little background might be appropriate here. Once a week at Capitol Records' main office in Hollywood, about five of us would meet in the twelfth-floor conference room to review the upcoming four or five single records that were due for release in the next several weeks. Typically this group consisted of someone from A&R (an acronym for artists and repertoire, the fancy words used to denote the music production team at a record label), promotion, merchandising, sales, and publicity. Although the meeting was informative to all, its purpose was not really for artistic input from the "suits" or for fostering inventive discussion concerning the proposed release's critical success; it had more to do with the creative aspects of the staff producers' recent efforts and their selection of material to be released. Therefore A&R pretty much dictated the actual titles for single releases. Occasionally there were times when promotion or sales would see positive airplay reaction coming from certain previously released album tracks, and this would be the basis for recommendation that those active airplay songs be considered for future release as a single.

These meetings were very interesting and had a really cool vibe. This was the very heart of Capitol Records, and the handful of executives in that room were really the guts and hopeful glory of the company. It all started and ended with this managerial group. Each one of us had achieved a certain degree of success in a very tough business by reaching these positions. It was hard to wallow in the glory of it all, though, because the responsibilities were big and the stakes were high. It wasn't like stocking shelves at Wal-Mart where, as long as you did what you were told, you knew your job was there tomorrow. Here you either delivered on your assigned tasks, or you were out. Our job descriptions were not written out in a numbered section of a corporate register—they were embedded in our beings as an integral part of our survival instincts. Everyone knew that there were always up-and-coming hot shots right outside the door, down the hall from our offices, or just outside on the street who were just waiting to push us out of the illusionary curved windows of the Capitol Tower.

Back to Brian Wilson. Because he produced his band, he was known as an independent producer as opposed to being a staff producer for Capitol Records. Because they were the Beach Boys, he pretty much decided what they released and when. The formal staff meeting had little meaning for the Beach Boys, and we basically bypassed it in their case. At Capitol Records, as in most business ventures, it is hard to argue with success. "Let It Be" hadn't been written yet, but that was pretty much the theme song that surrounded the label's approach to the Beach Boys' offerings.

In those days the executive offices at Capitol basically had only turntables for playback purposes. These clunky machines were almost akin to government issue and played speeds at either 45 or 33$\frac{1}{3}$ RPM (that's *revolutions per minute* for my younger readers). When we considered new recordings, we reviewed them from vinyl acetates that were hand-cut on huge disc-cutting lathes that were downstairs in rooms adjacent to the studios. Those were our demos in the mid-'60s. Most of the producers on staff, though, did have reel-to-reel tape decks in their offices so that they could make a "dupe" (tape copy) directly from the master tape in the studio when they finished a session and bring it up to their office on the twelfth floor for their personal review. Other than this, there was virtually zero portability, and you could only play your product in a room that had a tape deck. There was no little wire going from your shirt pocket to tiny earbuds so you could work and walk the dog at the

Here you either delivered on your assigned tasks, or you were out. Our job descriptions were not written out in a numbered section of a corporate register—they were embedded in our beings as an integral part of our survival instincts.

same time. Also, as a producer, it was hard to select certain songs or segments of songs when you were working on them because other than a built-in number counter that never really worked right, it was pretty much a fast-forward and fast-rewind procedure of seek-until-ye-shall-find the spot in the song you were looking for. In addition, the tapes were burdensome to carry around and susceptible to damage from heat and other outside conditions. I would love to go back in time with an iPod in my hand and walk into a '60s A&R meeting.

Back to Mr. Wilson again and his visit to my office. Brian handed me an acetate of "Barbara Ann" that had just been made downstairs by a Capitol staff engineer. I put it on my turntable with great anticipation. Was

I just about to hear another "Help Me Rhonda," "In My Room," or "Don't Worry Baby"? Much to my surprise, what came out of my hi-fi speakers was this ragged recording that sounded just like what it was—a party record that was recorded live in the simplest of terms when it came to recording technique. In my estimation, what I was hearing sounded like everyone was having a good time but obviously not too concerned about the artistry of it all. Beneath my trained and stoic exterior, my mind was screaming through its own shock and disbelief, *This is a Brian Wilson record, for crying out loud, and definitely not what I was expecting.*

The Beach Boys had already released two impressive albums, *The Beach Boys Today!* and *Summer Days (and Summer Nights!),* that year; both were filled with well-produced tracks like "California Girls," "Help Me Rhonda," and "Let Him Run Wild." With tracks like these, no one could deny Brian's increasingly sophisticated record production skills. To me it was clear: releasing a sloppy-sounding record like "Barbara Ann" was, for Brian, a major step backward.

As I listened to the playback, Brian was sitting in a chair in front of my desk while I had my back to him facing the speakers behind my desk. It ended as it began, much to my dismay. Gathering my best executive look, at my fine executive desk, with a learned executive manner with face set and practiced executive body language in position, I slowly spun around in my comfortable executive chair and took, I guess you could say, a counseling stance with Brian. As I look back now, I am sure Brian was expecting more of an applause and accolade response from the young hip guy at the label who always understood their music. "Brian," I said, "I feel this is a mistake and possibly your first stiff record [record industry terminology for an unsuccessful record] since you guys started having hits. I really don't think we should release this." I continued, "I know how you guys have had to fight to get Capitol's attention away from the Beatles, and I think this would be a setback in your friendly competition with them."

To me it was clear: releasing a "Barbara Ann" was, for Brian, a

Brian had been giving me this steady eye-to-eye unbroken stare the whole time I had been laying this out to him. During my learned discourse, he didn't move a muscle, almost like he was frozen in space. Then as my last words had the sense of reverberating like slap back in an old EMT echo chamber, and the syllables, paragraphs, and dangling participles laconically faded into the distance, he moved as if in slow motion to the turntable. With the utmost in unwasted motion and calm, he lifted the acetate from its place, carefully slid it into the dust cover he had taken it from a few minutes earlier, slowly turned, and walked to the door of my office in a manner worthy of any John Wayne exit into an eventual sunset. Placing his right hand on the doorjam and without hardly turning around, he looked back at me over his right shoulder, almost as if the earlier stare had never been unbroken, raised the vinyl outline of "Barbara Ann" high above his head with his left hand, and stated softly but clearly, "This is our next single." He then disappeared out the door and to the elevator that took him out of my life and away from the building.

I soon received a phone call from Nick Grillo of Julius Lefkowitz and Company. (Nick had come aboard the Beach Boys bandwagon in an accounting position, and we immediately became good friends through our day-to-day dealings concerning Beach Boys label matters. It wasn't long before he became the band's business manager.) Because of our personal relationship, Brian had asked him to relay to me that I would no longer be involved in the planning portion of future Beach Boys releases.

I can remember no meetings after this episode that did anything other than serve to fulfill Mr. Wilson's wishes. I can't imagine any of us going against him in matters such as these. My guess is that such a move on Capitol's part would have had Murray Wilson (Brian's father and the band's early manager) and/or Nick Grillo knock, knock, knockin' at our door. As hard and crusty as some of the record company executives were, after years of fighting their way up through the ranks, they all knew they

sloppy-sounding record like major step backward.

This picture was probably taken in Brian's kitchen shortly after he left our meeting. He ate the acetate but when "Barbara Ann" became a hit—I ate my words.

were the "suits," and it was very clear which side their bread was buttered upon. Ask anyone in the music business, and they will agree that once you dig down deep enough, it does all begin with the song and then the artist, and when the artist is a very successful artist, the tried and true way to keep your job is to just stay out of their way.

When you are a seasoned executive in the music industry, the business usually plays out to a positive conclusion (in our favor). We have the

Ask anyone in the music business, and they will agree that once you dig down deep enough, it does all begin with the song and then the artist, and when the artist is a very successful artist, the tried and true way to keep your job is to just stay out of their way.

Billboard Hot 100 record charts to prove us right when we (who, after all, are paid to make decisions like these) are challenged by the irresponsible, temperamental artists on the label. To wit: simple history works to our advantage because over 95 percent of records don't become hits, so one is almost always on the winning side of the odds by taking a negative stance. I was certain that once these percentages worked in my favor, Brian would see I was right and would return to me for guidance on future releases, so I wasn't that upset. In time this would all work out, and my position of knowledgeable authority with the great band would be reinstated.

As fate would have it, "Barbara Ann" was a worldwide smash. So much for me "delivering on my assigned task." Maybe if I ever speak to Brian again, I'll tell him it's clear my "reverse psychology" ploy worked. Or something like that.

As per the relayed request from Mr. Grillo, that November 1965 day at 1750 North Vine in sunny Hollywood, California, encompassed and included the last conversation I ever had with Mr. Wilson.

Hollywood
Paul 'e Would

» *Los Angeles, California, June 1968*

When the Apple Records label was conceived by the Beatles, everyone, including the other major labels, initially and incorrectly assumed that Capitol Records would distribute it. In actuality Capitol had no more rights to distribute the label than anyone else; we had to compete with the other majors for this prize. We did have one small advantage though: the Beatles were EMI/Capitol artists, and distributing Apple through Capitol Records was the only way the Beatles were ever going to be on their own label in America. This fact, coupled with rather substantial preestablished relationships and a common parent company (EMI), did give us a *slight* edge. By distributing Apple through Capitol, the Beatles were able to have 1968's "Hey Jude" as Apple's debut single release. Technically, the Beatles were not Apple artists. Although they released their records on the Apple label in the United States, the controlling documents, contracts, accounting, and record numbers were Capitol's.

We had a convenient coincidence working in our favor once the Beatles made the decision that Capitol would distribute Apple. We were getting ready to hold our annual convention in Los Angeles, scheduled for the third week of June 1968. Every salesman, field rep, district and divisional branch manager, as well as all promotion and field merchandising managers were going to be in one room at the same time. In addition, all the major executives and employees from the "Tower"* would be in attendance.

Wouldn't it be great if one of the Beatles were to come to the convention? After all, it was a fairly standard occurrence that when a major distribution deal is made with a new label, one of the owners would almost always appear to announce the new business relationship.

Which Beatle could we get?

Who would come to Hollywood?

Stanley Gortikov called and inquired—

Paul said 'e would!

'E would come!

Paul 'e would come to Hollywood!!!

We sneaked Paul into town without anyone knowing. No one except Gortikov, me, and the upper, upper echelon knew that we would be distributing Apple records. Gortikov had set the stage by announcing that we were going to have a special guest make a big announcement at the convention as a preliminary excitement teaser. I don't think anyone ever imagined that it was about Apple and would be made in person by a Beatle.

The convention was in progress, and the big day, Friday, June 21, arrived. Virtually every employee of any import was sitting in his or her seat waiting for the festivities to begin. It was totally dark in the auditorium— we secreted Paul from a holding suite at the Century Plaza Hotel to the convention room. We had arranged for a stagehand to bring the room lights slowly up as he started walking down the aisle from the back of the auditorium. A long gasp came out of the gathering as they began to realize that a real, live "in person" Beatle had walked into their midst. Paul, ever the diplomat, began waving, smiling, shaking hands, and giving

* Capitol Industries' main offices were located just off Hollywood Boulevard and Vine Street in Hollywood, California. Nicknamed the "Tower," this building housed the major executives and creative personnel that ran the company. Originally designed to look like a stack of records, the finished product was not that aesthetically pleasing, and window treatments and the "sundial" or "needle" on top were added later to give it dimension and alleviate the unplanned squatness of the building. Working in that building at first is a little unusual in that furniture never quite fits right on the slightly curved outside wall of your office, and there was something symmetrically and psychologically unsettling about having an office with no square corners.

'60s-style high-fives as he made his way to the stage. Simultaneously, as if by some cosmic cue, everyone started cheering, clapping, standing up, and shouting with joy. There was this incredible feeling of mutual affection between the men and women of Capitol Records and Paul McCartney. I stress mutual because it was a joy equally shared. The left and right brains of a phenomenon in the music business journey had come face-to-face. This was a case where them that makes the records got to meet them that breaks the records. Paul was a member of the group that had given these men and women great prestige, honor, and financial rewards in their professional and personal lives—and *they* were there before him: the men and women who had brought it all home for the Beatles in

A long gasp came out of the gathering as they began to realize that a real, live "in person" Beatle had walked into their midst.

America. It was so English *and* American—so much pride and hard work all mixed into an internationally cowritten song entitled "a job well done."

Capitol Records USA had done a great job for the Beatles. There was no debating that America was the most important market for them to break into. Looking back now, it would seem automatic; after all, they were the Beatles. But one must remember that acceptance in the United States was not a given in those days, and many famous European acts had gone before them to face dismal failure in the land of sweet American milk and honey. In fact, because Capitol Records was an EMI company, we had first right of refusal on all foreign EMI acts for the United States, *and* we had indeed passed on the Beatles more than once. Paul was aware of and thankful for the job that had ultimately been done here. As for the Capitol employees, because of a quota/commission system that was in place at that time, every one of these men and women became relatively wealthy in just one year. (The company was forced to revise the method it used to compute commissions in order to take into account the incredible Beatles sales volume.) The Beatles had essentially bought them new cars and paid off mortgages and were sending their kids to college.

Paul and me "in step" as we leave a Hollywood restaurant after a full-blown Polynesian food fest.

When the Capitol "gang" quieted down, Paul made the announcement about Apple. The place went absolutely berserk!

Later, Paul attended an outside cocktail party at the Century Plaza Hotel where he spent time with the field sales/promo/merchandising

As for the Capitol employees, because of a quota/commission system that was in place at that time, every one of these men and women became relatively wealthy in just one year. The Beatles had essentially bought them new cars and paid off mortgages and were sending their kids to college.

employees, taking pictures with each one, chatting with them, sharing his fame in an exquisitely common manner that endeared him and his bandmates to a group of hard-working people forever. They talk about that afternoon to this day. Paul rewarded their efforts with this encounter, and as a new record company co-co-co-president, he was accomplishing a powerful public relations push in a hands-on manner by enlisting and then fueling their enthusiasm for our new label—Apple Records. When they returned to their homes across the American landscape, you can imagine the effort they put forth to launch the new Apple venture.

A foreshadowing of the feelings and camaraderie that was to be experienced that day occurred when I was bringing Paul down the hallway from his suite to the convention hall. Just prior to the convention, I had returned from Atlanta after hiring a black man who sold class rings and Bibles to head up Capitol's R&B (Rhythm and Blues) promotion for the Southern states. His name was Sydney Miller, and he had one of those personalities that lit up a room when he walked in. Everyone immediately liked Sydney. He would give the biggest, and to this day I believe the most sincere, smile upon meeting you, and then Sydney would own you within minutes. He soon became one of my best men and a loyal friend. I had a sense about hiring new employees, and I knew from the beginning he would be a star on my staff horizon. (Good people working under you *always* make you look good to the people over you.) Sydney had an amazingly unique and powerful sense of self, and he offered that into his relationships. That was why he made everyone glad to be around him.

Anyway, he had gone to his room to get something during the break and was returning down the hall at the same time we came out of Paul's suite. They came face-to-face, and when Sydney saw Paul, his eyes got as big as saucers and he started grinning the happiest look I had ever seen. Paul had no idea who Sydney was or that he was a Capitol Records employee—all he knew was that he was standing face-to-face with this smiling, joyful black dude in the hallway of an LA hotel. Spontaneously, they embraced, neither saying a word. Sydney walked away in a daze, and Paul had this really serene look on his face before falling back in step and looking over his shoulder at Sydney dancing down the hall. This was simple respect and human nature at its finest. This was that golden thread that ran through the Beatles' nature and personal makeup—it is the thread that binds us all together when we get past all the stuff that conditioning imposes upon our natural goodness and love for one another.

The day ended with a round of meetings and dinner and then back to the hotel. I had booked Paul a bungalow at the Beverly Hills Hotel for the privacy and atmosphere conducive to writing songs for the *White Album*, the recording of which Paul had just left behind in London for a few days.

We entered the lobby of the hotel through the front, and Paul stopped at the desk to pick up messages. A young boy of about twelve was checking into the hotel with his mother when all of a sudden he realized that he was standing next to a Beatle. He was so stunned that he turned to

This was simple respect and human nature at its finest. This was that golden thread that ran through the Beatles' nature and personal makeup—it is the thread that binds us all together when we get past all the stuff that conditioning imposes upon our natural goodness and love for one another.

Paul and started pointing at him and stammering, "You're . . . you're . . . you're . . . you're . . . ."

"That's right," Paul interrupted, "Stevie Wonder!"

"Right," the young fellow quickly agreed. "Stevie Wonder!" As we walked away, the boy's eyes and mouth remained frozen in the maxed out open position until we walked out the door and into the garden paths that led to the bungalow outside the lobby.

Interestingly, Paul would always get this startled look on his face when he encountered the public's response as we would get out of a limo or walk into a restaurant. He would act genuinely amazed at the reaction of people to his presence. His worldwide fame at that time was about four years old, and it was all so out of whack with his upbringing that he still couldn't get a grasp on it. He would shake his head and say to me, "I just don't understand. . . ." This trip was different for Paul, traveling alone at times without entourage and all the customary hype. Although Ron Kass, Tony Bramwell, and Paul's childhood friend Ivan Vaughn (the classmate who introduced Paul to John all those years earlier) accompanied Paul on this trip, they often weren't around when we made the various personal and promotional rounds. Especially in the United States, Paul was not used to moving about in relative secrecy. This solo flight (that is, without the other Beatles) allowed him to see things from a different perspective. He commented one night in the hotel suite that for so long the Beatles always had to enter buildings like restaurants and hotels by the service entrances, basement tunnels, alley doors, and other inconspicuous passages that it was nice to see the front entrances and nice parts of the places he was visiting on this U.S. visit. American hotel lobbies and curbsides were new to him.

Saturday, June 22, 1968. (The next day . . .)

This postcard was written on a TWA flight from LA to London (via New York City) after I had taken Paul to the airport following the Capitol convention. Paul put it into an envelope and sent it regular mail from the Apple offices like a letter, thus no postmark.

Ob-La-Di, Ob-La-Da

I was hanging about the bungalow, being generally available, while Paul was writing new songs and rewriting others. Apple President Ron Kass had tried to convince Paul to carry a tape recorder of some sort around with him because he would write incredible song after incredible song and then totally forget them. He would sing an absolute stunner to us in the living room on Monday and then on Tuesday we would ask him to sing that great song he wrote the day before and he wouldn't have a clue what we were talking about. Anyway, because I was there, hanging around, he started including me in his musical constructions. I got wrapped up that afternoon in the words and intent of "Ob-La-Di, Ob-La-Da" and "Back in the USSR." On the way home over Mulholland Drive that night, I realized I had, in a sense, just spent the afternoon

On the way home over Mulholland Drive that night, I realized I had, in a sense, just spent the afternoon songwriting with Paul McCartney.

songwriting with Paul McCartney. Of course, later on when the album came out, I wasn't surprised when I didn't see my name as a cowriter. But I *was* surprised to see the songs listed as Lennon/McCartney compositions because to my knowledge John had nothing to do with them. It was several years later before it was clear to music lovers that the "Lennon/McCartney" songwriting credit was only occasionally accurate and in reality more of a showbiz, PR device. Although the public was still mostly unaware of the unique nature of the world-famous Lennon/McCartney songwriting team, it was then that I was vaguely able to grasp the unspoken part of the intangible structure of their business, as well as their musical and personal friendship. They told me that they considered each other, at that time, such an integral part of each other's influences that they were in some ethereal way writing songs together though apart.

For me it was a unique day that didn't necessarily pay well but was one that money can't buy (me luv). To this day, I wouldn't trade it for anything.

Got to Get You into My Life

That day had an unusual ending. We had taken a break, and Paul had gone into the bathroom. The suite was laid out with a dining area and living area on one side, separated by a hall that ran alongside with a bedroom at each end and a bathroom in the middle. The door to the hallway was midway between the dining and living areas. With Paul out of the room, I answered a knock at the door and met Linda Eastman for the first time. "Hello, may I help you?" I asked. Speaking through me, not to me, she vaguely replied, "Is Paul here?" Over my shoulder she saw Paul coming through the door that led from the bedroom/bathroom portion of the suite, and *wham!* She went past me like a Notre Dame football tackle. She full-force embraced him in the doorway, push-pulled him through it, slammed the door shut, and that was the last I saw of him or her that day. (I waited around for about an hour because I had this great idea for a line in "Ob-La-Di, Ob-La-Da" that I knew he was dying to hear.) I finally gave up and went home. I am not quite sure what happened that night, but I do know that Linda was with us until I put them on a plane heading east—man!

Linda in the Sky with . . .

The next day I drove Paul and Linda to LAX. They were flying to New York together, and then he was going ahead on to London. After we had checked in and secured tickets and seating arrangements, Paul announced that he was hungry and opted for a hot dog (he was several years away from being a vegetarian) from one of the little stands LAX used to have at the top of the escalators. Linda passed on the "decomposed cadaver tube on a roll" and opted to spend her last few minutes before takeoff capturing the sights of LAX with a new camera she had purchased on the trip. These hot dog stands were short-lived but were strategically placed close to the gates so that people in a hurry could grab a quick bite to eat. We ordered a couple of dogs and stood at the stand and ate them. Paul McCartney caused bedlam wherever he went, yet no one was even aware that they were standing elbow to elbow with a Beatle while they were grabbing their fast eats.

We were starting back toward the gate when we were gathered up by a group of airport officials who advised us that there was a bomb threat on the plane. They explained that they had set aside a special room for our comfort so that Paul wouldn't be mobbed by the crowds during an extended wait. The wait did become extended, and a couple of hours soon passed by. I later found out that the bomb scare was a ruse and they were going through Paul's luggage, searching for drugs.

The airport officials found no bomb (or drugs!), and it was finally time to board. During the long wait, we talked about England, and I told him how much I was looking forward to my first trip to London. At that time, I was acting in the capacity of Capitol's national promotion manager and director of the Artist Relations Department. I didn't know at that point how involved I would be with the Apple venture. Before leaving, Paul took a medallion he had worn during the trip from around his neck and put it around mine. I had admired it earlier in the week because of its uniqueness. "You'd better be wearing this the next time I see you," he said. He started boarding, stopped, turned around, and said, "In London!"

Ron Kass told me later that McCartney was mainly responsible for appointing me the official U.S. manager of Apple Records and had already made the decision when he left LA that day.

Those were the days, my friend, but that was *the* day as far as I am concerned!

Years later, I noticed something interesting in this picture that was taken during a Buck Owens photo shoot at a ranch outside Bakersfield shortly after I had put Paul McCartney on a plane back to London. This was the medallion Paul had put around my neck after his appearance at the Capitol convention when he had announced Apple Records would be distributed by Capitol.

Track 6

Hands Across the Water

» *Somewhere over the Atlantic Ocean, July 1968*

I peered out the little oval window into the clouds, searching for the coastline. Still in a state of disbelief at the recent dramatic upturn in my career (which hadn't been going too badly anyway), I tried to discern the transitional point in my life that had brought me out of a small town in northern Idaho into this moment and this airplane as it prepared for the approach to Heathrow Airport, London, England—and the Beatles!

Less than a year after the death of Brian Epstein, the Beatles were masterminding their own business empire. Ron Kass had by now notified Stanley Gortikov that he and the "lads" wanted me to become the U.S. manager of their record division, Apple Records. They asked that I join them in London for a dramatic and insightful series of Apple-related meetings. It seems that washing my feet, brushing the potato peels out of my hair, working my way through college, and then scrambling my way up through the corporate ranks at Capitol was paying off in a way I had never imagined. The world I was about to enter was precisely 6,071 miles and just as many light years away from my Idaho beginnings and the Nez Perce Indian reservation lands where I grew up: a world with no freebies, no frills, no backstage passes, no fish and chips wrapped in newspaper, no bobbies on horseback, no afternoon teas, and certainly no Fab Four.

I traveled with Gortikov and Capitol's head of press and publicity, Larry Delaney. Apple A&R man Peter Asher (of Peter and Gordon fame, an old friend of mine by now) was to pick us up at the airport. Gortikov's straightforward admonition on the way to LAX—that the Beatles currently accounted for approximately 50 percent of Capitol's business—kept running through my head. Fifty percent! As he subtly put it, "When it has to do with the Beatles—*there is no margin for error.*"

Later on, back at the Capitol Tower in Hollywood, Bob York, my immediate superior and the V.P. general manager of the company, summoned me into his office to discuss my new responsibilities. He let me know in no uncertain terms that I was to "keep it together" as far as the Beatles and the Apple staffers were concerned. In order to make my job easier, he informed me, I did not have to get approvals for my travel, expenditures, or schedules. In fact, I would not even be required to explain my whereabouts or what I was doing—as long as I "kept it together." At this point, I expected Glen Wallichs, the founder and chairman of the board of Capitol, to call me over to his home next and instruct me to "keep it together" with the Beatles, just to be sure I got the

Capitol had just handed me a first-class ticket to ride on a long and wonderfully winding road into the most amazing place and time in musical history.

message from the complete executive hierarchy of the company. I did get the message, but more than that, Capitol had just handed me a first-class ticket to ride on a long and wonderfully winding road into the most amazing place and time in musical history.

I stopped dream-staring out the window and began straining to see land. Suddenly I saw sparkling lights way off and way down below; I was seeing England for the first time. Then I realized that because we had taken the typical north-southeast approach, we were being blessed with a night view of portions of Scotland, Ireland, and northern England. The stewardess shook me out of my wonderment to ask if I wanted coffee or tea with my breakfast. "Coffee, please . . . no wait, I'll have tea." I better get used to it.

I twisted off the wind tunnel of air above me and pulled close the thin

Below, left to right: Larry Delaney, Neil Aspinall, Peter Asher, and George.

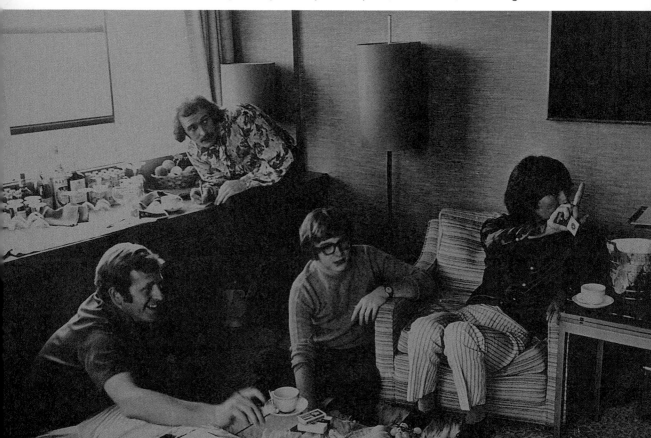

excuse for a blanket. Still searching for the coastline, I felt like a kid, excited, nervous, and gawking out of the window like I had never been on an airplane before.

As the runway came into sight, the view from the oval window looked cold, rainy, and bleak.

The airplane had hit the runway when it all suddenly *hit* me—this was real heady stuff, and this country boy was scared stiff!

Below, left to right: Back of George's head, Ron Kass, Paul, me, Ringo, Stan Gortikov, Mal Evans, and John's head in lower right-hand corner. Using George as the common point, the layout of the participants in the hotel suite becomes apparent in these two pictures. It still seems odd to me that at least one of these mega money groups, Apple or Capitol or the Beatles, couldn't have afforded a larger suite for these meetings. (It does speak for the purity of purpose within the Beatles' hearts, and besides, the long meetings in close proximity like this did help draw us closer together.)

Track 7

Hello Goodbye

» *London, England, July 1968*

Knock, knock. "Hello, my name is Peter Brown, and I am the chief of protocol for the Beatles, and I have come to give you your 'shejule' [schedule]." He then continued on officiously with outlining the said "shejule" without any response from me or even a little transitory chitchat. His approach was proper, clear of purpose, and veddy, veddy (very, very) English. There was no question that we would be spending quite a lot of time communicating with each other over the months or years ahead, but right now he had an agenda, and we were going to discuss my "shejule."

I was still in somewhat of a daze. Peter Asher met our plane at Heathrow, and after he and I had our mini reunion, which included my inquiry into the well-being and whereabouts of my friend and his ex-partner Gordon Waller, Peter adeptly ushered us curbside at Heathrow and presented us with our uniformed chauffeur, who snapped a curt salute as he held forth stiffly in front of our personal white Rolls Royce limousine. Apple had graciously provided us this classy perk on a twenty-four-hour basis for the entire visit. We were then driven (without our baggage because naturally someone would see that it was properly delivered) to our waiting suites at an exclusive Hyde Park hotel. Of course, we were preregistered, pre-checked in, pre-Fabbed in every way. Getting to experience this together was special to Peter and me because we had become good friends during the "Peter and Gordon" visits to California (they were signed to Capitol in the United States) where my responsibility as head of promotion and artist relations was to spend the entire time with them during their visits and tours. I would meet them at the airport in Los Angeles and cart them off to their hotel. Now he had just met me at the airport and had just delivered me to *my* hotel. There was a continuous irony in our relationship in that after Peter and Gordon and our Capitol records stint, Peter and I ended up at Apple. We next became vice presidents at MGM together, which was followed by us both leaving the loony lion to eventually become independent record producers. To give this sequence of events a perpetual feel, as record producers, we both scored chart-topping singles at the same time with similar artists (Linda Ronstadt and Jessi Colter). Coincidentally, but not surprisingly, we then found ourselves mixing our competitive hit albums side by side in the same town (Hollywood) at the same studio (The Sound Factory) for the same record label (Capitol).

I was still looking out the window at my beautiful view of the park and listening to the stereo system and complete selection of current English rock albums libraried in my room by the Beatles' personal staff when Peter Brown came to my door.

"We will begin with tea at 3 Savile Row (catered by Fortnum and Mason), next you will be having lunch with all four of the lads (and Yoko) at the Ritz Hotel in Piccadilly to get better acquainted, and then we will go directly into meetings for the rest of the day." He continued, "At approximately 1700 hours you will be returned to your suite and allowed time to freshen up. Tonight Ringo will be taking you to dinner and then to the theater to see the new Robert Morely play *Halfway up the Tree* written by Peter Ustinov and directed by John Gielgud. Tomorrow morning you will have breakfast with George. Afterward it's back into meetings, and then you'll be having lunch with all four of the lads in the private restaurant on top of the hotel that has been reserved for just our group. We will continue meetings for the afternoon, and then Paul will take you night-clubbing that evening." Peter Brown clearly laid out our whole itinerary for the entire visit with the perfect blend of subtly tourist things and hip insider jaunts that would help meld us into the organization.

There was also the obvious proper mixture of being with all four Beatles together and one-on-one time spent in various activities.

I liked Peter Brown a lot upon this first meeting. He reminded me of a regal rock and proper roll version of Peter Ustinov. I was to learn as time went on that his high-hat upper-class British snobbery had only recently replaced a common upbringing akin to the other members of the Apple corps. As a supporting cast member of this unfolding play on words and music, he definitely was an Academy Award winner. I was very disappointed in the slant on the Beatles' story he took in his 1983 book *All You Need Is Love*. Having read it I look back now and in retrospect feel that *act* was the

Peter Brown clearly laid out our whole itinerary for the entire visit with the perfect blend of subtly tourist things and hip insider jaunts that would help meld us into the organization.

operative word when referring to Peter Brown as a class act. I was in the room in different instances he wrote about in his book and found it odd that he would name everyone there except me. Although I must confess that my ego was a little miffed historically because of this discrepancy, I found I greatly questioned the validity of other stories in his book where I wasn't present. My greatest objection was to the dark-side approach he took to events and the Beatles themselves. I think there must have been two John Lennons—I never met his!

The chauffeur became a regular member of our visit, and as protocol dictated, he would never speak to us first—he would only respond when a conversation was initiated on our part. His answers would be to the point and always courteous. If he did need to make an unsolicited comment (like if my hair was on fire or something), he would always ask permission to speak before actually doing so—if that's possible. We would sometimes keep him going for twenty-four hours in a row, and he was always crisp, polite, alert, and available to serve us at all times—no complaints, just proper demeanor and courtesy.

The Apple Meetings

You would think that trying to schedule and hold formal meetings with the members of a successful four-piece rock-and-roll band would be like trying to organize fire ants into straight columns, but it was quite the opposite with the Beatles. They had accomplished about everything there was in the category of rock stars, and they took the Apple endeavor very seriously. Over the years, I have wished some of my other business associates could have been as punctual and attentive (and as enthusiastic!) to the matters at hand. Their fame and fortune allowed them to play businessmen. But like Joe Montana when he played football, they were not playing around. They really enjoyed this new career in the beginning and were truly into it on all levels. As crazy as the whole thing was, I defy any other group of this stature to be as focused and coordinated in effort and spirit as this one was at the outset.

Apple was fun. Apple had heart and a philosophy of good intent. It had good people and good music. Good grief, I wish it could have gone on forever.

A large suite had been reserved for the week in Hyde Park's Royal Lancaster Hotel, and that is where we met. The days were long, and we worked hard. We would break for lunch in the showroom on the top floor that was only open in the evenings. The room was a classic English supper club that featured dining and dancing to a four-piece band. We were able to be served our noon meal there without the obvious intrusion of fans during these needed breaks. Stan, Larry, Tony Bramwell, and a few other Apple staffers and I got a surprise musical treat one day. We were seated at a ringside table in front of the empty bandstand, and as we were finishing lunch, Paul got up and sat down behind the drum kit and started laying down a pattern on the drums. Before long, all four Beatles were on stage jamming on instruments other than the ones they were noted for and played a twenty-minute impromptu set for us—their delighted guests. Musicians sure do like music! Pickers sure do like to pick! We sure did enjoy watching and listening to our employers at work!

During the nonmusical portion of these meetings, we decided on a six-man promotion team that I would set up on a regional basis when I returned to the United States. This team would be drawn from the elite of Capitol's fifty-man field team that I had put together over the years. I knew every man well and had hired most of them personally. Gortikov approved this team as a Capitol expenditure and felt that the other six or seven small independent labels that I was responsible for could use this promotional SWAT team's efforts as well. We decided on the first four releases* and mapped out the original release campaign and decided it would culminate in the "Golden Apple" award** ceremony to be held in LA at the then happening Sunset Strip Playboy Club. The Playboy Club—times have changed.

Probably the most memorable part of these meetings was Paul's personal dilemma over the first Beatles release to be included in the "Our First Four." Although the "A" and "B" songs had been selected ("Hey Jude" and "Revolution"), Paul had serious misgivings about the acceptability of "Hey Jude's" length, which clocked in at over seven minutes.

We would adjourn to the new Apple building on 3 Savile Row where a professional tape deck and giant sound system had been set up in one of the large rooms. The building was carpeted in dark green and painted inside and out in white. There was no other furniture or accoutrements except for a table set with refreshments and snacks at the opposite end of the same room. We would sit on the floor for extended periods of time playing the two songs over and over trying to decide which one to release as the "A" side. We were playing by the rules that all new releases had the "A" and "B" side designated for Top 40 airplay purposes.

The mechanical reason for this was so that when a record company released an artist's new record, the promotion men would all work on the same song (the "A" side) for airplay in order to create a hit song. For example, if 100 percent of the important radio stations played one side of a record, it meant you had a hit. If 50 percent of the stations played one

---

* The first four records to be released on Apple were: the Beatles' "Hey Jude" backed with "Revolution," Mary Hopkin's "Those Were the Days" backed with "Turn, Turn, Turn," Jackie Lomax's "Sour Milk Sea" backed with "The Eagle Laughs at You," and the Black Dyke Mills Band's "Thingumybob" backed with "Yellow Submarine." The advertising agency of Wolfe and Ollins designed the "Our First Four" plastic 10" x 12" black matte box that encased hand-lathed versions of these records with handwritten labels by the Beatles. The outside top lid said, "Our First Four," 3 Savile Row with Stanley Gortikov, Larry Delaney, and Ken Mansfield individually listed on the front. This special package also contained photos and bios along with the records.

** The basic concept of the competition between Capitol's field promotion staff for this award was based on setting a formula for airplay and sales on a territorial basis. The promotion man who got the most airplay on designated key stations and caused the most sales on the first four Apple releases would be flown first class to LA. There he would be rewarded with a banquet in his honor and presented with a large beautiful gold Apple as a trophy. The icing on the cake, when we were planning this event at the Apple meetings in London, came about when the Beatles agreed that one of them would fly from London to LA and present the Golden Apple award in person to the Capitol employee who won the contest.

side and 50 percent played the other side, it meant you had a mediocre chance at success. The irony of this dilemma was that every station played every song the Beatles released. They were going to play both sides anyway, but Paul wanted to do it by the numbers. It was amazing to sit on the floor in front of the speakers and witness Paul's artistic insecurity. Somehow fear of rejection didn't seem an appropriate emotion in that room. (Looking back, one thing I find great joy in is the fact that I don't ever remember any of the Beatles suggesting that one alternative to this problem would be to shorten the record.)

It seemed the playbacks would go on forever until I came up with a suggestion that put Paul at ease. I volunteered to reroute myself on the way back to LA via a few key airplay markets if he would trust me with

It was amazing to sit on the floor in front of the speakers and witness Paul's artistic insecurity. Somehow fear of rejection didn't seem an appropriate emotion in that room.

one advance copy of the record. I would hopscotch my way to Philadelphia and play it for Jim Hilliard at WFIL, then continue on to Jim Dunlap at WQAM in Miami, and then head out to another location. These men and a few others at American Top 40 stations at that time were known and respected for their ability to "pick the hits." When I got back to LA, the plan was for me to call Paul and let him know the results. He liked the idea, and I really liked the idea because not only was it a very exciting first assignment but a great PR move for me with some major radio stations. Needless to say, the music directors fell out of their chairs when they heard "Hey Jude." Such a hesitant start to possibly their greatest record.

At the conclusion of the hotel meetings and the signing of the Apple contracts in the suite by Gortikov and the four Beatles, they presented Stan, Larry, and me with hand-lathed 45 RPM copies of the first four records. The labels were handwritten by the Beatles themselves. They had packaged them in black plastic boxes with our names, a green Apple, and "Our First Four" embossed on the front. (Many years later in Nashville, I had to decide between eating and looking at that package. This unique treasured gift from the Beatles represented a time in my life in which I felt very alive and vital. In Tennessee, I had to sell it for "vittles" to stay alive.) Gortikov had arranged to present them with a special crystal Apple that didn't make it to the meetings so he symbolically presented them with a real apple instead and a crystal rain check in return. On the table with the documents, the real apple had been placed in the center. After the contracts were signed, Paul picked up the apple and walked away from the others and ate it.

Years later after the breakup, I was rummaging through some old boxes in my closet and this picture fell out with Paul standing apart from the others—back turned to them, staring out the window and finishing off the apple. The symbolism and foretelling of the future rushed over me like a giant emotional tidal wave and made me wonder how far back in our lives we are given the metaphoric information to know things that will someday happen.

I've included this picture here—I don't think any of the Beatles have ever seen it.

Below: The signing of the Apple contracts giving Capitol the rights to distribute Apple Records and the agreement that the Beatles could release future product on Apple Records. Paul stands separate from the others eating the apple—a foretelling?

Track 8

A Is for Apple,
B Is for Beatle,
C Is for Comrades

» *London, England, August 1968*

We were sitting in a small meeting room, all four Beatles, Neil Aspinall, Mal Evans, and me. It was an Apple planning meeting, with the attendees being the four owners of the company and the three of us underlings. In all humility (yeah, sure), I always felt that being an underling with the Beatles was still giant steps above the rest of the blokes in the entertainment industry. It was casual yet serious at the same time. There were a lot of things on our plates with this gathering, yet even with all that pressure, there was also a sense of intense calm. Something kept happening in the conversation that caught my attention by the very fact of its repetition. This particular phrase was simply two words that were used by each one of the Beatles at one time or the other, not only during this meeting but also at other times when I would be one-on-one with them. That phrase was simply: "the Beatles."

As we discussed promotions, concepts, and upcoming releases on the Beatles and other Apple artists, each of the four in turn would refer to the Beatles as if we were discussing a band that was from another planet. I asked Paul why they kept referring to the band in the third person. He explained to me rather casually (and at the same time, I sensed, with a bit of bewilderment on his part) that the whole "Beatles" thing had exploded into this tremendous abstract anomaly that had gone totally beyond them to the point that it had become something bigger than they could comprehend. As we sat there in that room, there was a "them," that is to say, a John, a Paul, a George, and a Ringo. Then there was this other enigmatic thing known to the world as "the Beatles." Things like this really distilled the whole thing for me; I would be so amazed at how

I received these great Christmas cards from Neil, Mal, and many of the Apple staffers. I loved the concept. The left-hand outside were pictures of everyone when they were young and the right-hand outside were their current photos. The interior was striking in its simplicity and message. I liked Mal's note to me the best and have included it.

normal and easy it was to be with and work for these four guys. "The Beatles" was this giant superstar group, and they were, simply, themselves.

Years later, the band did a good job of demonstrating this point at the beginning of each *Beatles Anthology* DVD. Each disc starts with the four lads performing a few seconds of the song "Help!" The picture then begins a slow zoom out to reveal the band dwarfed under (and finally completely overtaken by) a colossal "Beatles" logo. The sound of the music is simultaneously drowned out by a cacophony of screaming fans. I liked both entities ("the Beatles" and those four guys) and found each totally fascinating. I really loved the Beatles, their music, the whole magical and mystical phenomenon of it all, but deep down I think the part I liked best was the really cool people in that band—the John, the Paul, the George, and the Ringo of it all.

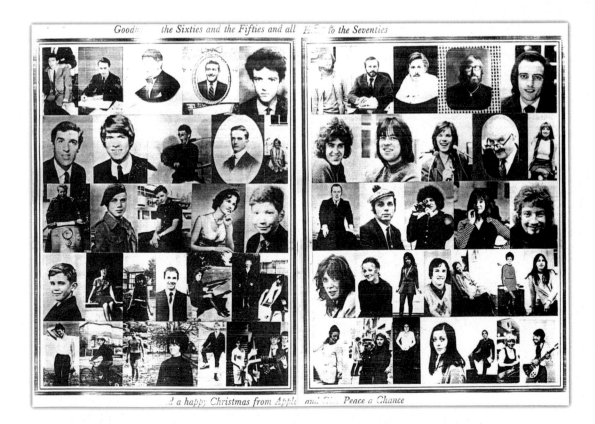

Good... the Sixties and the Fifties and all ... to the Seventies

...d a happy Christmas from Apple ...... Peace a Chance

None Bad Apple

» *London, England, September 1968*

One night Paul and I and a couple of Apple staffers, most likely Tony Bramwell and Jack Oliver (as habit would have it when it came to late night romps), went out for an evening on the town. We started with a light dinner at the Bag O' Nails before heading on to the various clubs, private and otherwise. One of the hangouts was Tramp, which was very private and seemed to be the place where the famous bands and their staffers hung out. Members of the Rolling Stones and their people would be there, a Beatle or two, and assorted hangers-on. It was fun to be an accepted part of this rarefied air and to see how much fun everyone had in this secluded setting. As the evening progressed and our spirits became lifted by the spirits we were lifting up to our lips, things really began opening up. The mood and milieu was one of increasing laughter as the evening wore on. Before things got too incoherent, I asked Paul how Apple came to be named Apple. He did give me an explanation, brief in content, so I am not sure if he told me the real reason; it is sometimes hard to see through that natural English sarcasm. His answer was, and I quote, "Have you ever heard anyone say anything bad about an apple?" I considered that position a "plum" to be savored and let it go at that.

We ended up at one club that I can't remember the name of sitting at a long table where a couple of Paul's friends joined us and started tossing ales and telling jokes. We went nonstop for about an hour, with each ale and each joke creating continuous knee-slapping laughter. Paul and I were sitting at the corner of the table, and it was almost as if we were old schoolmates who were new at tying one on. In time, we all actually got silly drunk together with lots of jostling and our faces literally falling into our beers.

It was getting late, but we proceeded out of there to another more private place. The time was nearing 5 a.m., and I was still suffering from a little jet lag. This was only my second day in London on this trip, and for me there was always a little bit of body shock when flying from LA to points across the Atlantic. I always had trouble the first day in London adjusting to the shift in time zones, meal times, and sleeping schedules and would really have to fight nature's intent with my body, which by this time just wanted to shut down for a few hours. Oddly enough, going back the other direction was never a problem. I could catch an early nonstop from London to LA, get off the plane, and hit the ground running. Anyway, the evening had narrowed down to Paul and me from the original group, and he was just getting up a head of steam. I had to beg off and put a cap on my part of the party. I couldn't believe that I was bailing out on hanging out with Paul McCartney—probably the most famous entertainer in the world at the time—at least one of the top four.

I asked Paul how Apple came to be named Apple. His answer was, and I quote, "Have you ever heard anyone say anything bad about an apple?"

I was duty bound to be in the Apple offices the next day, so it was with great effort that I dragged myself in for morning meetings. Sometime in the early afternoon, while I was still struggling through a British hangover (they do drink different concoctions there than we do in America so I am sure there were some forms of new body shock from the odd combinations that had entered my system), Paul sauntered in all bushy tailed after a good night's sleep and gave me that boyish look, which suggested that us Yanks just couldn't keep up with the big boys!

Bad Day
at Beach Rock

» *Los Angeles, California, September 1968*

When it comes to the Beach Boys back in the '60s, they were definitely a triple whammy when you combine the surfer attitude with youth and a ton of success. Things were never normal when it came to this band and its operation. A state of tsunamic turmoil was as calm as it got when any one of them or their team invaded the comparatively quiet hype and hysteria that surrounded the upper floors of the Capitol Tower. Keeping a handle on their affairs was like trying to organize frogs in a hailstorm.

One smoggy LA afternoon in 1968, I walked into the Capitol Tower after a series of stressful meetings held outside the building. Not only were these very intense times at Apple, but I was close to buckling under the weight of the rest of the managerial load I had taken on and was deep in thought when I stepped off the elevator onto the eighth floor. I had no commitments for the rest of the day, and I was going to head straight into my office, close the door, and catch up. My secretary greeted me with a look of sheer terror instead of words, handed me a stack of memos, and then headed for the ladies' room without looking back. National marketing manager Rocco Catena came out of his office as I stood there with this handful of urgent messages from every major executive at the label and gave me the male version of my secretary's deer-in-the-headlights gaze. Rocco just shook his head as he, too, headed away to the men's room without a word. All the secretaries on the floor put their heads down and started typing really fast as I walked by, while other executives quickly disappeared into their offices, shutting the doors behind them. I had the sense that I had just brought leprosy to the building and that nobody wanted to be in my general vicinity. I didn't have time to figure out what was going on because the phone on the empty desk outside my office was ringing madly. I picked it up and was summoned immediately "upstairs." (In the Capitol Tower, the word "upstairs" was a staff synonym for the offices of top management.) I dropped my briefcase where I was standing, turned around, and headed straight for General Manager Bob York's office where I was given "the news" before I could even sit down.

It seemed that Roger Karshner, my national field promotion manager, who was in charge of the day-to-day direction of our fifty-man promotion team, had managed to have a little run-in with the Beach Boys' management and had taken it upon himself to "fire" the Beach Boys from the label. Unfortunately, once having been "fired," not only was the band angered to a point just beyond repair, but they also took the legal stance that the firing was a formal notice by an executive of the company and that they were free from all contractual obligations with the organization.

In a nutshell I was to get this sad situation undone and the time frame was—now. Bob had just returned from an emergency meeting of the even more "upstairs" people, and the unified command from these highest-ups was concise and left no real need for me to have a side of the conversation—my job, to save my job, was to get on it—now.

I don't believe I used the elevator, the stairs, or even the hallways but immediately transported myself three floors into Roger's office where I was confronted with his hand held out toward me in the air, palm first, telling me to hold on while he completed a phone call. When he finally hung up the phone, I think I probably asked him something simple like, "Anything I should know about concerning one of our biggest acts—ROGER?" Standing up for emphasis and with cool composure, he explained to me exactly what had happened. These were his words, delivered in a clipped and clear manner:

I received a call from their manager complaining about my handling of the promotion on their current record. He was demanding and acerbic, using words that contained an inordinate amount of Fs. As the conversation continued, the anger between us escalated to the point where I told him that the Beach Boys were fired. Ken, you should have heard the stunned silence at the other end of the line. Then he replied, "Fired?" "Yeah," I replied, "Fired, off the label, pick up their final check, apply for unemployment! Fired!" The guy went bananas, couldn't believe it, told me he was coming to the Capitol Tower to punch me out. I told him to save his gas, that I was headed to Beverly Hills to return the favor. Before hanging up, I also let him know that from my point of view the Beach Boys were nothing more than out-of-work musicians!

As stunned as I was, there was that part of me that knew how Roger thought, and although I was sympathetic, my understanding was not going to run too deep or too silent. I had brought Roger out to Hollywood from the Midwest to this national position at Capitol. He was probably my best field man operating out of Cleveland, Ohio, and typically was overqualified intellectually no matter where you sent him or what job you placed him in. He also had a grassroots sense of right and wrong that let you know you could always count on him to do the right thing. Because of this, he felt he had addressed the current situation in the appropriate manner regardless of its political implications. The Beach Boys in general were not overly fond of us "suits," and their manager had been rude and uncouth and had truly insulted him on many levels. The wickedness and meanness of the terms used against him were totally unacceptable to Roger, and no matter how big a deal they were—they were "fired" for improper behavior. Cut and dried. Case closed.

It had been established years earlier that I was to have nothing to do with deciding anything regarding Beach Boys record releases, so even though my label involvement with them was slightly restricted on a creative level, one of the departments that reported to me was Artist Relations. In matters like these, the buck and the beach clearly stopped at my door. I wasn't about to fire Roger, which, by the way, was the basic inference from "upstairs" as to what part of my actions in handling this matter should be, because he was too important to the overall success of my operation. I am not sure what my basic instructions were to him as I ran out of his office, but I know he knew he was not to go near a beach or any of its boys from that point on. I spent the next few hours on the phones pleading, on the freeway scurrying, and on my knees begging, trying to turn this thing around with the successful surfer sons from the western edges of Orange County. In all honesty, I did it the Hollywood way—I sold Roger out. I let the band know how unimportant Roger's opinion and general position in the universe were and that he would be severely reprimanded with resultant bleeding and weeping. I had a lot to offer with increased promotions, pumped up advertising and marketing budgets, as well as special monies to be spent on their next two million records. When they were able to ascertain with certainty that I had nothing left to give, we finally agreed to return to the previous insane normality of a typical superstar–record label relationship.

I think the thing that got me was the calm way that Roger handled the aftermath of the whole thing. I don't think he really gave it another thought after his anger had passed. He knew he was in the right so—what's to discuss?

I wish it had been as easy for me—help, help me, Roger—help me Roger, yeah, git it out of my mind.

The Beach Boys performing on BBC-TV's *Top of the Pops* in 1968. It had been some time since Brian Wilson could bring himself to make a public appearance with the band. His replacement, Bruce Johnston, is at left.

Track 11

White Out

» *Hollywood, California, October 1968*

Things seemed to stiffen up in 1968 during the Beatles' "white out." George Harrison told me that the *White Album* had become a much larger undertaking than they expected. Creating a double album was just a bit much once it all got going, and its natural progression evolved into more of a cacophony of dilemmas as it gained its own monstrous momentum. Besides the enormous volume of musical work, there were all the unexpected inner-group conflicts (during which Ringo left the band for several weeks), heavy schedules, the mind-blowing logistics of getting the entire Apple enterprise off the ground, never-ending pressures from the fans, deadlines with the record companies, as well as the everyday demands of each Beatle's personal life. The music they recorded that summer and fall has stood the test of time, but outside of that, everything else had really become somewhat of a nightmare.

By mid-fall, the entire band wanted to put the *White Album* (as most know, the album was really called *The Beatles*) project behind them. Anxious for a little artistic freedom, George called me from London and told me that he wanted to come to LA in October to produce more tracks for Apple artist Jackie Lomax's album. (Jackie's only Apple album, featuring tracks recorded in LA and in London, was to be released in 1969 as *Is This What You Want?*) In a brief time, I had George set up with the digs and doings for a seven-week visit.

Production for the *White Album* was completed back in London while George was in LA. Capitol's engineers had tinkered with the mix, and when George heard Capitol's acetate pressings of the soon-to-be-released final product, he was unhappy with the sound. So while we (George, Jackie, Mal Evans, and I, among others) were holed up in Armin Steiner's Sound Recorders Studio (SRS), working on Jackie's album, George shifted gears and set about remastering the U.S. version of the *White Album*.

The music they recorded that summer and fall has stood the test of time, but outside of that, everything else had really become somewhat of a nightmare.

To Ken, something groovy love from George Harrison.

The BEATLES

0030032

George offered to sign my copy of the *White Album* as a kind gesture for me helping him while he was working on the album. He asked what I wanted him to write on it—actually George was offering to say whatever personal thing I wanted him to say so I could kind of show off how close I was to a Beatle. I bashfully replied, "Oh I don't know—just say something groovy and sign it with love from George Harrison." Well as you can see, that is just what he did. *Next time,* I thought, *I will be a little less vague.* In retrospect it has made the autograph more meaningful because of the personal humor he interjected into it.

George just wanted to get this Beatles project done and behind him. He felt the obligation to jump in there and get the thing finished. By this time, I had gotten a feel for things and how they fermented in the Apple barrel, and from watching the way they worked, I had gathered the impression that Paul would never really let go of anything. Somehow, though, I had the feeling that George grabbed away the reins on this stampeding horse of so many colors and became a creative detail man, and out of sheer necessity put a little methodology into effect just to get the project completed.

By this time, I had already spent considerable time with George both when I worked for Capitol and now for Apple. During this extended visit, I became more of a friend than a business associate. I spent quite a bit of one-on-one time with him, and this period away from the other Fabs

From Apple

Jackie Lomax
Under the sign of the Bull in the borough of Wallasey which lies upon the River Mersey in the North Midlands county of Cheshire, was born on May 10, 1944 John Richard Lomax, now known as Jackie, who grew to be a nine-stone weakling, and still is.

His father is John Richard Lomax, a labourer in a flour mill and his mother is Edith and his elder brother is Jimmy whom, when Jackie last heard of him, was thought to have been discharged without honour from the Royal Navy, later to work in a brewery.

Jackie Lomax has green eyes and is 5 ft. 9 ins. tall he says, and when you really look at him you see he is quite tall but when he walks he slouches in that Merseyside way and you would think he was shorter, say 5 ft. 7 ins. masquerading as 5 ft. 8 ins. or thereabouts.

He went to school, to Wallasey Technical Grammar School where he won three O-Levels, in Art, English, and Architectural drawing so you can imagine his surprise to find himself working as a motor mechanic in a scooter shop and then as a lorry driver and then as a time and wages clerk for the Mersey Docks and Harbour Board at the Pier Head in Liverpool.

Can you dig it?
In July 1962 he went to Germany with the Undertakers, a very good rock 'n' roll group from Liverpool of whom you will have heard.

To Germany.
To Hamburg.
To the Reeperbahn.
To the Grosse Freiheit.
To the Star Club.
To crazy days.
Jackie says.

Crazy for sure. Cruel days. The Reeperbahn. Sin Inc. Flesh and leather and ladies wrestling in the mud for men and for marks. Terrifying days. Terrible people in random uniforms from some Ruritanian hell parading the pavements as doorkeepers for clubs beyond your wildest nightmare. No place, no fit place, no fit companions for Wallasey boys just out of school.

However it must have been OK, because five times the Undertakers went to Hamburg and Jackie Lomax has nothing but rose-to-scarlet-hued memories of the Star Club and the Hamburg heyday when the Beatles swung with the Searchers, with Rory Storme, with Little Richard, with Joey Dee, with everyone who was there. Jackie had played with the Undertakers in and around Liverpool before the first Hamburg trip but the money wasn't great. It was better than great in Germany. Fifty quid a week, Jackie remembers. Fifty quid for playing eight hours a night and more.

Well that was fine, Jackie thinks because it was better than the Dock Board and there was a lot of craziness. Once, they got drunk—those were the days when you drunk and shouted out of the window, "we won the war you dirty krauts" and poured water over the population who didn't like it and called the police. Two members of the group were arrested, not Jackie. Oh no.

He was too young for arresting and too young to care anyway. One of the Undertakers was named Bugs (real name Warren; warren, rabbit rabbit bunny Bugs, yes) he dressed up as a gorilla and with a singer named Davy Jones dressed as an Arab, ransacked a shop, moved down the street into the whore's market-place and there caused considerable difficulties which didn't end until long after Bugs had been removed into hiding from the St. Pauli police, a force who to this day are not seeking awards for their scruples, nor given any.

JACKIE LOMAX

allowed more of the person "George" to be "about." By that, I mean I was able to get a better sense of not only how diverse his talent was, but I got a much deeper sense of his gentle personality and how he felt about everyday things. If there was an article in the *LA Times* that day about a man biting a dog, then that was what we would talk about. Being away from the band and England, he seemed to shed most of his "Beatle-George" persona. It came to be that I could be with a Beatle and actually kind of ignore him while I went about other things. He would hang out in my Capitol Tower office sometimes out of boredom, or I would be up at his rented house kicking back, listening to music sometimes, just drifting in and out like old friends.

It may be a semi-shocker to many, but there were basically very few drugs involved in our daily routines. There were times we would just kick back and have a smoke, but it was not an important part of what we were about. That is why it was so amusing when Mama Cass Elliot dropped by the studio where we were working during the production of Jackie's album and pulled out a joint the size of a giant knockwurst. We all laughed, including Cass, without pointing out the obvious, but each of us was thinking the same thing—that it was a Mama Cass-sized reefer!

By now I had become accustomed to (and thereby relaxed with) the people and events that would transpire inside the Fab Four world. So there we were sitting back in the SRS control room chairs on the corner of Argyle and Yucca (virtually a stone's throw from the back door to Capitol's recording studios), getting stoned, and listening to playbacks on Jackie and the *White Album*. Because of the way George presented me to fellow artists like Mama Cass, I always felt I was a validated part of these little gatherings. He had a way with his body language that would suggest we were good friends. This proved to be an unusual and, I might add, very enjoyable part of his character.

While My Guitars Gently Sleep

» *Beverly Hills, California, November 1968*

During George's working weeks in LA, Jackie, Mal, and I left him alone for a few days and headed out on a brief cross-country tour that I had set up to promote Jackie's debut single release on Apple, "Sour Milk Sea/The Eagle Laughs at You." We hit the road hard and heavy for a few days doing the obligatory and all-important TV shows, radio stations, cocktail parties, and press interviews. When it was over, we were pretty fried and quite happy to return to LA and the calm space that the "Quiet Beatle" seemed to create around his personal world. That night when the three of us got back to the house that I had rented for George in Beverly Hills, I collapsed on the conversation pit-style couch before heading home to the Hollywood Hills. It was like I didn't want to go to my place because that meant reality, and returning to reality included getting up the next day to face the giant workload that always piled up during my absence.

Jackie had gone upstairs and was on the phone, while Mal immediately

Opposite, left to right: Ricky Nelson, Kristin Nelson, me, Pattie Harrison, and George Harrison join me to celebrate the launching of my "Hometown Productions, Inc."

crashed in the back bedroom, totally exhausted from the road and his twenty-four-hour-a-day vigil as Jackie's protector. I had joined George and Alan Pariser, and we were just sitting there, kind of staring off in space—just lounging around downstairs, not really saying or doing anything. Nothing was planned for the evening, and we were all tired from our individual day's activities, but you could tell that we hadn't totally given up on the night. Amplifiers and electronic equipment dominated the living room as both George and Jackie were occupying the house and were working on a myriad of things related to Jackie's debut album on Apple.

Rock stars are like hyperactive children in a way, and they can only sit and be quiet for so long.

There was a time that George stored his guitars and things in one of the bedrooms at my house in the Hollywood Hills. I was always a little nervous about the responsibility of caring for these valuable items. The added fact that my house had become the first stop and layover for so many music people from England prompted me to always keep that bedroom closed off. When the house would get full and someone would wonder why they were sleeping on the couch, they would sometimes ask me who was sleeping in that bedroom. I would reply that Mr. Gretsch and his friends slept there.

Suddenly the doorbell broke the silence, and because it was his house, George voluntarily and methodically got up to answer the door. It was Jack Casady from Jefferson Airplane with his bass in hand. He and George had become acquainted along the way, and through mutual relationships between his Artist Relations Department at RCA and Capitol's Artist Relations Department, Jack had found out where we had placed George for his stay. Jack didn't have a phone number for this house, so he just decided to stop by. After a brief exchange of greetings, Jack joined us on the couches, and because he was tired from traveling, it wasn't long before he also drifted out of our non-conversation into the previous quiet.

Fifteen minutes had barely elapsed when the doorbell rang again, and this time it was Eric Clapton, in the very last days of Cream, with travel guitar in hand. Same scenario—hellos—light couch conversation—tiredness sets in—it gets quiet again. Twenty minutes later the doorbell rang once more, and it was Donovan! Now, I have been around a lot of stars, but this was a little different than my normal evening-at-home-on-the-couch routine. Enter Donovan—same format from door to couch except Donovan's guitar was acoustic. Once seated, it took him about ten minutes to attain the level of laid-back stupor we all seemed to have gathered together to enjoy that evening. No doorbell this time, but a few minutes later Jackie sauntered downstairs to join us on the now celebrity-ridden couch. Because he had been on the same whirlwind schedule that day as the rest of us, he immediately went from the hellos into the semi-silence du jour.

Rock stars are like hyperactive children in a way, and they can only sit and be quiet for so long. George finally reached behind the couch and pulled his guitar over his head and on to his lap. He then started quietly noodling on something he was working on, and as attentions and volume increased, he in essence gave us all a nice little twenty-minute performance. As he was winding down, Casady plugged in his bass, gently joined in, and then took over center stage (couch) as George faded back into the impromptu audience. Without hesitation or invitation, Jackie eventually joined in a few minutes later and took over from Jack. This thing was now becoming a full-fledged guitar pull.*

* Nashville, Tennessee, is famous for its guitar pulls. Here is how it works. Several artists, pickers, and/or songwriters will get together in a circle and start passing the guitar around. It usually starts out simple and low-keyed with each person playing a current work in process or new song he's just written. When he finishes his song, the person next to him "pulls" the guitar out of his hand and plays his current fave. This may sound blandly uninteresting and maybe not too exciting, but something always happens during a "pull." Given the artistic makeup and competitive nature of people in the entertainment business, something deep down inside each person in the "pull" makes him want to outdo the person before him. These gatherings eventually take on a life of their own, and by the time you go around the circle a couple of times, you are witnessing Carnegie Hall/Grammy Award caliber performances! All the stops are eventually pulled out, and everyone's best material begins pouring forth.

One other magic "pull" night was at my house in Laurel Canyon when four of us witnessed a "pull" that involved David Cassidy (whose musical talent has always been highly underrated) and Roy Orbison. There is something about sitting on the couch in front of the fire three feet from one of the greatest talents of all time while he is belting his heart out on "Cryin'," "Pretty Woman," "Blue Bayou," and the like. It makes today's "Unpluggeds" seem impersonal at best. My first and still one of my favorite blockbuster "pulls" happened the night I was a guest for dinner at Johnny Cash's house and an after-dinner "pull" developed that included Cash, Waylon Jennings, Jessi Colter, Guy Clark, June Carter, and Rosanne Cash. I have always said that when the cowboys party, they make the rockers look like choirboys with training wheels. This goes double when they start "pulling" the guitar!

Clapton plugged in and worked his way into Jackie's set, and soon he was flying solo. At first it had all been very laid-back, but now it was starting to heat up. Pariser and I were sitting right in the middle of this on the couch, and we quietly melted into the fabric and prayed that this thing wouldn't go away. The last act that night was definitely the headliner. Donovan politely took over and absolutely blew everyone away. His vibrant voice soared softly in that intimate setting; the songs he sang and the unique Celtic-folk-jazz-style on the guitar were beautiful beyond description. In the lighthearted portion of his set, he introduced us to part of an unfinished work—a song entitled "I Love Me Pants." He wound down his portion, easing us back into the state that George had "pulled" us out of with a soft Scottish ballad. Mr. Leitch then quietly set his guitar aside, and we returned to our thoughts. It ended as it began. No one said anything before, during, or after this little flurry of musical genius. The thing that was interesting about this event, and I think it was brought about by the friendships between the people in the room, was how each person communicated his roots that night through his music. No one played what he was known for but instead shared what was natural to them—an inside thing that few people ever get to see. Entertainers are not known as great communicators when things get down to a one-on-one level, but I think each of these friendships grew deeper that night as they shared themselves through their music and got to know a little more about each other. It was pretty and it was poignant, but most of all, it was personal.

When I drove home that night, I was in a trance. They say that big things happen in threes. The three most important musical events I have witnessed in my thirty-plus years in the music business all involved the Beatles: the casual noon cocktail set that they put on for seven of us at lunch during the Apple meetings; this night at George's house where I was in the audience of two; and unquestionably the event of events in my rock-and-roll life—the concert on the Apple roof. There were only about a dozen of us on the roof that day, and although it was their last concert—in my heart it will always be their best.

The next day George and I went to Fred Segal's clothing store to buy jeans.

Track 13

I've Just
Seen a Face

» *Hollywood, California, November 1968*

I think one of the greatest joys I experienced as a result of working for Apple and the Beatles may appear to be the most insignificant. It is somewhat of a personalized version of a steadfast trait I found so attractive about them as a group. It was their loyalty to old friends, being true to their background, and having a sense of who they really were and not what they had become in the world's eyes. I, too, have some old friends, and when I see them, they help me keep on track by reminding me who I really am through our memories.

During George's extended visit to LA, he found himself in Hollywood with an hour or so to kill before he was scheduled to go into the studio. He didn't really have time to go back to where he was staying and he had just come from a luncheon, so he didn't really feel like going to get something to eat to kill time. Instead he just decided to drop by the Capitol Tower and hide out in my office. It was safe there because of the downstairs entrance security and the protective attitude of the secretaries stationed outside our doors. My office was large, so I could continue on with my calls and work schedule while he just hung out in an easy chair in the corner at the other end of the room, reading *Billboard* magazine and making phone calls.

After about thirty minutes, I totally forgot about him being in the office. He had become quietly and totally absorbed in his reading, and as usual I was doing eighty things at once while playing my favorite sport—"catch up ball." The quiet and "game" were interrupted when my secretary buzzed me from outside. She said a Mr. Bing Drastrup was in the lobby, and the receptionist wanted to know if it was OK to let him come to the eighth floor executive offices. I said, "Yes, of course, send him right up."

Like so many of us, I got my start in the entertainment business as an entertainer. During the early '60s folk craze era, I was in a rather successful southern California folk group called the Town Criers. We were signed to a prestigious Beverly Hills management group called Artists Consultants, who worked with acts like Peter, Paul, and Mary and the Gateway Singers during the folk era. For recording, we were signed to Fred Astaire's hot new AVA Records (Elmer Bernstein's "Walk on the Wild Side," Pete Jolly's "Little Bird," or was it "Yellow Bird"?) and were appearing with everyone from Steve Allen and Mitzi Gaynor to Dick Gregory. We were the headliners of Hal Ziegler's 1961 "Hootenanny Tour," which sold out major auditoriums all over the country, and when it looked like the Limelighters were going to break up, we were RCA's top contender as their replacement. Fortunately for me, I knew I didn't have the performing talent or technical musical skills to make a living as an entertainer for the rest of my life, so I opted to put my

I—ARTISTS CONTRACT: VOCALISTS

äva RECORDS

CONTINENTAL BANK BLDG.
8730 SUNSET BLVD., SUITE 404
LOS ANGELES 69, CALIF.

THOMAS DEAN SCALI
ALFRED BING DRESTRUP, JR.
KENNETH FLOYD MANSFIELD
GARY LONG

NAME OF ARTIST

Date April 1 1963

Individually and professionally
known as the "Town Criers"

ADDRESS

Gentlemen:

The following will constitute the agreement of this date between FA Enterprises, Inc., doing business as AVA Records (herein called "Company") and yourself (herein called "Artist"):

1. Company engages Artist's exclusive personal services as a recording artist in connection with the manufacture of phonograph records, for an initial period of 6 months, as the same may be suspended, extended or terminated, commencing on April 1, 1963. Artist accepts such engagement and agrees to perform to the best of his ability at recording sessions conducted by Company at times and places designated by it.

2. Artist and Company agree to record a minimum of 4 7" 45 RPM single record masters, or their equivalent in playing time during the term hereof, and additional masters shall be made at Company's election. Materials to be recorded hereunder shall be selected by Company; each master shall be subject to Company's approval as commercially and Artist agrees to rerecord each selection until a commercially satisfactory master results.

3. Company will pay Artist a royalty based upon ninety per cent (90%) of its net sales of records for w... has been paid, embodying performances of Artist hereunder, as follows:

a. RECORDS SOLD WITHIN THE UNITED STATES:

4 % of the retail list price (less excise and other applicable taxes) thereof.

b. RECORDS SOLD OUTSIDE THE UNITED STATES:

2 % of the retail list price (less applicable taxes) in the United States of America manufacture, England, or the country of sale, at Company's election.

c. 4 % of the retail list price (less applicable taxes) on all sales in the Unit recorded magnetic tapes and all other non-disc type sound reproduction devices, containin hereunder.

d. Royalties on records sold in or as albums will be determined by the suggested for replacement records, exclusive of excise and other applicable taxes.

e. Royalties on foreign sales will be computed in the national currency of the co above provided, and will be deemed earned only when moneys from sales on which such re are received by Company in the United States of America, and at the dollar equivale exchange at the time Company receives payment. Company may elect to accept paymer foreign currency; if lawful, Company will, at Artist's request and otherwise may at its Artist's credit (and at Artist's expense) such foreign currency in a depository selected by royalties accrued in such foreign country. Company will notify Artist thereof promptly accordance with the foregoing shall fulfill Company's obligation under this agreement cable record sales.

FAE: F2(A) 2-63

Bing Drastrup is pictured here shortly after he joined the Town Criers.
Left to right: Steve Isaacson, Tom Scali, Bing with the banjo, and me seated.

Bachelor of Science degree in marketing to use and in time bid adieu to the Town Criers dream and headed for the business side of the music business.

Bing Drastrup was a member of the Town Criers and a good friend and someone I hadn't seen or heard from in a long time. I was so excited that he was in the lobby that without thinking I told them to send him up. A few minutes later my secretary brought him into the office, and it was great to see each other. Our mini-reunion consisted of the usual—hugs, "How are yous?" "Gee, you look greats," "How's such and such?" and other pleasantries. All of a sudden Bing stopped in the middle of our exchange and froze. His eyes got big, his mouth was hanging open, and

One of the greatest joys I experienced as a result of working for Apple and the Beatles may appear to be the most insignificant. It is somewhat of a personalized version of a steadfast trait I found so attractive about them as a group. It was their loyalty to old friends, being true to their background, and having a sense of who they really were and not what they had become in the world's eyes.

he was staring over my shoulder. I turned and remembered George sitting in the corner reading his magazine. He smiled, nodded "Hi" to Bing, and went back to reading. I honestly think that neither George nor I thought anything about it at first or realized how stunned my old friend must have been to walk into a room where a Beatle was casually relaxing in an easy chair in the corner. I introduced them, explained to George the relationship, and then typically, the stance George took during the remainder of our brief three-way chat was that if Bing was my friend, then he was George's friend, too. After about fifteen minutes we all had somewhere to go and walked out together.

I wish Bing could have seen the look on his face when he recognized the face he had just seen.

Track 14

There's a Place

» *London, England—Copenhagen, Denmark, December 1968*

"Let's go to lunch—*there's a place* I like to go." With that Paul McCartney stood up, slipped on a light jacket, and headed out of the Apple offices' front door and out onto the street with me following behind, stumbling like a small child trying to catch up. He had a favorite pub called The Green Man (there are several by this name in London, but there was one in particular that he preferred), and that's where we were going. The pub was actually a rather long way from the Apple offices, and we had to walk right through the heart of downtown London during the busy noontime midweek crowds. It is pretty amazing that he would do this because this was in 1968, and seeing a Beatle in person was a monumental traffic-stopping event in those days.

He set a brisk yet casual pace, which made us less noticeable and helped us blend more into the hurrying crowd around us. As we forged ahead, I would glance back over my shoulder, and it was like looking at the wake behind a speedboat. The people would hurry by, never dreaming they would be bumping against a Beatle, and then suddenly it would register. They would suddenly emerge from their thoughts, stop in their tracks, and then turn around and look after us in transfixed wonder.

We arrived at The Green Man, and inside and out it looked exactly like you would imagine a typical English pub: dark, worn woods, people playing darts and drinking dark pints of ale. In the center was the crowded bar with steak and kidney pie, shepherd's pie, and other rectangular heavy glass dishes and pans filled with hearty-looking foods warming behind the bar.

Our arrival was rather ordinary as far as the reaction from the patrons. Most of them were regulars, as was Paul, and he was able to go there and have a fairly normal lunch. The ruddy English lady behind the bar (Annie) was right out of a Dickens novel. As soon as Paul and I sat down for lunch at the bar, she ran upstairs to her and her husband's apartment above the pub to get something from the stove that she had just cooked. Paul ordered us something that sounded like "Brown and

Paul and me face-to-face at an Apple meeting.

Bitters" (whatever that was) and then spun around, leaned his back against the bar, and began watching the heated dart game that had been going on behind us. There was a relaxed, natural banter going on between the bar patrons, Paul, and the contestants. Compliments and friendly challenges were being issued back and forth between the Beatle and the boys as they would comment on how good his music was and he would note how badly they played darts.

Annie soon returned proudly with a large, steaming hot, glass bowl wrapped in a blue bath towel. Through the sides of the glass I could identify potatoes, carrots, and brown things. I had long ago learned not to ask that the brown things be identified in my English pub food. I smelled it, I tasted it, and if I liked it—I ate it and let it go at that.

She piled our dishes high like she was our mother, not bothering to ask what or how much we would like for lunch. She periodically returned to examine our plates and constantly chided Paul for not eating his vegetables. We were barely finishing our meal when I began to notice how crowded it was in the pub. I turned around, and the entire place was packed beyond standing room only. Paul gave me a couple of light taps with his knee, and as if on some cue based on the tempo of his knee tap, he was up and out through the crowd, out the door, and setting a fast pace streetward back to work. I am sure this was a common procedure and that he had an arrangement with Annie because we didn't pay before leaving. Although he had warned me between bites that a speedy exit was in the works, I still had to fight my way through the crowd, which quickly opened up and made way for him as he left and then quickly closed behind him leaving me to push my way out of the place. Again I was trying to catch up like a little kid running after his dad. By the time I was able to fall in stride with him, we were almost a block away, and the crowd oddly enough held back and let us disappear down the street. It seems that once we had entered the pub, the word started going up and down the road outside that Paul was in The Green Man, and soon everyone was crowding in to get a glimpse.

Once I had matched his pace and we were walking alone, I noticed that it was just like nothing had happened. He said that by this time he was programmed to know about how long he had in any given place, and it was almost like anyone else hurrying through a twenty-minute lunch.

In a way, Paul still couldn't comprehend his fame, and yet as time went by, he had almost unknowingly made subtle adjustments to his lifestyle to account for it. I sometimes feel like I am telling the same story over and over when I reflect on these mini nonevents, but the point is that these guys were such everyday, straight-ahead guys that it was almost easy for me not to be in awe of them when I was working with them on a day-to-day level. They seemed so normal all the time.

We returned to the office and picked up where we left off. This particular trip had a lot to do with our conversation the day I put him on the plane in LA after the Capitol convention. He hadn't forgotten my comment at that time about having never been to Europe. Not only was he largely responsible for me making my first trip to London to be involved in setting up the company, he also seemed to take it upon himself to see that I got over there often.

Before this meeting, I had been in Muscle Shoals, Alabama, with Ric Hall working with him on his newly formed Fame record company. Fame was one of the seven other independent labels distributed by Capitol that I was responsible for in addition to Apple. During lunch, a call came in from Stanley Gortikov in Hollywood. He said Paul needed to see me in London the next day and had set up a 1:00 p.m. meeting for us at the Apple offices. I told Stanley of my artist relations concerns—mainly that Ric could be offended if I just got up and left to go to another, "more important" record company. I also let him know I was a little behind on my rest as I had been on the road for over a month without being able to

In those days I would get out on the road on one assignment, and then crisis after crisis would arise and I would start running from one end of the country to the other for weeks on end.

find my way back home. In those days I would get out on the road on one assignment, and then crisis after crisis would arise and I would start running from one end of the country to the other for weeks on end. Now with London on my plate, I found the daily excursion requirements stretched from Hawaii to London and all points in between. I would get out there and lose all sense of time and location.

I also told Stan that I had no clean clothes and was out of money, and in addition to that, I didn't even know if I could get from Muscle Shoals, Alabama, to London in that short a time due to the limited flight schedule out of that semirural area. After a brief review of (a) my responsibilities, (b) the 50 percent of our business Apple factoid, and (c) the direct relationship between my next paycheck and the Beatles' happiness, I did agree that I could make it. He said he had to go to New York the next day so he would have his secretary ticket him on the "red eye" and have her book me a series of flights so I could hook up with him at JFK. From there I could continue straight on to London. He said he would call my

© www.musicpictures.com

Paul and Apple artist Mary Hopkin discuss Mary's new album, *Postcard* (in Mary's hand).

wife, have her pack for me a fresh bag with proper clothing for that time of year in London, and he would bring it and some cash for Europe. I was instructed to go to the local airport immediately and then call his office to get my flight plan. This was still the 1960s, and you did have to plan your liquid cash and flight schedules a little more carefully because things weren't automated like they are today. I was not only changing a lot of time zones on these trips, but I was also jumping from climate to climate and trying to plan ahead so I would have appropriate clean clothes that could keep me both warm or cool at least most of the time. Hotels do have valet laundry service but not when my typical schedule was to check in at midnight and check out at 5:00 a.m. the next morning.

Getting from Muscle Shoals midday to London and Apple by 1:00 p.m. the next day, with a New York City hook-up with Gortikov, did take some doing. I left Ric Hall wondering "what the hey" happened to our meetings and his record company, swung by my hotel, packed and checked out in ten minutes, and continued on to the first phone booth at the airport as instructed. I called Jane at Stan's office to get my itinerary and almost immediately flew out of the Tri-City airport there—about an hour and a half after receiving the phone call from Gortikov. My first stop was Atlanta, where I changed planes for a flight to Washington DC's Dulles Airport, where I again changed planes to New York City's JFK, where I had an almost Olympic relay hand-off between Gortikov and myself as I rushed to connect with my flight to London. I slept the whole flight, jumped into a waiting car at Heathrow, checked into Claridges, and then concluded this little journey by walking into Paul's office at three minutes before 1:00 p.m., rested and wearing crisp, clean, and warm clothes over a lot of deodorant and shaving lotion. We said "Hi" and proceeded with our meeting like I had just dropped in from across the hall.

The content of our meeting? Paul had the artwork to Apple's Mary Hopkin's *Postcard* album spread out on his desk when I walked in. He invited me to look at it and offer my comments and observations. I said it looked good to me. He said it looked good to him too. After this brief period of review, we decided that we both felt good about it. We were approximately thirty seconds into our 1:00 p.m. meeting when Paul stood up and suggested we should adjourn for lunch at his favorite pub, The Green Man. "By the way, Ken, have you ever been to Denmark?" he asked with an implied wink in his voice. As I followed him out the door, he told me there's a place he wanted me to go. He would like for me to meet with the head of the EMI office in Copenhagen and get his opinion of the album *Postcard* cover. He then said after I returned that I should probably hang out for a while around the Apple offices in case anything important came up. He told me he would notify Gortikov that he needed me for a few days to help him out on the Hopkin project and a few other things. Basically, Paul had just orchestrated a paid vacation in Europe for me. It was generous favors like this that made it hard to refuse him and the other Beatles when they would ask me to go out of my way for them.

When I got off the plane in Copenhagen, the mere fact that I was there on Apple business surprisingly garnered me special treatment. I was met by either royalty or high-ranking government officials and given the red carpet treatment for two days.

Nice town. Very clean.

Track 15

Norwegian Wood—A Separate Reality

» *3 Savile Row, London, England, 1968–1969*

In my opinion, the only person left today who has the right to write the complete Beatles' story is ex-head road manager and now Apple managing director Neil Aspinall. I am honestly beginning to doubt that he will ever be moved to do so, but it still remains that he is, other than Paul and Ringo, the only inner-circle player still here that was truly there for the duration.

There were definite insiders on various levels, of course, but anyone left today outside of Neil can only offer a partial or slanted view at best. (Former General Manager of Apple Records, Jack Oliver, could write the comprehensive Apple story, for instance, as he was there from the very beginning to the very end—but it would take a lot of prodding.) Because most visitors only momentarily occupied an inside position of involvement, they would be subject to the overriding rule of the woodland domain— "unable to see the forest for the trees." I do know one thing: in these woods it wasn't always good—like "Norwegian Wood."

I was not a full-time insider. I wasn't around in the beginning, and when I was around, I wasn't necessarily in a position of everyday confidence. But also I was not weighted down—brought to my knees by the day-to-day intensity of the whole thing—unable to see past, through, around, or into things because it was all so incredibly big. As U.S. manager of Apple Records, I had my own forest to stand in—the corporate world of Capitol Records, Hollywood, USA, where I held the additional title of Director of Independent Labels. The Apple position placed me there in the UK, but I was only inside for days at a time by conditional circumstance or revocable personal invitations from one of the major participants. (Analogically I considered myself an entertainment industry gardener. I had a purpose inside a private place and had a specific job to do, so I was allowed to witness the activity therein as long as I did my job up to their expectations. I was welcome and treated well while I was there but was expected to remain discreet when I left.) The Beatles didn't write these rules—those are the rules for this business.

I would sometimes, by default, get to briefly wear Mal Evans's hat as sidekick because he and Neil couldn't be in four places at one time. It always amazed me how much Mal and Neil had on their plates. They seemed to be responsible for a million things from the mundane to the intricate. Their work was personal, and it was also quantitative. My observation was that they were able to pull off the impossible by making it qualitative. So little time—so many Beatles!

During George's extended visits to Los Angeles during the Jackie Lomax sessions and the remastering of the *White Album*, or the completion phases of *The Concert for Bangla Desh*, I was the guy who received guests at the door, the one on the phone, the person screening the requests, and at the end of the day, I would be the one who rode home with the "Quiet One." Life with George in these situations was always comfortable and natural—almost everyday-like—he made it that way. He was easy to be with, gentle, kind, and caring. Although I was supposed to be taking care of him, he would always concern himself with how I was doing. He had a bashful, soft-spoken manner with friend and stranger alike and always appeared to care about others.

Years later, when I was producing Waylon Jennings, I would join the honky-tonk hero on the road for a few days. I wasn't aboard for the whole tour or a member of the band, but I was traveling on the bus, in the hotel, and hanging out backstage as one of the gang. I had a title (Waylon's producer) and therefore owned a validated spot inside Waylon's superstar world. But when I would begin to sense that I was starting to believe it was all real, I would, figuratively and actually, jump off the bus. After four or five days of the craziness, my internal gyroscope would start spinning out of control, and I would metaphorically emerge from the mist and seek the world for what it really was—a place without the deception of the glad-handlers, screaming crowds, and unending sensual indulgences.

In my metaphysical days, I was a big fan of Carlos Castaneda and was particularly fond of one of his most famous books—*A Separate Reality*. I would always reflect on its central message as a lifeline I could hang on to when it became time to disconnect from the misconception of existence the road can bring. I took away from the book the simplistic interpretation that things are not always as they seem. From there I projected into my life in the entertainment world the operational knowledge that I should never let the abstract become the front line. Real things are not real if their basis comes out of an unsubstantiated nowhere. I call it the "believing in skyhooks" syndrome. Accolades and adoration for being able to sing and whip your hips in a suggestive manner all at the same time do not make someone a master of all

An informal meeting on the floor of the newly decorated but unfurnished Apple offices at 3 Savile Row. Clockwise from the top—Ringo, Peter Brown, George, Apple staffer, Stanley Gortikov, Larry Delaney, me, and Peter Asher.

intelligentsia. Some of my most bizarre, clinging-to-the-edge friends were sought out for their wisdom just because they were famous. If these same people broke a shoelace in the morning, they were lost for the day, and yet the words that literally escaped from their numbed brains were taken as gospel truth and lives were shaped after their insane verbiage. When I was out there with a famous entertainer or group, I found it was easy to get caught up in what was going on, especially when that fantasy-in-motion world began to seem like the real world. Eventually it became hard not to believe that this separation from reality had something to do with actual life on planet Earth.

If there ever was a separate reality, I experienced it the minute I walked through the doors at 3 Savile Row. The only thing that kept me from biting on the inviting Apple-illusion that lay therein was the mere fact that I was coming and going. I knew it would take more than a kiss to wake me up out of that dream, and fortunately I was never there long enough to completely succumb to its mesmerizing altered state of rock

When I was out there with a famous entertainer or group, I found it was easy to get caught up in what was going on, especially when that fantasy in motion world began to seem like the real world. Eventually it became hard not to believe that this separation from reality had something to do with actual life on planet Earth.

and roll. But I was there, both as an observer and a participant, and so I can more than imagine what it was like for the full-time staffers. They spent the whole of their semi-waking hours in a Mersey beaten vortex pressurized by the intense focus of a sociopolitically shipwrecked youth screaming to be heard above the sound of real social revolution and the deafening heartbeat of this hard driving band.

How can anyone wake up, fall out of bed, run a comb across his head, and work those long hours under that extreme pressure without losing touch with the reality that surrounds the dream that he "went off into"? Individually, the Beatles were incredible people. Collectively, they attracted a sterling staff—an improbable gathering of rock-and-roll angels that graced the core of the Apple. On a street-level analytical basis, I would also like to lovingly add that the members of the Apple crew were the oddest flock of ducks I had ever met.

I walked away from that building many times, but I will never be able to leave behind the memories of those people and events.

Real or unreal, it will never happen again.

Individually, the Beatles were incredible people. Collectively, they attracted a sterling staff— an improbable gathering of rock-and-roll angels that graced the core of the Apple.

Imagine There's No Heaven

» *Los Angeles, California—London, England, 1965–1976*

I am constantly asked if I had the chance to get to know any of the Beatles individually and personally during the years I spent with them. I always respond that, yes, I was fortunate to spend time alone and share a comfortable and personal relationship on some level with each of them, except for John Lennon.

In the early years, he appeared distant and shy but never difficult in my presence. I look back now at pictures of us taken at the August 1965 press conference when we first met, and remember what an intelligent and relatively pleasant fellow he was then, even though he may not have been as accessible as the other three. By the summer of '68 when Apple was cranking up, I noticed a dramatic change. Yoko was encouraging him to get involved in world visionary projects, basically expanding his perception of the powerful social dynamics of rock and roll; by the beneficial utilization of his fame in promoting change. One thing didn't change though—John carried his heart on his sleeve, and from that same sleeve there was always a gentle hand extended that willingly and naturally wanted to reach out to everyone around him.

Occasionally I would find myself positioned next to Yoko at a meeting or an event. (That's me in the white trench coat sitting on the bench with her, Chris O'Dell, and Maureen Starr in the *Let It Be* film and in photographs of the January 1969 rooftop concert.)

While John would always converse normally with me, she would not give me the conversational time of day. I always felt that maybe I was too common or that she was too intellectual to exchange ideas with just anyone. Whether this observation came out of her reality or my own insecurities was of no import—she was with John, I was with Apple, and my instructions from Capitol were crystal clear: "keep it together!" In retrospect, I simply think she may have just had a lot of things on her mind, and also these were pretty heady times in which she and John were under a lot of scrutiny and hurtful criticism. I can avow at best to be a total non-authority in matters of "The Ballad of John and Yoko." In fairness to Yoko, I must confess that she always treated me courteously and with respect, albeit subdued in enthusiasm. The one thing I can avow is that when she was in the room, she definitely never went unnoticed! She could do more with being quiet than anyone I have ever known.

As the curtain began to be drawn on the '60s, on Apple, and on the Beatles as a working band, John seemed to grow increasingly bitter, angry, and cynical. It was probably more apparent to me because of the length of time between my short visits. At times it was hard for me to be

John wanted confrontation to have its own page in the dictionary. When he looked for an apartment, as the joke would have it, he wanted one with a dissenting view.

around him, especially when he and Yoko would team up on me. If you wanted to see what a guy from Idaho looked like when he was wishing he was back on the banks of the Clearwater River, all you had to do was walk into the room when they were two-teaming me with their sociopolitical worldviews that I couldn't even begin to comprehend. While I was wondering where I was going to get my Cadillac convertible waxed when I returned to LA, they were proselytizing about world hunger. I honestly believe that balance should be one of everyone's great goals in life; John and I were obviously at opposite ends of the philosophic playing field. Spiritually and politically, we knew we weren't even close enough to muster up the content for a meaningful discussion. I knew about Carnauba (car wax), and they knew about Sai Baba (a famous Indian guru). I thought they needed to lighten up. I know now that I needed to get a clue about what was going on in the world around me.

Early on in the game of life and especially in the Super Bowl of mind games, the entertainment industry, I decided there were two ways to approach matters: be naive or be cynical. I chose naiveté because it was a lot more fun, and one of the perks was that you never had to take anything too seriously. Being a cynic was a full-time job and a downer. Also, you could never take any time off. I avoided conflict at all cost; John wanted confrontation to have its own page in the dictionary. When he looked for an apartment, as the joke would have it, he wanted one with a dissenting view.

Mind Games

One day in early 1969, John and Yoko called me into their ground-floor office at 3 Savile Row to talk about a record that George had brought to Apple's attention. John wanted it released in the United States and wanted me to explain my negative position on the record. Because of his passion for the project, I assumed it was his baby and didn't find out until later that he was championing the cause of his bandmate. I wondered why George wasn't in on this meeting, but looking back I now realize the deeper content of the day's dialogue was really John's department; John and Yoko sat shoulder to shoulder behind one long desk that dominated the whole end of the room. My chair seemed smaller than most, and I'm sure to this day that they had the legs shortened so their guests/victims would feel even smaller than they already did in their presence.

The recording in question was "The King of Fuh" by an American singer who called himself Brute Force. Unfortunately the lyrics, due to creative repositioning, were so blatantly objectionable by American standards that Capitol Records would have been crazy to consider releasing it.

Apple

Dear Ken   re. Life with the Lions

We'd like the Zapple label
to be SILVER not white - it's
more subtle! o.k?

Also it must be out sooner
than June 2nd. Yoko and I
hope to be there (N.Y.) MAY 20th.
— don't spread it round (too much)
until you hear from Derek Taylor.

∴ MAY 15th — U. CAN DO IT!
love
John + Yoko xx.

This letter and drawing were mailed directly to me at the Capitol/Apple offices in Hollywood, California, the first week of May 1969.

Of special note:

- The letter is handwritten by John Lennon on original Apple stationery.

- It includes a line drawing self-portrait by John of him and Yoko.

- It is possibly the only personal document written by Lennon concerning his pet project—the Zapple label. (The Zapple series was conceived as a subsidiary of Apple Records which would accommodate spoken word, avant garde, and experimental recordings. Zapple's first two releases were George's *Electronic Sound* and John and Yoko's *Life with the Lions*. Names like Ken Kessey, Lawrence Ferlinghette, Charles Bukowski, Charles Olsen, and Richard Brautigan were also batted about as potential artists for the label.)

- Lennon shows in this letter his personal involvement with Zapple and his availability to further the project.

- This letter was written by John Lennon during a time of heightened activity in his life (April 21, 1969–May 16, 1969). He had just formed his and Yoko's film and production company, Bag Productions (April 21, 1969), had changed his middle name from Winston to Ono in a formal ceremony on the roof of the Apple (April 22, 1969), bought Tittenhurst Park, a mansion in Sunnydale, Ascot, Berkshire (May 4, 1969), and signed a business management contract with Allen Klein, along with Ringo and George—Paul refused (May 8, 1969). John was also applying for a United States Visa in preparation for his trip to New York (referred to in this letter) to stage a "bed in." The visa was rejected on May 16, 1969.

- Of special interest is the additional Apple/Zapple historical aspect of his request to change the label color and what could be considered as Lennon shorthand (rond for round, U for you), or simply misspelling.

explained that I couldn't release a record in the United States on Apple or any other label with that kind of lyric. It would be a "brown paper bag under the counter" type of thing at best. Then they started in on me: "We thought you were one of us, Ken . . . but it looks like you are just one of the establishment like everyone else, after all. . . . We thought we could trust you of all people to understand the concept behind the whole Apple enterprise. . . . We didn't know you were sent over here from the 'land of the free' to act as Apple's personal tight-assed censor!"

Mere words can't explain how intimidating they were. From a cowering position it was hard, but I tried to explain it had nothing to do with me or Stanley Gortikov or Capitol Records or any of our personal beliefs. It had to do with FCC regulations, other legalities, and the like. I never quite got the sense in this particular matter that I totally convinced them that I was indeed "one of them." Looking back over this lyric debate really makes it easy to see the separate worlds we lived in and how times have changed since then. These days no one would probably even comment on this lyric or the *Two Virgins* album cover.

Tell Me What You See

I will never forget the first time I saw the picture for the *Two Virgins* album jacket. It was 1968, and London was beautiful that summer. We were ensconced in a private suite in a Hyde Park hotel, holding meetings with all four Beatles, Neil Aspinall, Ron Kass, Mal Evans, Peter Asher, Stanley Gortikov, Larry Delaney, and Yoko. I left the meeting for a few minutes of attitude adjustment with Mal and had just returned to take my place that particular day on the couch with John and Yoko. Quietly, John leaned over, put his hand on my shoulder, placed a packet of photos on my lap, and asked me to "check 'em out." I pulled a dozen or so 8 x 10s out of the envelope and went into executive shock. "Just keep it together, the

Kass said the reason John
because he felt comfortable

Beatles are 50 percent of Capitol's business," and other Hollywood job security related admonitions began ringing loudly in my ears. I became transfixed, staring at an armload of nude pictures of him and Yoko. I incorrectly thought John was making some kind of perverted sexual move on me involving his mate, and I didn't know how to respond. Following what I thought was John's lead was totally out of the question, but being so focused on "keeping it together" made me very sensitive to possibly offending him through rejection and thereby losing my job. The wheels were spinning at warp speed in my head. I suddenly became acutely aware that I was just a simple, inexperienced young man in a strange, foreign place. I didn't have a clue as to exactly what the ground rules were in matters such as these. I certainly wasn't equipped to handle it. I guess my reaction was fairly noticeable because when I looked up in desperation toward Stan Gortikov for help, Paul started laughing and came to my rescue.

It seems that while Mal and I were out of the room, John had brought up the subject of his desired approach for the *Two Virgins* artwork and had shown the nude photographs to everyone in the room. Mal and I had missed this presentation, and so I was shown the pictures without any advance instruction. Paul picked up on my dilemma, and after letting me sweat it out for a little while, he finally decided to interrupt my imagined fall from corporate and mop-top grace and filled me in on what transpired while I was out of the room. I thanked him later, in private, and I asked him, also in private, what he thought of the nude photos bit. He responded that he was totally with John in the matter. He didn't understand John's thinking but figured that John was intellectually ahead of him in this area and that he would just have to catch up. He said he was sure at some point that he *would* catch up and *then* he would be in complete agreement with John. Why haven't I ever had a friend like that?

was so aggresive was being open with me.

Day Tripper

I was always nervous about what John was thinking and if I was "keeping it together" as far as he was concerned. He used to call me, write me caustic letters, send obscenity-laced transatlantic cables to my office in Hollywood, and constantly badger me on a variety of topics, especially those concerning projects on his beloved Zapple record label. Zapple was Apple's experimental sound sister label, which was only to release two albums, John and Yoko's *Unfinished Music No. 2: Life with the Lions* and George Harrison's *Electronic Sound*. He would communicate encouragement to me when he wanted something done and relay his devastating disappointment in me when he thought I wasn't performing up to speed on Zapple matters.

One time, a person that resembled my image of a raving lunatic more closely than any person I had ever seen parked himself in the Capitol Records lobby and informed the receptionist that John Lennon had sent him to see me. He wasn't leaving until he had a proper audience with me as John had instructed and intended. By this point in my relationship with the Apple crew, nothing surprised me. I knew I would have to give this whole scenario a 50-50 chance of being exactly "as John had intended." I told them to send the fellow up to my office where he uniquely occupied a large easy chair without completely bending at the waist. He had, after much practice I'm sure, accomplished a 45-degree liquid linear approach to being seated.

He was more than wild-eyed; he was what we called in Idaho "wall-eyed." He eventually organized his one man free-for-all into the following pitch: According to him, John had prepared a list of two hundred names of Southern California musicians, artists, poets, and miscellaneous free spirits. He was in possession of this list, and I was to immediately buy first-class one-way tickets to London for this elect group. It seems that John had advised this abstract ambassador from a real nowhere land that the whole of Southern California was going into the ocean in two days, and he wanted to have this particular group preserved for his personal jam sessions and round-about intellectual gatherings in the UK. The only thing odder than the wall-eyed's presentation was the fact that, until I could confirm otherwise, I absolutely had no other option but to entertain the possibility that John was actually behind this, although I did have serious doubts. The question in the back of my mind was: "Why wasn't I on that list? If California was going into the ocean, why wouldn't he want the guy that was working on his Zapple project saved?" I was the one on this side of the Atlantic with all the information in my head, I had the artwork for the covers on my desk, I had been in all the meetings, and I was working on a deadline for him that very day. If I went into the westerly waters, he would have to start all over again with a new boy and lose a lot of time.

Fortunately I was able to track John down while my new friend took advantage of the kind attentions of my secretary by enjoying about twenty-three cups of coffee with seven sugars each. He seemed surprisingly undisturbed when I told him that John had never heard of him or his ideas. He wished me a nice day, asked my secretary if she had a paper cup for one more coffee to go, and simply walked out to the elevator and left. At first I marveled how good-natured he was about the whole thing. He was so intent of purpose and clear of mission when he walked in. Later on I decided he had probably forgotten what he came to see me about in the first place. I also felt a lot better knowing that John hadn't left me off the list.

I Should Have Known Better

Not all of my memories of John are of an angry young man. In the fall of '69, the Beatles were riding high on the crest of the phenomenal success of the *Abbey Road* album. I felt as though I knew him well enough by this time and had been through enough with him throughout the years to ask just one fan-type question about one of his more oblique lyrics from that album. He was in a particularly receptive mood one day, so I thought I would ask my first Beatles trivia question. The reason I was so hesitant was because I had seen how incessant the fans and writers were in asking the same incredibly dumb things over and over again. Even though each of the Beatles usually handled them graciously, I could see it was irritating, and they didn't need the people who worked with them doing the same thing. Anyway, I saw an opening, and after all, I had been saving up for this: "'*She's well acquainted with the touch of the velvet hand like a lizard on a window pane,*' (from "Happiness Is a Warm Gun"). What does that *mean*, anyway?" I asked off-handedly, hoping that a casual approach would better my chances of a comradely-type response.

He grinned and replied, "Nothin'. I just made it up." Smiling gently, he continued softly as if he were confiding a secret with me. "We've learned over the years that if we wanted we could write anything that just felt good or sounded good, and it didn't necessarily have to have any particular meaning to *us*. As odd as it seemed to us, reviewers would take it upon themselves to interject their own meanings on our lyrics. So, why 'strain me brain'? Sometimes we sit and read other people's interpretations of our lyrics and think, 'Hey, that's pretty good.' If we liked it we would keep our mouths shut and just accept the credit as if it was what we meant all along."

It is unfortunate, but I fear most people never got to see this casual, lightness of being aspect of John Lennon. I am personally offended by the disproportionate amount of negative verbiage written about other areas of his brilliant life.

Tomorrow Never Knows

Years later I was sitting in a London café with former Apple president Ron Kass. We were reminiscing about the Apple days and the four "lads." When I mentioned that I felt I had never quite gotten to know John, he seemed very surprised. Kass said that out of the four, it was John who had been the most expressive to him about liking me. Kass said the reason John was so aggressive was because he felt comfortable being open with me. In his way, it was his manner of trusting me.

Up until then it would have been easier to imagine there was no heaven than to imagine myself as one of John Lennon's favorites. The funny thing about this revelation was in how I perceived John Lennon's music after that. I became a bigger fan and developed a greater appreciation of his lyrics, and now I actually become uncomfortable listening at times because it all sounds so personal.

I Don't Want to Spoil the Party

On June 12, 1976, I unexpectedly ran into John at Ringo's house in Beverly Hills. I had just finished producing Waylon Jennings's new album *Are You Ready for the Country* for RCA Records Nashville. Ringo, who was a big fan of Waylon, had called and asked for an early listen. When I walked into the living room at Ringo's house, I was surprised to see John slouched moodily on the couch. Knowing what I know now, he must have really liked me that day because he had never been meaner. He was in LA for his last recording session for almost four years, playing piano on his composition "Cookin' (In the Kitchen of Love)" for Ringo's Atlantic album *Rotogravure*. No doubt he had dropped in to relax and be alone with his old friend and bandmate. I had unwittingly been cast as an intruder by Ringo's invitation that day. As it happened I needed a lyric change approval from at least three of the Beatles on a female version of "Hey Jude," which we retitled "Hey Dude," that I had cut with Jessi Colter ("I'm Not Lisa") for Capitol Records.

I had bribed Ringo for his signature with a private, exclusive playback of Waylon's album.

I bribed Paul by sending him a pair of sunglasses from Rodeo Drive that he had seen in a fashion magazine.

I took advantage of John's mood and bribed him by leaving Ringo's house. I never saw him again.

(Why Couldn't They Just) Let It Be

» *London, England, January 1969*

I had the good fortune to go to various Beatle recording sessions, but going to *their* sessions was a little different than most. Even though we Appleites were among the privileged few who got to attend a Beatles session, usually we were never actually in the studio with them. The privilege of attending one of these happenings basically consisted of being invited to hang out in the halls and the lobby of the studio where they were recording. Occasionally, one of them would come out on a break or hang out with us for a while. You could hear the muffled music behind the doors get loud and clear during the few seconds it would be open as they or the recording team would go in and out. It was still an elitist event being seen by the fans as we were going in and out of the heavily guarded entrance to the studio.

This was not the case in the *Let It Be* sessions. Because the studio was downstairs in the basement of the Apple building, the Beatles would more or less merge into the studio from within the building, and the whole atmosphere was a little more relaxed and natural and conducive to a creative mind-set. One day George interrupted a meeting between Kass and me with a question on a personal business matter. As he apologized for the interruption and quietly made his exit, he stopped and turned in the doorway and asked if I would like to come "down" to the session. I looked at Kass—he looked at his watch as if to say, "Why don't you go ahead—I've got a lot to do." I think I saw an exchange between them in a glance. I know how Ron Kass thought and did things, and I know how he always treated me special. I am sure to this day that he had prearranged the interruption and invitation with all four of the "lads." It was just an experience that he wanted me to have, and George was the soft-spoken messenger.

The day I was invited into the *Let It Be* sessions at the Apple studios was second only to the concert on the roof when it comes to experiencing rock-and-roll genius. I was not only blown away with being one of only two people in the studio (not the lobby, not the control room, but the actual recording studio) with the four Beatles, but through this experience I was given the gift of understanding the very essence of this four-piece band. I never realized how good they were until I sat on the floor leaning against the wall for hours and watched them just play their instruments. Every one was, as we would say in Nashville, a really great picker. I was especially impressed with Ringo—he was the perfect drummer for this band. He laid it right in the pocket and knew how to weave his rhythms in and out and behind and in support of the raw

I never realized how good they were until I sat on the floor leaning against the wall for hours and watched them just play their instruments. Every one was, as we would say in Nashville, a really great picker.

intricacies of his bandmates. In simplistic terms, he knew how to stay out of the way when it was appropriate, the true sign of a confident, professional drummer. Paul had the appearance of an eternal force pushing the band all the time; John's genius would surface, and everyone knew when to fall behind this expression; George, like Ringo, knew how to be supportive of the band as a whole and then would, like everything else in his life, present his unique style gently into the mix of creative musical Liverpuddlian stew. Even when George was blazing forth with electronics seething and screaming, it was always right on—like righteous sonic anger.

The *Let It Be* sessions were an incredible experience for me and the other invited guest in the room—an old friend and associate who was just as surprised to be there as I was—Billy Preston. Billy was a Capitol artist and had a very aggressive manager who would virtually camp out at my office in the Hollywood Capitol Tower in the days/years before this time. Gene Taft was his name, and Gene was an "in the trenches, in your face" manager; nothing was ever good enough for his artist. He was even critical of the way I dressed when we were doing promotions for Billy Preston to the point of paying to have my suits altered so they would fit better and getting me ties to match my wardrobe. Billy and I knew each other as an eager young rising executive (me) and an unknown struggling artist with a lot of promise and a major recording contract (Billy). Now, instead of sitting in my office at Capitol with Gene, we were sitting in the most famous room in the musical world—that is, whatever room the Beatles were recording in at that time. I sat there with fixated eyes and my mouth hanging open (I hope I wasn't drooling). I was transfixed by what was going on and in total awe of just how good these guys really were. Off to my right and seated about six feet away, Billy was leaning over his keyboard, hands in his lap, with the biggest grin on his face. Every once in a while, he looked over at me with an even bigger smile and a look on his face as if to say, "Wow, did you just hear that?"

As the sessions unfolded in front of me, the Beatles played, argued, and worked on something for days only to throw it out. The recording concept was unique and a pleasure to watch unfold. In the studio, lights

Opposite page: Me and Ringo chatting at the Apple offices at 3 Savile Row. That's Jackie Lomax's promo picture on the wall. The two ladies are Apple staffers.

were glaring and film cameras were rolling. In the control room, the tape was rolling all the time. The walls were stacked almost floor to ceiling with two-inch master tapes. Theoretically, Glyn Johns was engineering and George Martin was producing, but in reality it looked like their roles were a little less defined. To an observer it would appear that they shared the production responsibilities for the project. I find it interesting that when the "Get Back" single was released, no producer credit was listed at all, making George Martin's official involvement a little more unclear, even though he was there and he was their producer.

The Beatles took the approach of recording the songs from beginning to end in the studio. Writing, arranging, rehearsing, recording, and

acceptance of final takes were one continuous process. I would see a song grow from inception to the point that one of them would turn around and look in the booth for George's approval and then say, "Let's hear that one." If they liked it, then that was the album master. The idea was to have "live" takes. Looking back, I find it ironic that the album from these sessions, *Let It Be*, which was issued more than one year later, featured music that was anything but "live." It wasn't until the Apple-approved *Let it Be . . . Naked* CD arrived more than thirty years later that the intended "bare bones" approach to the music was finally heard. I will never forget hearing the newly released *Naked* version for the first time. It was a Christmas present from my kids shortly after its release. Decades had

It was a special time in the recording business because everything was changing—music, mores, and mankind. I wish we could "get back." For some of us, it's hard to just "let it be" in the past.

passed since I'd sat on the studio floor in the Apple basement hearing the sweet rawness of this fabulous band, and I honestly couldn't believe I had forgotten how incredible the intent and concept of the original recordings had been. I was taken aback by my reaction and surprised to find myself crying. Those days and those sounds flooded over me in a dreamy retroactive rush as I began remembering what it was all like back then. The jagged expressions that lived in the original sessions came alive, and I was so glad that others would finally get to hear what it was really all about when the greatest rock band of all time was getting back to where they once truly belonged. I miss who we were and our innocence; I miss that special time and the music that was so possible then. I especially miss them.

Pressing schedules and commitments back in my mother country pulled me off the floor, away from the wall, out the Apple door, down the street, and up to my hotel room to pack. It was cold and gray outside, and the huddled hurrying people rushing by in the streets that seemed to be the unreal ones. I felt like I did when I was a kid coming out of a Roy Rogers movie. I always felt like the hero for the first ten minutes or so after walking out of the dark theater into the mundane hometown street. Didn't these people know I had just been in a Beatles session and what a major big deal it was? How can they be concerned with daily financial matters, political concerns, and daily routines? I slowly decompressed into their reality, knowing that it was time to return to mine.

It was Tuesday in London and time to go. I would walk into my Hollywood office Wednesday morning relaying instructions on the go and piling papers on my secretary's desk. Rocky Catena, Maurie Lathower, Jack Snyder, Lew Marchesi, Hal Rothberg, Larry Delaney, Fred Rice, Roger Karshner, Bob York, Al Coury, and Brown Meggs, my executive cohorts in Capitol crime, would all drop into the office within the first hour, say their quick hellos, ask how it went, and then dump responsibilities in my lap that had piled up in my absence. We had a really special group of executives at that time (the late '60s) that genuinely liked each other and liked working with and for one another.

As I look back now I feel so fortunate not only to have been part of this special team but to also have been part of the record business in all its shallow crassness when it still had a sense of purity about it. I knew I was the hot dog of this group, but they excused me for my youth, tolerated my humor, and respected the giant load of my responsibility by pitching in, covering up, and taking up the slack in my long absences. We were not that well paid, and for the most part we were there because we were drawn. You could still believe in something just because you had a feeling and then jump headlong into the project feet and heart first with all your energies, money, and time devoted to some new artist's music. Now the machinery is so big and so complicated, the stakes are so high, and the overhead so gigantic that it is no longer a business based on creativity and heart but one run by accountants, investors, agencies, powerful management teams, and lawyers. I am tempted to interject the word *ruthless* somewhere in the preceding sentences but will leave that up to you.

In those days the eighth floor of the Capitol Tower housed the marketing, merchandising, sales, press, and publicity departments and my whole operation, which included artist relations, promotion, radio and television services, and internal management of the independent labels. This floor and the twelfth floor, where all the producers and A&R execs lived, were really the throbbing creative centers of this odd round building located at the once cool Hollywood and Vine intersection of Hollywood, USA.

It was a special time in the recording business because everything was changing—music, mores, and mankind. I wish we could "get back." For some of us, it's hard to just "let it be" in the past.

••••●•••

I received word a couple years ago that one of "the gang," Rocco Catena, was not well and was living in an assisted-care facility and was fading away to the point that we did not know how much longer he would be with us. I was able to track down Mauri Lathower and Roger Karshner and arrange for us to go pick up Rocco and take him to an Italian restaurant not far from the "home." It was one of the sweetest gatherings I have ever attended. We had so much history between us and had shared such a special time, and the fact that we all really cared about each other back then meant that there were no bad memories to get in the way. The only downer was having to accept the fact that eventually we were going to start losing members of our group. Rocco now lived much of his current days in a world of his own, and you could see recognition go in and out as we spent the afternoon together. There were times that we would try to recall past events and highlights of our years at Capitol, and it was easy to see that "Rocky" didn't have a clue what we were talking about. It blew me away, though, when Mauri started telling an obscure story about a jazz band that he and Rocky had something to do with a thousand years ago in Chicago before the Hollywood Capitol days and Rocky stopped him, corrected him, named every band member, what instrument he played, and the exact year and day that the event took place.

Rocky wasn't allowed to drink anything alcoholic as part of his residency rules, so we had agreed that there would be no drinking at lunch.

When the waitress took our order and asked if we would like anything to drink with our meal, we all ordered a soda or plain water out of respect for Rocky's restriction. When she got to him, he got this look he used to get on his face forty years ago when it was "mischief" time with this crew, and he ordered a glass of Chianti to go with his pasta. Something about this breaking away from the routine at the home seemed to clear away so many things, and for the entire meal he totally joined us in our reunion. When we took him back to the lobby, he changed, and it was almost as if at that point of disconnect he didn't remember us as we tried to say our goodbyes. As an attendant took him by the arm, he seemed to lower his head and shuffle as he walked away.

Rocky passed away not long afterward.

I am not trying to make a real analogy here, but I think to Roger, Mauri, and me, the feeling we had as we walked away from Rocky is similar to when John Lennon was taken away from the other three Beatles. There are things that just can't be replaced in our lives. I am personally glad that at least we had the chance to say goodbye.

Capitol gang reunites around Rocco Catena.
Left to right: Mauri Lathower, Roger Karshner, me, and Rocco.

Track 18

Up on the Roof

❱❱ *3 Savile Row, London, England, January 1969*

As I mentioned earlier, if I had to single out one event that stood out above all the others during the time I worked with the Beatles, it would by far be their last concert. That event presented the end of a time warp, an intimate gathering, a worldwide event—I'm referring to their concert on the roof of Apple Records during the cold midday of Thursday, January 30, 1969. The fact that I ended up becoming a small part of the historical musical phenomenon called the Beatles began with being in the right place at the right time. The fact that I was working at Apple in London when this event took place is probably the penultimate example of the good fortune in my entertainment business life.

The *Let It Be* recordings (which were called *Get Back* at that stage) were wrapping up, and we still hadn't accomplished the live footage segment that was planned for the movie. Apple executive Jack Oliver, who, at that time, was the head of the production department and the foreign department, told

Opposite page: I (in the white trench coat) huddle from the cold against the chimney between Yoko, Maureen Starkey, and Apple staffer Chris O'Dell, while the Beatles perform "live" for the last time.

The Apple Building
3 Savile Row
London, England

me that they had tried to schedule a club in Germany by booking the Beatles in under a different name—"Ricky and the Red Streaks." (Jack revealed to me recently that the reason he and I spent so much time communicating with one another was because *I* was a foreigner and therefore was *his* responsibility.) The idea was to sneak the lads in, and when the local patrons showed up at this small club to see this new group from England, they would get the surprise of their lives when the Beatles walked out on stage and did an "à la Cavern" show. This club gig would be filmed for footage in the *Let It Be* film. Of course, this was a great idea, but as you can imagine, it was in reality an unkeepable secret. Word would always get out before the show date, and the usual media madness would begin.

Then came the craziest and most short-lived idea for a concert: Mal and I had been given the brief assignment of scouting out deserts for a giant, one-time, free Beatles concert. Mal was to check some African deserts, and I was to look at locations in our southwestern United States. The idea would to be to set up in the middle of nowhere, announce a date, and then invite anyone and everyone who wanted to come see the Beatles perform live—for free! It didn't take long to come to the realization that the logistics and realities of this idea were preposterous to say the least. First of all, every kid in the world would be trekking to this location, and the mass numbers would be overwhelming. Forget about staging, sound systems, accommodations, and travel. It was the stark reality of not having enough toilets that killed this idea. Besides, who was going to pay for all this? How would you like to look for an insurance underwriter for this Fab Four fiasco? We figured only about half the people would return alive from this adventure. It would end up being every concert nightmare rolled up into one, multiplied by the tenth power. The Rolling Stones' Altamont concert would look like a prayer meeting in comparison.

The Beatles had a frustrating problem. They were a performing-live-in-your-face-rock-and-roll band. Their immense fame swept them up and away from the very thing they did best and loved the most—rocking out in the purest rock-and-roll sense to a breathing, sweating live audience with a front row only a few feet away. I can remember conversations that addressed their performance issues all the way back to the original Apple meetings. They were in the awkward position of suffering from their own colossal celebrity. John expressed it best when he said that "people have built us up so big in their minds that there is no way that we could go out on stage and live up to their expectations." *Sgt. Pepper* only made matters worse. A formal "live" concert tour was out of the question no matter how many times they brought it up, but they still had the need and desire for a live show.

The roof was a last-minute and logical answer to getting live footage for the film. Apple staffers, stage crews, and carpenters readied the roof surface and the film and recording electronics. It was an actual gig. There was a time and a place and a band. There was no advance publicity, but we definitely ended up with an audience. As zero hour neared (I think it was Mal who locked the downstairs doors), staffers, stagers, and stars alike all became willing prisoners of the love of history and music that wonderful day at 3 Savile Row. A sense of calm mixed with anticipation filled the air once the doors were locked, and there was no doubt that it was a go. We were just kids playing with things bigger than we understood. It was just us and it felt good; it was personal; it was special, a gathering of rock-and-roll angels expecting to fly. Words and music soon soared out of the very heart of the staid financial district and into the ears and souls of the unexpecting people on the streets. London was the center of cutting-edge music, and in the neighboring buildings of this vibrant city, secretaries, bankers, and deliverymen alike were jolted alive by the rockin' that was rollin' off the Apple rooftop. Everyone within a mile of that place that day will proudly state for the rest of their lives that they were there the day the music came wafting down the streets, echoing and slamming up against the red brick buildings; melodies and rim shots blew in through the cracks and into board meetings, while Lords and loonies alike stood frozen up and down the row, necks craned upward to the rooftops. They knew immediately who it was—they were just trying to work out what was happening. These were not the usual sounds coming down the roads of London's staid financial district at lunchtime.

Soon the streets and sidewalks were clogged by voluntary standstill, open windows started dotting the sides of the once sealed buildings, and bodies started lining the ledges of the adjoining structures. It was all so unexplainable yet so incredibly wonderful. For a while I stood a few feet from George with four lit cigarettes between my fingers so he could reach over and warm the tips of his fingers. Chris O'Dell (Peter Asher's assistant), Yoko Ono, Maureen Starkey, and I huddled together against the smokestack on the roof for warmth. I had an unlined white raincoat that became frozen stiff and offered little protection from the cold. I was a total Southern Californian who hadn't experienced a real winter in many years and hated it when the weather started dipping down into the low fifties, but you could have hosed me down in my shorts with ice water and I wouldn't

I'm in the white trench coat talking to Apple staffer Kevin Harrington. To my left (behind George and John) is *Let It Be* film director Michael Lindsay-Hogg. Yoko is still huddled against the chimney trying to get warm.

If you ever want to find out just single unit, a live, four-piece, live recordings of the concert

have left this "happening" on the roof for all the money in the world.

If you ever want to find out just how good the Beatles were as a single unit, a live, four-piece, rock-and-roll band, just listen to the live recordings of the concert on the roof that day. Almost every conceivable obstacle was set before them. Forget about the pressures of the Apple empire, but just consider that this was a band that hadn't done a live show since August 29, 1966, at San Francisco's Candlestick Park, *and* this was a group of still idealist young men who were dealing with some very heavy internal business problems and dissension that touched each of them deeply. They also had a deadline, and I might mention that it was windy, damp, and frighteningly cold up on that roof that day. Just listen to how well they played and sang in those conditions. After thirty years in the heart of the record business, and off stage, on stage, and backstage with everyone from Roy Orbison to Don Ho, I personally feel that this was the greatest rock-and-roll band of all time. Their fame wasn't a Milli Vanilli happenstance. They made it because, as Ringo simply mused, "We were a good band."

It was maybe the smallest event inside this day that I remember the most. We had set a "lunchtime" show time, and the Beatles all showed up in time to be on stage at that time. I walked into the office that they were gathered in as a dressing room to give a message to John and saw before me a young group of rockers going over their set and showing signs of nervousness and pre-stage jitters just like any other band. All of a sudden it was time, and they came out of this dressing room and through the door onto the roof stage just like all the bands I had seen do a thousand times. There is that unique moment for entertainers when they are told "It's time," and they journey that strange distance from the dressing room out onto the stage. Until you know you've connected with the audience, there is that deep-down indescribable fear of not pulling it off no matter who you are. (Andy Williams told me that even after decades of super success and

how good the Beatles were as a rock-and-roll band, just listen to the on the roof that day.

thousands of concerts he always wanted to throw up just before he went on stage.) Football players experience it until they have had their first physical hit on the field—at that point they are finally in the game.

The rules to this game had changed somewhere along the way for the Beatles—confused and un-amused, these players decided to just play one more time—a whole note—a final chord.

The Beatles burst through the door to the stage and did their last concert.

When it was over, I wanted more. I still do.

Here It Is—
Come and Get It!

» *London, England—Los Angeles, California,
March 1968–1969*

One of our early Apple releases was from a young McCartney-laced group called the Iveys. Actually, although they are often best remembered for their first hit single, Paul's "Come and Get It," Mal Evans was really the first Appleite to get behind the band. It was Mal's enthusiasm that brought them to Apple's attention. I met the fellows on one of my early trips to London, and before hearing their music I was very impressed with their youthful innocence. They looked how I must have looked in the beginning days of my employ with the Fab Four—there was this appearance of wonder in their eyes as if they were still puzzling over what was happening and wondering how they came to be standing in this incredible place. When I returned to LA and later that fall was given an advance copy of the first Iveys single so I could plan a launch for the band, I was totally knocked out with what I heard on the acetate. Guitarist (he later moved to bass) Tom Evans's "Maybe Tomorrow" absolutely blew me away. The beauty of this situation was that I had an incredible machinery at my disposal with the Capitol Industries distribution network, and no one from the president on down would question my moves concerning anything related to Apple and the Beatles. I think some of the executives were a little jealous of my position, while others wouldn't trade places with me for the world.

I felt the Iveys *were* our next Beatles. (It seems every new band that was offered to Capitol was trumpeted as our "next Beatles," a phrase I often hear to this day and one that still makes me take a deep breath in fear I will throw up.) I really wanted to cement my position as a power broker on the label and felt "Maybe Tomorrow" was my opportunity to lay claim to being the founding father of a new superstar band at Apple *and* Capitol. It was Capitol's money and my career—a golden opportunity lay before me. I jumped into the project feet first and with an open checkbook. I put our entire promotional team and budgets on this one record. I put the regional guys on a nonstop road blitz to all the major stations in order to back up the local promotion team's efforts as well as a personal national push on my part. My relationships with the top radio stations were effective because not only was I the Beatles guy in the United States, but I was the one and only who had come from London a few months earlier with "Hey Jude" in my hand, making the rounds to some of the major stations for a first listen and asking their opinion about whether we should release it as the Beatles' first Apple single.

The initial feedback on "Maybe Tomorrow" from the Top 40 stations was very encouraging, and the fact that it was an Apple band didn't hurt. As far as I was concerned, my first feelings were validated at the very point in the hit record food chain that was necessary for success, and so I shoved a giant pile of chips into the pot. I ordered 400,000 initial pressings on their first outing, an unheard of move in the industry at the time. Upon doing so, I made sure that all the inside scoopers at the trade rags knew of the move so that it would create a buzz about how excited Capitol/Apple was with this new group. Because of the hype and honest response from music directors at Top 40 radios, airplay was almost automatic, as well as plentiful. Because of all the tremendous airplay, we placed every commercial piece we pressed into the various chains, music stores, and "moms and pops" around the nation. I was thrilled at my incredible expertise and visionary prowess.

We ultimately got back close to 300,000 of those 400,000 records in returns! We had the airplay. We had the inventory. We had the distribution. We had the prestige. We had the company enthusiasm. We had a Beatles connection. We had a great group. We had a great record. We were missing just one thing—the ability to go out and pick up people at their homes, drive them to the record store, and convince them to put their money on the counter and ask for "Maybe Tomorrow" by the new group from England called the Iveys! Amazingly, we couldn't seem to get this band off the ground.

Maybe a name change would help to overcome the failure image—how does *Badfinger* sound? You know the rest. The Iveys became Badfinger and Badfinger became one of our biggest success stories.

The Iveys drama was not the only time we experienced this happenstance at Apple. Let's look at James Taylor. I defy anyone upon hearing our releases on James for the first time (or at any time since the day they were recorded) not to listen in awe, knowing that they were

Apple

Ken Mansfield,
Capitol Record Distributing Co.
The Capitol Tower,
Hollywood,
California 90028.
U.S.A.

20th March, 1969

Dear Ken,

With reference to the Iveys album front cover, large cameo with the 4 cut-out heads.

Further to seeing a first proof from the original art-work we are making certain corrections to ensure that the general background in the cameo should now be, say, 90% of the fifth colour green with the existing black which will automatically come from the grey background. Regarding the heads being in two colours green and black we found that the black and green gave a strong blackish contrast. We, therefore, decided to reduce the black on the heads to 30% (approx) with the black at the (bust-line) (neck-line) totally reduced. The effect of this would be that the hard lines which appear at the base of each head will blend totally with the background which is now practically solid green.

We will send a proof of this showing these amendments as soon as possible. We enclose the first proof for your attention.

Yours sincerely,

Jack

JACK OLIVER

Apple Corps Ltd., 3 Savile Row, London, W.1. 01-734 8232. Cables Apcore London, W.1. Director, N. S. Aspinall.

MAYBE TOMORROW
IVEYS

hearing something magical. Talk about a slam-dunk! This one took no work. Everyone at almost every level raved over this product. Multiple radio formats welcomed it with open arms, and the "picks to click" and press reviews were unanimous in their response that this was major stuff. Our initial retail orders for the *James Taylor* album in late '68 and the "Carolina in My Mind" single in early '69 were beyond our expectations. The single was constantly being played on the air. Everybody loved this artist and his music. Apple A&R man Peter Asher had done an incredible job in presenting and producing James. The Beatles themselves were absolutely behind their new artist, and on a personal level they really liked him.

Another home run? Well, for some mysterious reason we couldn't even get to first base when it came to sales. The stations played it, and the stores bought it in anticipation of great things. Everyone on the business end of the project loved it, but once again, nobody brought their pennies in and plunked them down on the counter for it.

Finally, after James skyrocketed to fame in the early '70s, his Apple debut was rereleased and sold well, just as it should have all along.

Another Apple artist that was George's pet project and one that he became very deeply involved in creatively, financially, and personally was Jackie Lomax. Jackie had been in the early '60s Liverpool band the Undertakers and then, during the "British Invasion," moved to the United States and kicked around the states for years in various musical

Wow, the ups and downs of it all. Those were the days in the record business.

aggregations before catching Brian Epstein's attention in 1966. Jackie moved back to England and began work on an album with his band, the Lomax Alliance, but after Epstein died in 1967, Jackie's career stalled for a while. When we geared up Apple in 1968, I think George saw in Jackie his first real opportunity to produce another artist. Jackie had a great street background, had paid his dues, and was a very viable commodity.

As in the cases of the Iveys and James Taylor, the Apple/Capitol partnership went all out in putting their money, time, and hard work into establishing Jackie as a superstar. I really liked him and spent a lot of personal time with him, especially on the long promo/road tour that Mal and I took him on across the United States (see more about this in "Mal" in Track 30). Jackie definitely fell into the mode of the celebrity. He was handpicked by George and Apple and carried himself as a star during this period. His first record, "The Eagle Laughs at You" and the George-penned "Sour Milk Sea," was really a two-sided hit in many people's estimation. That was good news in terms of acceptance and initial response to an artist's first offering, but it actually turned out to hurt the release. In order to create a hit, you need to have everyone (the radio stations and record reviewers) on the same side. As I explained before, 100 percent of the action on just one side, the "A" side of the record, can give you a No. 1. Fifty percent on the "A" side and 50 percent on the "B" side can give you two No. 37 records even though you have the same amount of airplay and sales. Although the response was good and the tour was extremely rewarding, we couldn't get Jackie's career off the ground. In time, the whole thing fizzled out. George and Apple soon lost interest, and since the Beatles were busy breaking up by this time, the whole project seemed to quietly fade away. Jackie continued to record as a solo artist and band member for projects on Warner Brothers, Epic, and, ironically, again with Capitol. The big difference between Jackie and the others mentioned here was there was no successful aftermath.

Wow, the ups and downs of it all. Those were the days in the record business.

Speaking of such a thing: regarding Apple artist, Mary Hopkin, and her McCartney-produced, worldwide gold record smash hit "Those Were the Days"—none of us on the upper floors of the Capitol Tower in Hollywood really thought that one had a chance. Fortunately, because of Paul's incredible track record and the necessity for Capitol to keep the relationship with the Beatles pristine, perfect, and pleasant at all times, we followed the greater wisdom.

As for Apple's Black Dyke Mills Band? Well, that was a whole different story.

Track 20

The Games People Play

» *Beverly Hills, California, August 1969*

When Allen Klein made his move to take over Apple, Ron Kass had to go. Klein knew that this would make the well-documented Klein/McCartney contention even more precarious because McCartney wanted nothing to do with the brash New York accountant and music business manager, even though the other three thought Klein was the answer to all their needs. Somewhere in his research and planning phase, Klein had gotten a mistaken and overblown impression of my relationship with Paul. He found out that initially Paul, along with Kass, was the sponsor of my position at Apple. Because Ron Kass and Paul McCartney were close and Ron and I were close, Klein came to the conclusion that Paul and I were close. Wrong! I did have a good relationship with Paul but not the kind or one of such depth that would allow me to sway his opinion in a matter such as the leadership of Apple.

Once Klein had decided he wanted the Apple in his basket, he put into operation, what I am told, was his standard modus operandi—creating mass confusion within the organization. He knew that an Apple divided against itself could not stand. I was told that he did this by sowing seeds of confusion, bitterness, doubt, and insecurity among the Apple staff. When he could, he would subtly pit them against each other. He then did the same thing with the Beatles, convincing three of the four that, among other things, the music business as a whole had been cheating them. He assured them that many in Apple's inner circle were against them. He insisted that Kass was to blame for much of the band's troubles. Then, because he was the inventor of the problem, he came forward as the genius with all of the answers and obviously the only person who knew how to solve the problem. The outcome? They let Kass go and put Klein in, against Paul's stern objections. Simplistically, this was like secretly setting a building on fire and then becoming a hero by arriving first on the scene to save the damsel in distress from the flames.

So, according to Klein's plan, Kass was out at Apple, and Klein was in LA and on the phone to me. He said he had flown in *just* to talk to me about the new Apple restructuring and to discuss my recent resignation from the company. What happened was that shortly after Klein's takeover of Apple, Ron Kass was appointed president of MGM Records, and one of his first official acts was to offer me a vice presidency of that division. I immediately accepted. Kass and I knew each other's moves by now, and we were very comfortable working together. He had decided to locate to Manhattan in order to keep his European liaisons more accessible. He would commute to the West Coast offices and movie lot, while I would head up the Hollywood complex and commute the other direction, where I would occupy a plush executive corner office at the MGM building in New York City on a part-time basis. (Growing up in Idaho, my family didn't have an indoor bathroom until I was a senior in high school. I found that I adapted to my new life easily though, and insisting on a better suite at the St. James was a lot more fun than hiking one hundred yards down a frozen dirt trail to a frosty outhouse behind the barn. This proves the old adage—you can take the boy out of the country, but you can't do it unless you offer him a better suite.)

Of historical interest is the fact that at that time, the MGM roster of English, country, jazz, and pop artists had a serious morale problem. Somewhere deep within the corporate MGM lot it had been decided that the executive staff from the Beatles' Apple Records could possibly be prestigious enough to keep the singing lion alive in the music business jungle a little while longer. My musical and marketing background made me uniquely qualified to communicate with these lost souls. The fact that the company had literally just gone through five presidents in little more than one year with no successful records rather loudly suggested that a good marketing push might be in order to help solve a slight image problem. The label's stable of artists, which included Eric Burdon, War, Michael Parks (from NBC TV's *Then Came Bronson*), Tommy Flanders (Blues Project), John Sebastian (Lovin' Spoonful), Tompall and the Glaser Brothers, Hank Williams Jr., Petula Clark, and Bruce Palmer (Buffalo Springfield), to name a few, were starting to feel a little bit insecure, and it was beginning to look like the good ship lollipop had just about had its last lick. So Peter Asher (A&R) and Mike O'Conner (publishing) headed out of London and jumped into the lion's den with newly appointed president Ron Kass and myself (VP marketing and artist relations). We were all soon eaten alive by these magnificent movie men.

I'm not going to tell you exactly how this musical lion sufferari adventure turned out, but you may have noticed that there is no longer an MGM records.

When Klein called, I knew he was responding to my resignation and that he deemed it necessary to sabotage my MGM appointment before I officially left Apple. I was not friendly to him when he called, but he was persistent, and executive protocol did dictate a severance conference even in the madness of this situation and the associated turbulent times. I agreed to meet him at the Beverly Hills Hotel for lunch and/or whatever. After all, he *had* flown in from London to meet me, and there were transitional matters to discuss. Even this concession made me feel a bit disloyal to Kass, but I knew how I felt about Klein and knew Kass knew.

It was beginning to look like the good ship lollipop had just about had its last lick.

It seems that every action-packed, earth-shaking meeting that had to do with my career and future always took place at poolside, in the Palm Room, or in the lobby of the Beverly Hills Hotel. Guess where Klein asked me to meet him? We met in the lobby of the Beverly Hills Hotel in order to have lunch in the Palm Room. Afterward he suggested we could have drinks poolside to finish our conversation. At first meeting, I wondered how anyone could be so singularly unattractive and pleasant to meet at the same time. Our introductions were cordial, although a bit reserved on my part, and brief. Based on the misguided information about my influence on Paul's thinking, Klein wasted no time in getting to the point. He was up to full speed before we had cleared the lobby on the way to the restaurant and had made it very clear that he wanted me to stay on board.

More than that, he was willing to sweeten the pot more than I could ever imagine. His opening statement was: "I am not sure what kind of money you are making, but if you will continue on as U.S. manager of Apple Records, you now earn three times as much as you did thirty seconds ago!" (Kass had negotiated Capitol into paying my salary and benefits so no one at Apple knew how much I earned as U.S. manager of Apple Records. Before Klein had made this offer, I was basking in the warmth of Kass's generous doubling of my previous salary to come to MGM.) While I was still recovering from this and hanging on for dear life to my loyalties, he added that not only would the Beatles remain my responsibility, but he would give me the Rolling Stones and Donovan responsibilities as an added inducement and a few more bright career feathers in me skullcap.

I had been warned about Allen Klein in more ways than one—I had heard all the horror stories, and even as we sat there I knew I was living in a newly altered world that was personally and adversely changed by his methods and personal aspirations. I loved working with and for Apple and the Beatles, and I really believed we had a good thing—organization and peoplewise. Then along comes this squatty New York accountant who had more bad press preceding him than "Der Fuehrer" himself. He had individually derailed my and a lot of other people's worlds by upsetting the Apple cart—and here I was being beguiled. You couldn't help being taken in by this guy. He was charming and disarming in some obtuse, off-the-wall way that just didn't fit into all my learned responses. I didn't like anything about him, but I was enjoying listening to him and I liked what he was saying to me.

Because of his honed persuasiveness and my cultural unpreparedness, he was the kind of guy who was almost impossible to say no to. He knew I was a total tennis nut, and as part of his personal endearment plan to me had made the mistake of bringing up his tennis game in our conversation earlier in the meeting. What happened next, I admit, is absolutely crazy and yet true. To this day I can't figure out my mind-set or understand my actions. I think too much time in airplanes reading fiction novels may have contributed to my unreal approach to this situation. In complete denial of my arbitrative cowardice, I took what I thought was an adventuresome way out by acting cavalier about the whole thing. I challenged this odd-shaped little man to a tennis match. He looked like he spent all his time sitting at restaurant tables or in meetings in windowless rooms. At that particular time, I was playing every day of my life and was beginning to win some local California country club tournaments. This was my way to get even for Kass, maintain all my loyalties, and get out from underneath his super salesmanship spell. In a manner of veiled sarcasm I told him I would accept his offer if he could beat me in one set of tennis. I would arrange for us to play at the Bel Air Tennis Club the next day, and if he could beat me, I would be on the plane with him the day after that on my way to London and 3 Savile Row. He agreed. Let the games begin. I couldn't wait. I was going to send him home red-faced and with his tail dragging behind a whipped ass!

I went to see Kass that night and told him what had transpired. I was honest with Ron and told him how tempted I was: the money and prestige

I am standing with Ron Kass (right), President of MGM Records and Bo Polk (middle), President of MGM Pictures on the MGM back lot the day after the "the tennis match from hell." Although Klein's offers were attractive, the picture of my new life as an executive at this historical institution with a trusted friend as my boss was much more inviting.

and all. I told him how I was torn between my loyalties to him and to doing what was best for me and my family and career. I sought his advice as a friend and someone I greatly trusted and admired. Ron totally understood, and I knew as a friend that he wanted the best for me and would have advised me to stay at Apple if he thought it was the right choice for me to make. He then discussed with me the challenge we would undertake at MGM, my responsibilities, and the unique opportunity I would have in the overall corporate scheme of this very prestigious company. He had very little to say about Klein's proposal to me and simply offered one small piece of wisdom as I walked out of the door of his house that night into the sweet-bougainvillea-scented Beverly Hills air. "You lay down with pigs and you get up dirty!"

I went home that night with those words and all the wisdom they carried with them ringing softly in my ears. (I truly loved Ron Kass and feel I learned more from him and Stanley Gortikov than anyone else in the record business. Ron's early death probably affected me more than any one of the many associates I have known who has passed on. He seemed to give me special care from the very first.) After his comment, I knew that even risking the long-shot chance that I might be forced to keep my word and go to work for Klein was absolute personal—and in some ways, moral—madness. The position Klein was offering me may have been great for the moment, but someday it *was* going to be over with Apple and the Beatles, and then for the rest of my professional career I would be known as one of Klein's guys.

I met Klein on the tennis court the next day prepared to back out of my challenge, and then I saw him in his tennis outfit. He looked like an egg on rejected drumsticks. All worry left me as I knew this would be a snap. I could wrap this whole thing up without breaking a sweat.

His form may have not been the greatest, but I had overlooked one thing—this was not really a tennis match—it was a negotiation, and Allen Klein was virtually unbeatable in negotiations and was not about to lose this one no matter what form it had taken. His business dictionary had only one word in it: win! A picture of Klein's smiling face followed as the definition.

I never played better, but I couldn't get the ball past him. He couldn't have looked worse and yet couldn't have been more formidable. The ball just kept coming back no matter what I did with it, regardless of how hard I hit it or placed it out of his reach. I thought I had gone to tennis hell and that this match was eternal and was never going to end. (For those who don't play tennis, a set consists of games, and whoever wins six games first wins the set. There is one caveat, though, and that is that you must beat your opponent by two games. Therefore if you get to six games and he has five games, then it is necessary to get the game score to 7–5 in order to win the set. So basically, if you reach six without being ahead by two games, then you just keep going until one of you accomplishes that two-game spread.)

I finally beat Allen Klein that day by the score of 15–13. I learned the meaning of tenacity looking over a sagging net into a face and will set like flint. I saw firsthand what a tough negotiator looked like. I understood that when I extended my arms into the air to serve the ball that the tennis racket wasn't the only thing that was over my head. *I* was in over my head.

The whole time we were playing, he was talking. First he would sweet talk me, compliment me, review his awareness of and respect for my past glories. When that didn't work, he would fill me with fear of the future and how this would be the great missed opportunity of my lifetime and how my mind would come back to this point in time someday in the near future as I lay desolate and devastated, wallowing in the sad sewer of my wasted career. He upped the ante, appealing to my greed. He took me visually to the mountaintop of fame, let me look over the edge, and like the very devil himself, presented the world of fame and fortune that would lie at my feet when I joined him and his organization. When all else failed, he virtually threatened me in myriad unkind ways.

I beat him, and then it was over; it was like it never happened. We said good-bye, shook hands, left, and that was it. All intensity dissipated when this person and his mission walked off the tennis court. As of thirty seconds earlier, I no longer worked for Apple or the Beatles. His next stop was 1750 North Vine, Hollywood, California, the "E" floor of Capitol Records where he would seek my replacement. I never saw him or talked to him again.

Fall 1969. Apple chief Neil Aspinall (right) questions newly installed Apple business manager Allen Klein, probably about how Klein could have let me slip away from Apple as the result of a tennis match.

Track 21

I'm Only Sleeping

» *London, England—Hollywood, California,*
October 1969

A few years ago in London, over lunch, I finally got the opportunity to tell Neil Aspinall what I had to go through in the United States when someone at Apple would let a copy of a new Beatles song slip out of the Apple building before its official release. I was also able to explain to him the dilemma I faced when the Apple Corps would plan some new event without filling me in ahead of time. While they had a building full of dedicated employees at 3 Savile Row, I was flying solo as the only Beatles/Apple Records contact in America. This carried on to the point that even after I left Apple and moved to MGM with Ron Kass and Peter Asher, things like the "Paul is dead" rumor would virtually shut me and my office down for days just because of my prior association. I could only imagine what was going on at the Capitol Tower down the street.

I think World War III could have started during the "Paul is dead" period and no one under the age of thirty would have noticed.

I was fielding calls right and left because, since my move from Apple was virtually only days old, I was still the go-to guy as far as most people were concerned. Of course my pals, the few remaining Apple execs in London, took the sophisticated approach of dealing with the situation by simply hiding out and/or shutting off their phones and locking the doors. This was great for them, but like everyone else, I also couldn't get through to anyone at Apple UK, plus I didn't have a clue as to what the deal was on the whole issue. Meanwhile, my phones were ringing off the hook, and everyone in the world and news media wanted to know the scoop. I was supposed to be an inside guy, but because I was no longer "in the loop," I didn't know if it was a promo ploy, an aberration, or the truth.

Professionally, I needed to tackle the myriad tasks at my new job, but I also knew that helping the media solve this "Paul is dead" mystery was a good move in establishing new kinds of relationships and developing return favors for my new artist roster. The restructuring of MGM was not going to be an easy task, and it was important to build up "capitol" with

Paul and me with an apple at an Apple Records function.

the people whom I would need to win over to our side in the future as the new product releases hit the street. Left to my own devices and with definitely no help from my friends on the British Isles, I found a quick solution to the problem. From 1965 to points in time beyond his supposed passing on, I had Paul's signature on various correspondences, documents, and autographed items. We flew these to a leading criminologist and handwriting analyst in Chicago; he verified that all the writings and signatures were from the same man (Paul), and we were able to confirm that the dates of these signatures were before, during, and after the rumored death event.

This whole scenario was a little strange in a nice sort of way because for a few days it was almost like I was still at Apple, especially because Kass and Asher were with me during this dilemma. We documented, reproduced in leaflet form, and distributed the newly gathered information to all my new staff members at MGM. I instructed them to simply pass this info on in a very matter-of-fact manner in answer to the many calls coming into my office. Of course, being a quick learner and following the lead of my English mentors (or should I say in this case, "tor-mentors"), I locked my office door, ceased taking calls, and moved on from there to clean up the lion's cage.

I could have killed Paul for not letting me know if he was dead or not!

I think World War III could have started during the "Paul is dead" period and no one under the age of thirty would have noticed.

Track 22

Homeward

» *Laurel Canyon, California, April 1970*

I saw a common thread that ran through the very fiber and being of the Fab Four. It was the indelible impression left with me after first meeting the Beatles on Sunday, August 29, 1965, at the *Help!* press conference held in Capitol Records Studio A in Hollywood, California.

I honestly believe that the childlike quality of the Beatles is what people, starting with their fans in the Cavern days, sensed from the very beginning. I also believe that this attribute is what eventually attracted the mass affection of young and old followers worldwide. This band had a purity of purpose in their music that has remained unrivaled to this day.

Unfortunately, once they had reached the phenomenon stage, modern mankind in its predictable nature had to create a media version of this rock-and-roll innocence. This version, which only occasionally crossed paths with the truth, had a life of its own.

Mass hysteria, mass media, mass marketing, and mass messing around with a magnificent mixture of acumen and mesmerizing musical magic eventually turned it all into one major money machine of mass misery. Unfortunately, at that time, the Beatles ended up with most of the misery; most of the money ended up somewhere else.

What the establishment had built up now had to be dismantled because the Beatles weren't cooperating. They insisted on defining their own parameters, musical and otherwise.

The inevitable industry intervention and interjection of its own limitations and frailties into their makeup, in time, cut deep into the natural core beauty until nothing was left but a corroded outer shell, a fragile facade erected by everyone except the Beatles. Of course, what was left was unacceptable and simply had to be torn down.

As time progressed, I was privileged to meet and get to know each of Apple's primary supporting players one by one in this unwritten play. I was surprised to find that they also possessed this kindred inner quality that the Beatles had. "Like unto like," it is often said, and Neil Aspinall, Mal Evans, Ron Kass, Jack Oliver, Tony Bramwell, and Derek Taylor in particular

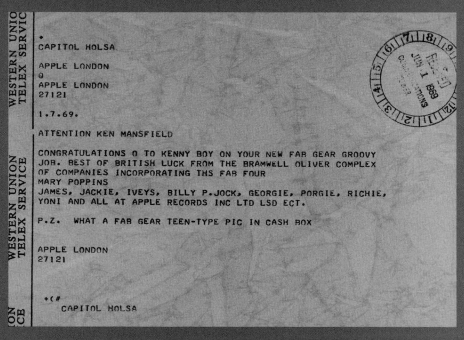

I received this telegram (most likely instigated by either Tony Bramwell or Jack Oliver–Apple, London) when Capitol Records announced in the trades that, in addition to the U.S. Manager–Apple Records position, I had just been appointed "Director of Independent Labels" with similar responsibilities, as with Apple, to all of Capitol's independently distributed record companies.

Sending their congratulations via their telegram code names, in addition to Tony Bramwell and Jack Oliver, were: Mary Poppins (Mary Hopkin), James (Taylor), Jackie (Lomax), Iveys (Badfinger), Billy P. (Billy Preston), Yoni (Yoko Ono), and the Fab Four (Jock, Georgie, Porgie, and Richie).

seemed to carry the unusual attribute of being aloof, occasionally a little crusty, yet immediately likable. Each had an acceptable eccentricity that drew people into either being a fan or a friend or both. All were extremely capable of carrying out their given "devoir," but above all, and to a man, they were fiercely loyal and dedicated beyond any normal human call to duty. They became inextricably swept up in the task at hand and soon were hanging on for dear life to that little bit of existence they once called lives of their own. I don't know if I was invited inside because I was like them or because I was different. I do know that from the day I walked through the Apple doors at 3 Savile Row, I was aware that in the midst of this musical banquet there were worms gorging themselves on the phenomenal fruit that these dedicated men were frantically trying so hard to preserve.

The eventual browning around the edges and rotting of the corps of the Apple due to repeated exposure and intrusion (the greeds and needs) of the outer world was predictable and unavoidable.

My eternal naiveté and potato-bred simplicity saved me. I looked for and found only their goodness and gentle natures. I found them idealistic and still able to dream, vaguely unaware that they were being pulled deep into an externally induced nightmare. Like the proverbial shot that was heard around the world, the sound of this musical monument breaking apart was deafening. This was the day the music died the second time.

I was only a visitor, and for that I am glad. I am particularly blessed to have been visited by them. I feel fortunate I was able to hop on a plane and take sanity-saving side trips into my other executive responsibilities. This allowed me to perform reality checks between those brief excursions in and out of their world.

I saw what I saw, heard what I heard, and felt what I felt, and I may have even forgotten what I don't want to remember. I always felt that they liked me. I do know they trusted me, and in order to dig up dirt or caustic observations about these times and these people, I would either have to become a fiction writer or betray that trust.

I admit that my view of the Beatles and Apple is totally jaded, but I love jade; fine jade is so beautiful and enduring.

I treasure my times in and around the Beatle Empire: a mystical place that I or time can never return to. My tour was a mystery to me and definitely magical.

Only a few of us were there. It will never happen again. You can never go back home!

Track 23

You Can Call Him Roy

» *Madrid, Spain—Azores—Miami, Florida, Spring 1970*

I was finishing up a combined business-pleasure trip to Europe and thoroughly enjoying the last days of the pleasure portion of an excursion in Spain. Ron Kass felt that he and I should keep our Apple/Beatles relationship alive as a good business move, so Europe was still on my plate. I did have to be in Miami for our big MGM Records national convention in two days though, and in those days, the early '70s, the suggested routing for flying from Madrid to Miami was a convoluted course that included either Rome or London, then New York City, and then Miami.

In order to spend an extra day in Madrid, I booked passage on Aeronaves de Mexico. A Miami stop wasn't on the schedule, but they stopped there for fuel on a flight from Madrid to Mexico City. Word was that I could simply disembark during the brief layover. Although friends warned of the dangers of flying with a little-known (until that point it had been *unknown* to me) carrier, I was really enjoying the hiatus from stressful company matters and felt I deserved an extra day in Madrid. One more day in Spain, or book with a more reliable carrier? Gee, I think I'll take my chances.

Being a know-it-all was especially pleasing on the day of departure as check-in, boarding, and take off from Madrid's Barajas International Airport were on time, and it wasn't too long before we cleared the west coast of Spain and headed out across the Atlantic Ocean for southern Florida. I was seated in a window seat in the first-class cabin next to a charming and air-travel savvy fellow from Peru in the aisle seat. He was easy to talk to and soon revealed himself to be a fascinating person. I learned that his father owned several airlines. In fact, he had been given Peruvian Airlines as a twenty-fifth birthday present.

We spent the whole time in conversation. All of a sudden, he stopped me mid-sentence and asked me to turn toward the window and look outside. As I did this, he asked if I could see the water. I looked down and was very surprised because it looked like we were about two hundred feet above the sea, and the perception was one of almost skipping along the surface of the water at breakneck speed. I told him what I could see, and he then asked me to look out at the wing tips. I did so, and as I peered outward and slightly forward, he then asked if there were any liquids coming from the wings, to which I answered yes. Without hesitation he said, "We're going down. They are jettisoning fuel, and we are going down!" It was clear he knew what he was talking about, and it was apparent that growing up around airplanes had made him acutely aware of the sounds one makes when it is in trouble. Sure enough, they were bringing the plane down even lower. There were no announcements over the PA until almost the very last minute. We were informed that we were going to make an unscheduled stopover in the Azores and to brace ourselves as the landing might be a little bumpy. All I could see out of the window as the plane descended even lower was an abrupt piece of parched and barren land directly ahead, jutting out of the ocean. We were soon bumping and swerving on a broken and weedy stretch of concrete that I learned later had served as a layover spot for naval airplanes delivering supplies to the various troops during World War II.

After what seemed like hours on a blisteringly hot airstrip, during which time the pilot and other crew members essentially had the hood up on our air-bus and were talking fast and gesturing like mad as they peered into what I took to be the operational part of the machine, we were told we could return to the mainland on a later flight that was being sent to pick us up or get back on the plane and continue on to Miami while holding our breath over a long stretch of ocean. I made the decision to carry on, mainly because I had no choice if I wanted to arrive in Miami in time for the event. It helped that my airplane industry wizened seatmate had also decided to continue on; I honestly think that if he had declined I would have had a really hard time convincing myself that there was a chance that the "Band-Aid Express" would make it.

My participation in Miami was key to the event, and my not being there would, to others, clearly be because I had decided to play a little longer in tapas-land instead of putting my business priorities first.

I was the VP in charge of promotion, marketing, and all exploitation activities for MGM, and the convention was to be one of the signature events of the year. Success or failure, it was my baby to put together and manage. A lot of money is involved in putting together a gathering like this where all the employees are flown in from all over the country. To add to the pressure, rumor had been bubbling recently that a buyout of MGM by Kirk Kerkorian was in the works. Further rumor had it that he already had Mike Curb lined up to come in and take over the presidency of the label from Ron Kass. I needed to join Ron in Florida as soon as possible to find out what was happening, what he knew, and what we were going to do. This was not good news as we were in the early stages of getting the label back on track. The news and timing couldn't have been worse. Of special importance to me personally was the entertainment segment of the convention. I had begun developing what would become over time a beautiful friendship with possibly the most special person I had ever met in my life, someone who unquestionably was then and still is to this day considered by almost everyone in the music industry to be one of its greatest artists: Roy Orbison.

As I mentioned earlier in this book, one of my prime goals when taking on the responsibilities of the Artist Relations department for MGM was to try and restore a rather incredible artist roster back to having some sense of belief and trust in the company. Roy's situation was quite different from the rest of the roster. They were disgruntled because of long-suffering through one bad management team after another and watching their recording careers nosedive because of it. Roy, on the other hand, had recently lost his two eldest sons in a tragic fire at his home in Nashville while he was on the road. His parents were supposed to be taking care of them, so the loss was magnified by a mixture of guilt and blame between family members. Roy had been hit by a double whammy because this tragedy was preceded by his wife, Claudette, being killed in a motorcycle accident two years prior to the fire. Needless to say, Roy was pretty messed up over these events and had essentially bowed out of the business, a business that in some ways he felt was responsible for his sons' deaths because he was out of town performing when it happened.

Fortunately, Roy and I hit it off immediately. He was naturally a reclusive person but fairly open with me and was receptive to us being friends quickly. Roy often smugly reminded people that the Beatles had been his opening act on a British tour years earlier. I liked that about him. (Roy conveniently left out the reality that the Fabs replaced him as the

I had begun developing what would become over time a beautiful friendship with possibly the most special person I had ever met in my life, someone who unquestionably was then and still is to this day considered by almost everyone in the music industry to be one of its greatest artists: Roy Orbison.

headliner shortly into the tour. I liked that about him too.) We shared the experience of knowing the Beatles and maintaining a friendship with them. This unique fact was also a bonding element in our relationship.

I felt enough time had passed since his tragedies and honestly believed the best way for him to heal was to become active in both his performing and recording careers. He had met a beautiful German girl, Barbara Anne Marie Wilhonnen Jacobs, in Leeds, England, after the fire, and they were subsequently married in Nashville in March of 1969. Barbara and I were definitely on the same page regarding Roy's return. A plan was developed that Roy was willing to try. He agreed that the safest place to explore getting back on stage, to feel it out, would be appearing before a small industry crowd in a private setting. Roy would be the special entertainment for the convention. Everyone at MGM knew how special this concert was, and they were very excited to be among the first to see Roy come back.

For me to not show up for this event was not an option. If there had been no alternative to getting off that island in the Azores, I probably would have started swimming west really fast.

The day of Roy's concert was a typically hot and beautiful Miami day. Roy rested up in his hotel suite and mentally prepared for his upcoming

© Corbis

performance. It was a very emotional thing for him, and he really had to get his head around going back on stage. Meanwhile, on the beach, his tall, gorgeous wife, Barbara, was sunbathing. My national promotion manager, Ron Saul, decided to take a break from meetings and get a few rays that afternoon on the beach. As luck would have it, he found himself within yards of this seemingly lonely European beauty. In his best California dreamin' manner, he proceeded to "hit" on her, not having a clue who she was. Barbara's response to his affections was less than appreciative. Typical for Barbara, she made it very clear about how she felt about the unwanted intrusion. Unfortunately, Ron used the fact that he was an executive with a prestigious entertainment company (MGM) as his opening come-on. She was rather insulted, and her distaste had the potential of spilling over into her opinion of the company. The planned event featuring her husband that evening was immediately in jeopardy.

I should have worked for Fred Astaire because of all the fast dancing I had to do that afternoon. I bounced and tap-danced between Roy, Barbara, Kass, and Ron Saul for about two hours, without an intermission, trying to get things smoothed out and back on track.

Amazingly, once resolved, this melodrama drew us all closer and in the long run became a favorite story for all of us. It was the perfect tale of a "Pretty Woman," an executive who was "Running Scared," and a whole lot of "Mercy" from my man the big "O," Mr. Roy Orbison.

Roy's performance that night was magical. The room was intimate, and the makeup of the audience (fellow industry associates) was perfect for what Barbara, Roy, and I had wanted for our experiment. You could see it in Roy's demeanor; it was one of those unique moments before an entertainer "hits the boards" where he knows he is coming home to where his heart and genius belong. It wasn't a long set, but he offered up his best songs with so much heart that it made everyone in the room feel special. This was also a smart business move because that night every salesman and executive with MGM records felt a unique bond with this great man and flew home ready to go to the wall for him.

Opposite page: Roy and Barbara in London 1970, around the time of the MGM convention in Miami.

Track 24

Blue Suede Suits

» *Las Vegas, Nevada, August 1970*

I loved my unique association with my friends at Apple, a relationship that happily continued long after I had moved on career-wise. I had a special place with them, being the young man from California as well as the executive who was brought aboard from abroad to be the focal force in launching and overseeing their pet project in the international music world's most important market. In those days the United States was (in fact, still is) the whole ball of wax, and without success in the land of the free and the home of the brazen, the potential and rewards were minimal. We were curiously mixed together, similarities and differences magnifying the moment we were in. Here we were, a mildly confused gaggle* of young men at the very top of our game *and* the world, but through it all we had an awareness and the common sense to know that we would never be able to totally shake loose from our common

* gaggle n (from the Encarta Encyclopedia)

    1.—a flock of geese
    2.—a group of people, especially a noisy or disorderly group

beginnings. This unique juxtaposition of civilizing realities gave us an innocence that was only faintly overshadowed by our out-and-out ability to shamelessly take advantage of the whole phenomenon before we woke up from the dream of it all. Not only was I fascinated with them and the interesting British culture I found myself immersed in, but also at the same time they were by their own admission very intrigued by the dude from the land of surfer girls and little deuce coupes. Apple promo chief Tony Bramwell once told me that I was exactly what they imagined a typical cool guy from California would look like. There I was, tan and young, driving a Cadillac Eldorado with a half-acre secluded home in the Hollywood Hills complete with a large swimming pool and an acute reverse sagacity of my own importance in the scheme of all things.**

So this continuum once again traveled through the phone lines via an early 1970 call into my office at MGM Records located on the Sunset Strip in the aforementioned Tinseltown, USA. It was Peter Brown, still enjoying his role as chief of protocol for Apple (a title that I am sure he came up with—definitely not one that Ringo would propose for any man working for a rock group), and he needed a favor and some help. Ringo, Peter informed me, wanted to see Elvis's show in Las Vegas at the International Hotel where the King was making his grand comeback. It was the hottest ticket of the universe at the time, and that, coupled with a Beatle wanting to go into a crowded showroom, would definitely take some inside and outside planning. Las Vegas had become my second home of sorts after five years of promotion and artist relations at Capitol, and now as the VP-director of exploitation at MGM (another title definitely not suggested by Ringo), I spent a lot of time in and between there and LA. It doesn't take long for a working stiff to get bored with the Vegas scene, yet this was an exciting undertaking and a guaranteed good time. The last time I had seen Elvis in person was in early 1956 when I was an eighteen-year-old navy seaman apprentice stationed in San Diego, and there was no question that I was going to have better seats this time.

** acute reverse sagacity/ intellectually vacuous

n, adj, adv, v—a combined condition that when its prolongation becomes apparent is a dead give-away for someone in the Hollywood entertainment business.

After a few well-placed phone calls, limited finagling, and restrained sublevel bargaining, the following scenario was prepared to deliciously unfurl.

All the arrangements were in place for Ringo to be secreted into Sin City. I had gotten permission to bring a limo out onto the tarmac, and a separate exit from the plane was arranged so that Ringo and Peter were able to avoid going through the terminal and the obvious melee that would happen at Las Vegas's McCarran International Airport innards. Peter had perfected this swishy Peter Ustinov accent, which belied his common upbringings, and when he saw me standing at the foot of the stairs with the limo door open, he stopped to acknowledge my very current and hip outfit, which consisted of as much leather as a happy

There was a price to pay for setting up special favors with the Las Vegas hotel to help us secret Ringo in to see Elvis. We agreed to this post-concert dinner with hotel insiders. I don't have a clue who these other people are. We are on the upper left side of the table.

California dairy cow. "Oh, there you are. Look at you, a vision in suede!"
Quick handshakes and manly hugs and the three of us piled into the limo
and headed for the Las Vegas Strip. (It would have been perfect if they
had searched us at that point because then I could say I went from the
Sunset Strip to an air strip where I was strip-searched before going to the
Las Vegas Strip.)

We entered the hotel from the back via the delivery entrance and were
escorted to our suites via the service elevator. Once we were situated, we
agreed that the three of us would meet in Ringo's suite half an hour
before the time someone from the hotel security staff would come to get
us and take us down to see the show. This gave us about an hour to
freshen up and get dressed for the evening. Something funny and very
unexpected happened that night. I had just returned from Italy where I
had bought a brand-new, deep dark blue velvet suit and had decided that
this was the perfect time to show it off. No way was I going to be outdone
by my compatriots who were famous for the flamboyance of their
wardrobes. The following sequence of events could only happen in the
movies or with members of the Apple Corps. Peter arrived first and let
himself into Ringo's suite and then met me at the door when I showed up
for my grand entrance. He opened the door, and we stared at each other
like two catty women who had worn the same dress to a cocktail party.
There *he* stood, a vision in black velvet in a new suit he had just purchased
for the occasion. Before our stares could dissolve into normalcy, Ringo
came out of the bathroom in a brand-new brown velvet suit that he had
just had custom made in London shortly before the trip over to see Elvis.
It was one of those hands-on-hips moments as the three of us surveyed
the sumptuous threads that we had draped about us. As the visual
cacophony of the velvet vapor that filled the room sunk in, we all cracked
up and decided we looked like a lounge act for the hotel we were staying
in. Peter took the picture of Ringo and me. It was taken in Ringo's
bathroom where the light was much better, using a cheap Polaroid
camera Ringo had picked up at an airport somewhere along the way.
Unfortunately, Polaroid film does fade over time, so it is now a little fuzzy.

The people in charge of the showroom and our seating arrangements
waited until Elvis had actually taken the stage, the house lights were
down to total darkness, and all eyes were focused on the King before
quietly sneaking us into the showroom and to our table. I suspect that the
reason the tables were jammed so close together was because Elvis was

charging so much for his appearance; we were virtually shoehorned into our seats. Even though we were shoulder-to-shoulder with the other patrons, no one noticed that they were touching a Beatle as they watched Elvis. We would have gotten away with our subterfuge of secrecy except that Elvis announced just before his closing number that he was proud to have a Beatle in the room and introduced Ringo. To make matters worse, the stage manager directed a spotlight to be aimed at our table to highlight his location. The fact that we were jammed into a central section of the showroom and had thought we would sneak out during the last song had left us without an exit strategy. Not only did the people who were already touching Ringo without knowing it become more intent on their proximity to one of the five most famous entertainers in the world,

but what seemed like about a thousand other people tried to move into a similar position. It was already rather stuffy and hot in the room, and fighting through the crowd one hundred feet to the exit was as physically demanding as the workouts held on the first day of high school football practice. We were drained and soaked by the time we cleared the room. Velvet smells when it is wet and loses a lot of its luster in the process. But we made it, possibly motivated by what we knew was about to happen.

Not only had I looked forward to spending this special time with Ringo, and admittedly it felt good to be able to once again pull something together for an old friend and former boss, but I also had a mini ulterior motive. I was going to meet Elvis because I was with Ringo! Within moments, one of the Memphis Mafia gathered us up from our safe position in the freezer area of the kitchen and escorted us out a back way into a private hallway. This was just how I imagined it was all going to happen. Then to both Peter's and my surprise, Ringo was whisked away from our presence and taken up to meet Elvis—he was the only one invited up to the suite. Peter and I looked at each other in our soiled and wilted prom outfits and were left to figure out how to get out of the kitchen because even the hotel security staff had abandoned us. Later, back at the suite, Ringo revealed to us his true playful nature as he kept rubbing it in and relating to us about his time with Elvis and, "Oh, by the way, what have you guys been doing since the show?"

Opposite page: Peter Brown was supposed to be in this picture too, but the hotel employee cut him off when taking it on Ringo's Polaroid camera. We are standing in the bathroom of the hotel suite where the light was better. I forgot I had it, so over the years the picture has faded due to its Polaroidness.

Bits and Peaces

» *Up and Down California—London, England,
Late 1960s–December 2001*

I always found it to be the little things that intrigued me the most about
George Harrison. These things were not only intriguing but were the light
that softly shone through his gentle countenance. In days of old, some of
the folk entertainers would do a little segment in their concerts called
"Bits and Pieces," where they would pick a little ditty, sing a single verse,
tell a simple story, and show off how they could, for example, make their
eyelids fold back while crossing their eyes. These interludes were usually
bits and pieces of themselves that gave the audience insight into the
makeup of these entertainers, a way to show just how real they were.

I offer some bits and pieces of my observations of George that came
about during the times I spent with him. There are no stories here with
fascinating endings or bone-chilling events to depict: just little stuff that
to me define the man more than his celebrity does.

Poolishness

Later in these ramblings, I'll tell of the day that George told me the
Beatles were leaving Allen Klein, a day that started with the two of us

hanging around the pool with our wives. Although we had made plans to be together that day, we hadn't set an exact time, and there were no scheduling pressures or business commitments on either one of us. Our only plan was to get together in the early afternoon, so the timetable was very loose by design. It was one of those days where it was nice to make plans to do nothing. This was in the ancient days before cell phones, so I called from our house to see what time he and Pattie had decided upon. No one was answering the phone at their house, so we figured they couldn't hear the phone because they were out by the pool. Anxious to set about doing nothing with them, we decided to grab our swimming suits and drive over and join them. We walked through the gates and saw George and Pattie lying by the pool sunbathing. We yelled our hellos from a slight distance on our way across the large lawn into the pool area. Upon seeing us headed in their direction, George suddenly jumped up and grabbed a long-sleeve shirt from the back of a nearby chaise lounge and quickly put it on. I didn't think anything about it, figuring it was an act simultaneous to our arrival to cover up from getting sunburn.

Later, while George and I were in the kitchen and the wives had gone shopping, Pattie confided to my wife that George was bashful about his slenderness and was embarrassed to be seen without his shirt on. When she told me this, I realized that I had never seen him in anything but long pants and primarily long-sleeve shirts before. It all goes to show how we think of celebrities as so invincible, and yet here was a normal person with normal little insecurities like everyone else. If you want to see how slim George was, just check out the *Bangla Desh* film when he isn't wearing his coat. Did you ever notice that rock-and-roll guitar players never have any butts?

Something in the Way She Moves

I always loved it when I would be in a big meeting with other executives, managers, artists, and agents, and I would get a phone call from one of the Beatles. Even though it was years after leaving Apple, one of them would occasionally call me (their unofficial personal liaison between the UK and the United States) when they needed something. Imagine what it must have been like when the receptionist would interrupt a studio session I was producing to tell me that Ringo was on the phone, or my secretary would slip into a meeting with potential clients to whisper to me that George Harrison was calling. The best part would be to put on an air of exceptional everydayness to the ensuing conversation for my stunned listeners. I would actually do things like say to my secretary, "Tell him I am tied up right now and I will get back to him—oh, never mind, put him through." I would then apologize to my startled visitor for the intrusion! Usually the Beatle on the other line was asking me to do him a favor, but for my captive audience it appeared that, from listening to my side of the conversation, he desperately needed my help.

George and Pattie
Harrison

© www.musicpictures.com

Such was the case when George called me at my MGM office while I was in a meeting with MGM president Mike Curb and the "Gold Dust Twins," the name we affectionately laid on Steve Gold and Jerry Goldstein, the managers of one of our most important acts, Eric Burdon and War. (Incidentally, not many people know this, but when MGM released Eric Burdon and War's 1970 Top 10 smash "Spill the Wine" single and the accompanying *Eric Burdon Declares "War"* album, Mike Curb had inexplicably neglected to put the funk band War under contract to us. We had Eric Burdon under contract, but his star quickly faded while War's career soon soared. War's MGM efforts established their career, but without a contract, they had no obligations to us, and consequently we weren't able to cash in on their success.)

Back to George and the reason for the call: Pattie Harrison heard that MGM was having a closed auction on the MGM movie lot of famous items from the sets of their biggest films: things like the bed from *Gone with the Wind* and the Wicked Witch's broom from the *Wizard of Oz*. She had asked George to call me to see if I could set her up to attend the private affair. I think she wanted to get some things for their home in Henley-on-Thames, Friar Park. Also George asked me if I had the time to watch out for and take care of Pattie during her five-day visit. I could hear the kind sarcasm in his voice because he knew from our previous conversations that I thought she was the single-most beautiful woman on planet Earth. I agreed over the phone to take care of everything, making sure that my arrangements for George (including pacifying the hierarchy of MGM, and subsequent travel for personal and business matters) sounded like major stuff between him and me. I ensured that my carefully chosen words for those listening to my side of the conversation suggested something of great importance and not the reality of me agreeing to be a roadie for his beautiful wife for a few days.

I easily made arrangements for Pattie to attend the MGM movie lot sale, made reservations for her at the Beverly Hills Hotel under my name to secure her privacy, and agreed to pick her up personally from the airport and watch over her during her stay. As a vice president at MGM, I had great leeway in my activities; Mike Curb actually liked the status within the label and artist roster that my continued association with the Fab Four offered on a prestige level. It was no problem taking the time to deal with these matters, and Curb figured the more I was seen with the Beatles et al., the better it looked for him and the MGM image. The day and time came for Pattie's arrival, and I decided to pick her up in my car instead of hiring a limo. I felt it was more personal and low key and would help downplay her entrance at the hotel as there were often photographers and reporters of the *Hollywood Reporter* gossip-column types who seemed to be in the lobby area of the Beverly Hills Hotel on a fairly regular basis.

In those days when you picked up international arrivals from LAX, you were able to see them through glass partitions as they came into the immigration area for clearance before being let into the country. Pattie was hard to miss; we exchanged waves and silent hellos through the glass, and I followed on my side of the partition to the point where she disappeared into the formalities of the procedure. I stationed myself outside the doors where she would exit, expecting to see her in a few minutes. Much to my displeasure, it was almost an hour before she came through the door, and it was a much different Pattie Harrison than the one who had smiled and waved at me through the glass. She had obviously been crying, and she was very distraught. She wouldn't talk to me until we had picked up her baggage and were driving away from the airport grounds. I kept trying to engage her in conversation while we were in this process of getting out of LAX, but she would just look straight ahead with a stoic, blank expression. Her only communication was to make it very clear that she wanted to get out of there.

Once we had cleared the runways, so to speak, she informed me that she had gone through the single most horrific ordeal of her young life: a strip search and complete body cavity inspection for drugs—just because she was married to a Beatle. I knew she needed to collect herself, so I opted not to take the freeway route to Sunset Boulevard and instead turned off into Beverly Hills and headed for a slower, more picturesque and less harried route on the side streets. Being in the entertainment business means you benefit from the fact that you travel so much. Eventually you learn all the back roads, short cuts, and alternate routes to and from the Los Angeles airport; you can customize the trip to the needs and moods of any given day. Pattie needed time and no freeway madness, so I chose the scenic route, if it's possible to describe any of the roads out of the immediate area of the airport as scenic; but in time we were driving through tree-lined residential streets.

George had this great peace with himself that allowed him to live on the outside of his phenomenal celebrity in such a natural manner and simplicity of being.

During the drive from the airport to the hotel an incredible thing happened. We listened to her husband's beautiful musical tribute to her on the radio almost nonstop the entire trip. "Something" aired on the Top 40 station and seemed doubly beautiful contrasted to the other songs on the playlist. As soon as it was over, I changed the dial and picked it up on an easy-listening station. At its conclusion I went to another format, and we heard it playing again. What made it really special was when most of the DJs "back-announced" the record, they spoke so glowingly of it and its writer/performer. Tears and discontent were magically swept aside, and Pattie seemed to sit up in her seat, gaze out the window, and lose herself in the beautiful surroundings of the fabulous Beverly Hills mansions and landscaping found in some very private areas of 90210 as we drew nearer to our destination. Soon she was smiling and virtually smelling the roses. She was a proud wife who had just flown eight thousand miles to a faraway land and heard her husband finally get the accolades and recognition she felt he not only deserved but that were long overdue. I was able to confirm for her how warmly the record had been received here, and by the time we arrived at the hotel, she was ready to go shopping.

Buy George

George had this great peace with himself that allowed him to live on the outside of his phenomenal celebrity in such a natural manner and simplicity of being. He carried himself so that you could probably sit down next to him on a bus, ride the bus route, and get off at your stop without noticing that you had just ridden with a Beatle. This is similar to what would happen when I went out to lunch with Paul in London: there would be this recognition time lag of sorts from people when George would run. into a 7-Eleven for a pack of cigarettes. Most times we would be in and out of a place before people would catch on to who had just been in there, and as we drove away we could look back as the stunned customers came to the door of the store scratching their heads in disbelief when the realization set in of who had just made a purchase.

Such was the day at Fred Segal's jean store on the corner of Melrose Avenue and Crescent Heights in Hollywood. At the time, this was Fred Segal's first enterprise that drew the music business people into shop for upscale jeans. Besides that, Fred had a very eclectic offering of hip clothes and had become the place to go when record companies and bands needed stage outfits. There was a great insider feeling at Fred Segal's in those early days. George and I decided to go try on jeans and probably were in the place for about half an hour taking turns with one of the small dressing rooms before someone caught on to who was trying on the really small-waist-size jeans. I remember that it was George's turn in the small changing room, and the store seemed to start tilting our direction. In a matter of minutes, customers who were casually grazing through the store were all now crowded outside of George's dressing room; each person all of a sudden had an article of clothing that he needed to try on, and this particular dressing room was just where he wanted to be. I saw what was happening, and it was obvious that we would have to abandon our original (optimistic) plan to simply try to buy a couple pairs of jeans.

I began planning an escape out of this small, crowded space—a blue jean bailout, I guess you could call it. Once the autographs started, it became a never-ending event, and we knew that. George was usually an extremely kind and courteous person and very considerate of people when they asked for his signature and although it was uncomfortable to be caught in these situations, he never wanted to disappoint anyone. This is a nice characteristic to have for most people, but here is where the rub comes in: Let's say there are ten people in the store, and they all line up for autographs. Figuring thirty seconds per autograph, it would take roughly five minutes to accommodate the fans and we would be on our way—right? Wrong. During this gracious five minutes on George's part, the word is getting out on the street and over to the people in the shops next door. Even the employees at Fred Segal's are frantically calling nearby friends and relatives to hurry down because a Beatle is there. Soon the location of a Beatle would cross area codes and into radio station newsrooms, and potentially within less than half an hour there could be TV trucks, reporters, and rubberneckers clogging traffic. Those who have been there know this is definitely not an exaggeration. I had experience in these situations, and I knew that my role was now to assume the position of being the bad guy.

I hustled George out of the place by literally grabbing him by the arm and pulling/pushing him out of the door while he protested that he wanted to stay and satisfy the gathering group's requests for autographs. We both knew our parts, and we both acted them out with great aplomb. Once we were in the car and pulling away from the curb, George continued his act by waving and smiling at everyone with a look that said, "Oh darn, I wanted to stay and sign your arms, T-shirts, store receipts, and whatever else, but my mean friend wouldn't let me."

Drinks Are on George

When I resigned as president of Barnaby/CBS, I launched my new company, Hometown Productions, Inc. The kickoff party was an unusual affair when it came to attendees. We decided to hold the party in a large meadow that bordered a grove of trees along a small stream in the middle of a seven-thousand-acre ranch in the Malibu mountains. I had just sold my Hollywood Hills digs and was hiding out at this ranch where I had rented and refurbished the groom quarters in the barn. The contemporary country music scene was beginning to explode, and I found myself being thrust into the heart of its emergence. I had willingly placed myself in a position of self-imposed limbo because although I felt Nashville's powerful call in my life, I was still a California kind of guy. I became somewhat torn between my comfortable existence in LA and the unnerving idea of moving to Tennessee. Deep down, though, I sensed that I needed a change, and that is why I made the quiet decision to seclude myself for a while at the Malibu ranch while I thought through this quandary. The rolling hills, streams, and open meadows were the perfect place for this country boy to chill out while warming up to the decision about where my new offices and I would eventually land.

In the meantime a choice location became available in Hollywood, just in case I gave in to my "surf's up" side, I went ahead and leased a suite of offices in a little complex that had once been part of one of the old movie complexes on Sunset Boulevard just off of Sunset and Vine, called the "Crossroads of the World." The courtyard was surrounded by what looked like Hansel and Gretel cottages, and the various offices were occupied by those in the music or film business. I rented the suite until the lease ran out without ever occupying or furnishing the place. For whatever reason, probably having to do with just leaving the corporate world after twelve years, I was having a problem with committing to the formality of "office space." Nashville was winning out, and I think my new relationship with Waylon Jennings had also instilled in me a somewhat free-spirited attitude; I just wanted to hang loose and make music.

I ended up traveling through a vibrant desert on a horse with a lot of different names for a five-year "Outlaw" ride I will never forget.

My only concrete plans the day of the launch party were to take off the day after the party and head for Nashville, where I was scheduled to start an album with singer/songwriter Rick Cunha for Atlanta's newly formed GRC Records as well as work on projects with Waylon Jennings, Tompall Glaser, and Jessi Colter. Once I headed out on that road trip, I ended up traveling through a vibrant desert on a horse with a lot of different names for a five-year "Outlaw" ride I will never forget. As I talked about earlier, Waylon and I merged our music, lives, and families and followed our dreams of a new country genre to the extreme, which resulted in a whole lot of new and incredible music. The suite of Hollywood offices became unnecessary because most of the following years were spent in the studio or on the road. I kept an LA address but split my time just about equally between Nashville and Hollywood.

Back to the party. In attendance were George and Pattie Harrison; Jack Oliver; and Mal Evans from my Beatle/Apple days; Claudine Longet, Ricky Nelson and his wife, Kris; the Hager Twins from my Andy Williams/Barnaby days; Waylon Jennings and Jessi Colter from the upcoming recording projects; and a bouillabaisse of famous people from the broad industry that were in and out of my life for various reasons— Leonard Nimoy, Penny Marshall, Rob Reiner, Jennifer Warnes, Karen Valentine, and others.

This was early May 1973 and the first time that many of these celebrities had ever met a Beatle, and they were quite surprised when George showed up. People in the entertainment industry know how to act around each other and honor the rules that have to do with being cool when a really big star enters the room. Everyone in attendance, being well trained in this little soft shoe of a routine, adhered to the unspoken guidelines of this order. Except for Jessi Colter. Waylon, who was so used to being the center of attention in every situation, was not to be upstaged, so he coped with the second banana position by doing what came easy and

Far left: Pattie Harrison (facing), Jack Oliver (back), Waylon Jennings (side view— partially covered) and me (side view). **Middle:** Claudine Longet (facing), Mal Evans (facing), Pattie Harrison (back) and Jack Oliver (side view). **Far right:** I just noticed this picture of Jack Oliver, the former General Manager of Apple Records and the one who was there running the label 'til the very end, is eating an apple at the launch of my Hometown Productions, Inc. It seems oddly similar to the one of Paul eating the apple at the beginning of Apple Records.

fell back on his aloof Outlaw cowboy persona. No problem. On the other hand, his wife and star-to-be, Jessi, having had a bit of the bubbly on a very warm day in the woods, became a little enchanted with George's presence and proceeded to virtually gush over him, and in the process managed to impart some of her liquid refreshments down his front. Not only was this embarrassing, but it was a bit uncomfortable for just about everyone because Jessi chose to ignore the booze baptismal she had just bestowed on George and kept prattling away as if nothing had happened. He didn't react as one would expect; he let the moment sit just long enough for Waylon to remove Jessi from a party that had suddenly become very quiet.

Luckily, the hot sun did its bit, and it wasn't very long before George's shirtfront dried out, and he was able to head back to the recording session in the city that he had left in order to attend this occasion. I can rarely remember seeing George with a beer or a glass of wine in his hand, so I'll bet the musicians at the session probably wondered where he had been. Fortunately it was champagne, so the stain was barely noticeable and the smell would soon be normalized in the smoky studio.

I left the next morning for Nashville as planned and became the producer part of the Outlaw era with Waylon, Willie, Tompall, and yes—Jessi Colter.

Golden Slumbers

I was on the road somewhere in the states on late '60s Capitol Records business when I got a call to drop everything and get to London

Far left: Me, Rick Nelson, Kris Nelson, and Claudine Longet (back to camera). **Middle:** Rob "Meathead" Reiner (*All in the Family*) and wife Penny Marshall (*Laverne and Shirley*) **Far right:** Leonard Nimoy became more than a well wishing guest that day by becoming the unofficial photographer for the affair. We caught him catching the action.

and the Apple offices as quickly as possible. This was not the first time this had happened, and I knew the routine. I headed out for the airport after having called my office with the instructions for my secretary to start booking me out of that airport on the most direct route to the UK. One of the main problems with this sort of bouncing around the universe was that things were always crucial in how I handled matters at Apple. If I had a chance, I would always try to rest up in some manner before heading eastward to Savile Row so I could be on my toes when I got there. No matter how many times I have flown to Europe, I don't think I have ever felt well the first day of arrival. This particular time, I was on a rather grueling tour in the American heartland and definitely had no chance to catch up on some much needed sleep. By the time I landed in London, dropped my luggage off at a hotel near the Apple offices, and walked into the building, it was already early evening and I was fried. It was as if I hadn't stopped from the moment I got the call until I stepped into an upstairs meeting room at Apple. I hadn't slept well on the plane and was virtually days into the clothes I was wearing when I walked in.

I remember that when I finally came to a full stop, all energy drained out of me, and all I could do was lean against a desk and hang on with my hands at my side clutching the front edge of the desk. I could barely keep my eyes open while my whole body just wanted to shut down! I hadn't seen the *Magical Mystery Tour* film yet (it had up to this point received very limited theatrical release in the United States, and these were the days before VHS tapes and DVDs), and they were racking up a 16mm copy of the film for my review and pleasure. People were coming in and out of the room and, upon seeing me there, would give me a pat and a "hi," ask a question or two, and then carry on like I had just walked in from across the street. We were all used to rolling in and out of each other's lives on both continents, and I don't think it ever crossed their minds that I had just spent about eighteen hours in motion getting to that point in that room and that I was totally exhausted. I got away with one or two word answers and started getting queasy and unsure of being able to stand up. I was afraid if I opened my mouth too far and tried to say too many words that my insides would come pouring out. There was an acrid aroma that permeated this space, and I am sure this added a downward descent to my unintended freefall.

The ever-present admonition from the president of Capitol Industries always started its rounds in my head at an amplified level in moments like these: "Ken, when it comes to the Beatles, there is no margin for error. Keep it together at all times." Fine—he wasn't the one staying up for days and eating bad food for a living. To make matters worse, George Harrison entered the room and walked straight over to where I was standing and started a full conversation with me.

George: Hey, Ken, how ya doin'?
Me: Fine.
George: Ya just get in?
Me: Yeah.
George: Whuja think of the film so far?
Me: Cool.

I was fading and panicking and holding on for dear life at this point when all of a sudden George squared off directly in front of me, put his hand on my shoulder, put his face really close to mine, and whispered so

No one has ever seen this picture of George, Ringo, Mal, and Bud O'Shea taken in Monterey, California, in 1968. Bud was my promotion manager for the San Francisco area at the time and filled in for me at the last minute when I couldn't get a flight out of St. Louis in time to take care of my West Coast artist relations responsibilities. Bud shares this from his private collection for the first time.

no one else could hear: "Come on, mate, I am taking you to your hotel and putting you to bed." With that, he quietly led me out of the building and took me to my hotel, helped me to my room, and actually sat me on the edge of the bed and pulled off my shoes. With the assurance that I could manage the rest, he told me to get some rest and that all business matters could wait until the next day.

One thing that was a little rough about working with Apple was the fact that with four bosses you could get into quite a spin when caught in the middle of some divergent creative juices and melodic dreams. On the other side of that ha'penny coin was the fact that if one of the Beatles took you on and covered, cared, or sanctioned you, then you had no worries. George did just that. He saw how beat I was. He knew my situation, and he instinctively knew that he needed to give me a break.

I didn't even hear the door slam when he left the hotel room. I was already in dreamland. To this day, I can't remember why I was called there in such a hurry. By the time I showed up the next day, I think they had forgotten too. I am not sure what we did for the next few days. One of the main activities at Apple oftentimes consisted of just hanging with the corps and going with the ever-changing flow of madness and mesmerizing moments.

There Goes the Sun

It was November 30, 2001, and the phone began ringing at about 3 a.m. I always hate any phone call between 10 p.m. and 8 a.m. because it usually means something urgent or something bad has happened. I have never received a phone call at three in the morning with someone giving me good news.

It was Fox News, and they told me George had died and wanted to know if they could do a live interview with me over the phone first thing in the morning. They would show footage from previous appearances I had made on the network with my voice-over. Then they asked if they could send a car for me in Bodega Bay to bring me into the San Francisco studios to do live interviews with East Coast anchormen James Rosen's and David Asmans's respective shows, as well as participate in a George Harrison special being put together by Laurie Dhue. This was not a good day for me because I had not been doing well dealing with my own cancer, and I had an important meeting with my oncologist that very morning to see what my latest test results were. I was expecting bad news, so I had already had a very sleepless night. I agreed to do the early morning phone-in piece but wanted to reserve any further commitments until after my 10 a.m. meeting with the doctor. They agreed. I did the interview as requested at about 6 a.m., California time. I did the best I could with the conversation considering that I was in a very groggy state of sadness as well as being a little short on sleep. I then got ready for the twenty-five-minute drive from Bodega Bay into the clinic in Sebastopol, a small town just west of Santa Rosa. My wife, Connie, drove, and while I looked out the car window at the sweet Sonoma County countryside drifting by, I finally allowed myself to open up a space deep down inside where I could let the heartbreaking news sink in.

I was diagnosed in December 1996, almost exactly five years earlier, with an incurable and very rare bone marrow cancer that was simply called Waldenström's macroglobulenimia. I had been ill for about two years, and the malady's identity had evaded a bevy of doctors until a specialist sorted it out and the diagnosis was made and then confirmed. They told me I had one to three years left to live at that time. I was also informed that it is so rare that in addition to being incurable, there is virtually no research, so outside of some experimental options, my silver future had a dark, cloudy lining.

While I was in the oncologist's office, Fox was calling Connie on the cell phone as she was waiting in the lobby to hear the results of the tests and my prognosis. In all honesty, she was not into the TV bit; she was worrying about how I was doing and fearing the worst. I had spent the previous month of August in chemotherapy, and it appeared that it wasn't working. I was not getting good news inside the hospital, and the newsroom was pestering her outside. She could tell when I came out into the reception area that I had just received a bad report, and she was getting upset at Fox's persistence. She had just received another call from them saying that time was of the essence for scheduling and that they were going to send a limo to our residence in Bodega Bay just in case I would agree to come to San Francisco to do the series of live shows. They said I could think it over during the drive back to the ocean. If I did not want to do it, I could just send the car away.

We pulled out of the parking lot of the clinic and headed west on Bodega Highway toward home. She was dealing with our personal crisis and was getting a little irritated by the media push. She was totally taken off guard when I told her I wanted to do the interviews. As hard as it was for her to understand, I had reasons, and they all made sense, at least to me. I felt it was a way to honor my time with George and pay respect to a particularly warm and rewarding relationship. No matter what they asked me, I knew my responses would do him well. I also really wanted a diversion from our own reality that had daunting parallels to the one I was going to be addressing on national television. I felt that if I thought about someone else instead of my own problems, I could come back to them in a day or so with a better perspective.

It was a proper goodbye on my part, and I know that if George had cable where he was that he surely liked everything I said.

We pulled up in front of our house, and I made a Pony Express transition from our car to the waiting limo because by now time was extremely short. Typically it takes about an hour and a half to drive from Bodega Bay to San Francisco city center with light traffic. As you can imagine, someone like myself who had spent a good share of his life in the fast lane is not easily frightened by risky actions, but I have never seen anyone drive like that limo driver did that day. I think I was on camera within fifty-five minutes from the time I got into the car. It was a long day, but I felt good, and the tension of doing three different shows live and on the natch totally took my mind off the home front issues. I did a live CBS interview from the car after we left the studio, dozed on the ride home, and fell into bed totally exhausted.

It was a proper goodbye on my part, and I know that if George had cable where he was that he surely liked everything I said.

Track 26

Bangla Desh on the Banks of Moon River

» *Los Angeles, California—New York,*
New York—Nashville, Tennessee,
August–October 1971

One of the most totally "out there" experiences during my time spent in the entertainment business happened shortly after I was hired by Andy Williams to be the president of his CBS record company, Barnaby Records. I had just resigned from my vice presidency at MGM Records under president Mike Curb to set up my own production company, Hometown Productions, Inc. Less than a month had gone by when Dennis Bond, my attorney at that time, called to tell me that Andy was looking for someone to head up his label. Mr. Moon River's long-term and very successful relationship with Alan Bernard had come to an end. Alan had not only served as Andy's personal manager for many years but also as president of Barnaby Records and its associated publishing companies. The position was a real plum in the record business, and many top execs with other record companies were vying for the gig, some even willing to leave the top position at much larger labels. It was a sweet job with beautiful offices on La Cienega Boulevard, a location that was perfectly situated between Hollywood and Beverly Hills. Andy was as big a star as there was in those days; the money was good, and the perks were many.

My interview with Andy was very brief. Within minutes, our meeting became more of a chat; it was obvious that I was going to be chosen for the job. Success does have a smell, and I could sense in the air the sweetness of the impending outcome. I knew his search ended the minute I walked through the door of his combination office and art gallery that occupied the entire top floor of his two-story building. The bottom floor held the record company offices that looked out onto the boulevard in one

One of the many trade magazine articles announcing me as the executive chosen by Andy and Clive Davis to head up this CBS imprint.

Ken Mansfield Is New President Of Barnaby

HOLLYWOOD — Ken Mansfield, one ... man- ... bel in

Mansfield New Barnaby Chief

Andy signs me on as the President of his Barnaby/CBS record company (1971).

REMINDERS!

ANDY WILLIAMS

Dear Ken —
Thanks for
the Xmas
watch:
I'm practicing
my draw.
This is our
year!
Andy

Christmas 1971 holiday thank you note from Andy to me.

confident the combination of Ken Mansfield and Mike Shepherd will be instrumental in bringing about this expansion efficiently and rapidly."

Williams, Mansfield, Clive Davis

direction and onto the beautifully landscaped courtyard out back. The center of the first floor was very open with offices on each side. The office I was to occupy was at the back end of the building where ten-foot windows, which filled one side and the back of the office, looked out onto the courtyard. An interior decorator was hired, and my new space was designed to my specific taste and colors using most of a handsome budget, a nice little touch-up for a space about the size of an average living room.

At the time, I was the perfect choice to run this classy little label that featured Ray "Everything Is Beautiful" Stevens as its lead artist, not just because I was the "Beatles guy" but because I had also been deeply involved in (or at least a part of) much of the previous decade's music industry innovations. The label was definitely ready for contemporizing, and the direction it needed to be taken in was totally open to the resourcefulness and imagination of its new leader. Among other things, the gig gave me: (1) a lot of room for creativity and (2) the clout that the combination of Andy Williams's name and the CBS distribution powerhouse gave me to get things done in the industry.

Andy and I did have one major, albeit somewhat enjoyable, problem: we really clicked with each other personally and had this propensity to party a lot. From day one we seemed to fall into a groove as pals. We were both single now, and shared the wonderful fact that neither money nor opportunity was ever a problem—ah yes, the world was truly our oyster. He had just wrapped up his very successful NBC TV series and had the time, fortune, energy, and out-and-out desire to have a good time. His marriage to Claudine Longet was over, but the relationship wasn't. They carried on in a way that showed that although they couldn't handle being husband and wife, they still really liked each other. (They were separated for almost four years and didn't finally divorce until 1975.) I became friends with both of them, which made things comfortable and uncomfortable depending on the current status of their relationship.

The two years I spent with Andy evolved into an unexpected roller-coaster ride of events and emotions, and unfortunately, things ended badly. I wanted to take the label heavy into the emerging contemporary country market, and he had a hard time wanting to commit over 50 percent of the label's resources to this kind of direction. I felt very strongly about where I saw the industry was headed and eventually resigned over this dispute, which didn't sit well with Andy. Fortunately, I did like how our relationship started and the way I was introduced to the company by my predecessor.

Me and Claudine Longet in session at Hollywood Sound Recorders. The album entitled *Let's Spend the Night Together* was released in 1972.

Alan Bernard had called and invited me to lunch almost immediately after I accepted the position to run Barnaby. He offered to help me transition into running the company by bringing me up-to-speed on projects in the works when he left. This kindly offer from the person you are replacing goes a long way in describing the good character of a fellow warrior in a very tough business. Over lunch at Cyranos on the Sunset Strip, he also gave me an inside tip—there were two immutable ground rules with Mr. Williams. One was that you never pick up the check at a restaurant when you were eating out with him. The other was that you don't quit on him. I broke the second of these two rules, but he had to like me for never breaking the other! My leaving the label changed our relationship so dramatically that I was truly stunned—not only were we no longer business associates, we were no longer friends. I always liked Andy and still do to this day.

As I mentioned earlier, I finally set up my own production company (Hometown Productions, Inc.) when I left CBS/Barnaby. I went on to produce the acts I wanted to bring to Barnaby—Waylon Jennings, Jessi

Colter, Tompall Glaser, and other cutting-edge and Outlaw country artists that I could have signed to the label. In time I also produced under the Hometown moniker such internationally famous acts as David Cassidy, Don Ho, The Flying Burrito Brothers, and Nick Gilder, so it actually turned out better for me financially. Now I was able to keep the money myself instead of making it for someone else's company and just drawing a salary.

Hollywood

As I started out telling at the beginning of this story, and yes, it is a Beatles story, one of my most bizarre happenings in the business took place with Andy in August of 1971 during the time I was in his employ. Late one night we were sitting in St. Germaine, a very tony Hollywood restaurant, having dinner. After about three hours of fine wines, we were deep in the bag. Both of us were brought up real simple and real country (I am from Idaho and Andy is a native of Iowa), so there was a shared innocence about the two of us when we would get smashed. Simplistically speaking, everything was really funny, and we laughed at everything each other said; pretty soon the surrounding tables were joining in and enjoying the fun with Mr. Andy Williams himself.

At some point during that August evening at St. Germaine, while we were in that elevated condition, someone came up to the table to mention that George Harrison's Bangla Desh concert in Manhattan was taking place the next day, and they wanted to know why we weren't going. (At that point it was simply known as the George Harrison and Friends Benefit Concert. There were going to be two shows: one at 2:30 p.m. and the second at 8 p.m.) That inquiry, although somewhat pointed, was not intended as a challenge, but Andy responded to it as such and immediately turned to me as the "Beatles guy" and announced to the restaurant in general that I was going to get up from the table and call George and get us tickets. I still had all their personal phone numbers and glowed at the thought of how impressive it would look to those around our table if I got up and did just that. What followed was an exercise of futility and what seemed like an hour of me sweating in my suedes in a phone booth just outside the men's room. I was desperately trying to get in touch with someone from Beatlesville! I couldn't find George, Paul, or Ringo or Allen Klein or Neil Aspinall or Mal Evans or even Ron Kass or Peter Asher or anyone else who could remotely have the ability to get me last-minute tickets to the hottest event on planet Earth at the time. So I had to suck it up and go back to the table and tell Andy and the onlookers that I had failed.

Upon hearing this bad news, Andy got up from the table and (with an air of total confidence coupled with a secondary look of disdain at my obvious ineffectiveness) stated that *he* would make a couple of calls and take care of the matter. With this announcement, he walked off in the direction of the men's room. Within five minutes he was back, and I noticed for the first time how I didn't like the way he looked wearing a smug smile. "I have our tickets," he announced and further stated he had called his secretary to make early-morning plane reservations and that she had already booked a pair of suites for him and me at the Warwick. Of course, we were all looking at Andy with incredulous disbelief written on our faces as we asked the obvious question—how did he get the tickets? As he slowly poured himself a fresh glass of wine, he really sketched out in great detail the simple manner in which he accomplished the task at hand. A sip, a sentence, a sip, a sentence—I wanted to strangle him but was also spellbound by what he had to say. He had called Ted Kennedy and told him the situation. Ted Kennedy then called Charles Bluhdorn, the founder and chairman of Gulf and Western. Gulf and Western owned lots of entertainment properties, including Madison Square Garden where the event was being held. Andy said that Mr. Bluhdorn then called the manager of the Garden and that our tickets would be waiting at will call! Of course, Andy had to add that they were very good seats just to turn the knife a little more. Anyway, we were on our way, and it only got better—in a bad boy sort of way. In order to enter a little false sense of sanity to this outing, it was decided that Andy and I would head to Nashville afterward to check out our company offices there.

This was the beginning of the most lost five days I have ever spent in my life. One thing for sure, it was one of the most hilarious.

New York

Unbelievably, early the next morning, Andy and I made it on to what was probably the first nonstop out of LAX to Kennedy International where upon arrival, we were immediately picked up by limo and Andy's brother, Dick Williams. We were taken straight to our suites to change, freshen up for the evening concert, and use the limited time left after the flight to make plans for later. While we were getting ready, I was able to get in touch with George at his hotel to find out what was happening after the evening concert. He told me that arrangements were being made to take over a popular Italian restaurant after hours and that there was going to be a very cool post-show party. He didn't know for certain where the party was going to be, and wouldn't have told me the location if he did. After years of the level of celebrity he had inherited, he knew that paparazzi and fans would overrun us if the word did get around. He told me to call him at the hotel after the concert because he was going to return there before going on to the party. He gave me a private room extension to ask for so I could get through to him for instructions. I had now redeemed myself in Andy's eyes by finally getting in touch with George and receiving the after-show party invitation, so we were back on track with all egos intact.

Going into the concert that rainy evening with a superstar of Andy's caliber was rather intense. It was the first time that I got a real sense of the magnitude of his celebrity as he made his way through the mass of people. In the past, I had always admired how he handled the fans, even the very troublesome ones who had no reservations about disturbing us when we were sitting down to dinner at a restaurant or trying to watch a movie.

When we finally got to our seats at the Garden, the strangest thing started happening. Everyone was passing joints and drugs of all kinds down the rows in a Woodstock/Monterey Pop Festival kind of sharing, and when they came down our row and people saw Andy Williams take a hit, everyone started sending their drugs down our row just to see America's "mom and apple pie" guy joining in the fun. Needless to say, the music sounded great to us that night. We probably would have had a good time no matter where we were sitting or who was playing.

The concert was indeed special. We went back to the Warwick, and as planned, I called George at his hotel. When I gave the private room number code to the hotel operator, I was told that no calls were to be put through to Mr. Harrison unless they were on a special list, and my name was not on that list. The fact that I had the private code carried zero weight with the phone naziette. I figured this happened because it was a last-minute arrangement with George, and after he had given me the information, he had probably forgotten to tell someone to put my name on the list. I politely suggested that she just call the room for verification, but she refused. No matter how hard I tried to convince her, she remained immovable in her position as unofficial guard of the phone waves that wended their way to George's suite.

Upon seeing me hang up the phone in defeat, Andy once again got that look on his face that he had when he came back victoriously to our table at St. Germaine, and said matter-of-factly to hand him the phone and he would take care of it, like always. He dialed the hotel and gave the operator George's room number and, just as had happened to me a few minutes earlier, was told that she was instructed not to ring anyone through that was not on the list. Andy then proceeded to tell her who he was, knowing his fame could move mountains. First, she told him that the name Andy Williams was not on the list and, second, that she knew he wasn't Andy Williams anyway. He replied yes, I am; she said no, you are not; he said yes, I am and I will prove it, and began singing "Moon River" over the phone to her. "See? I knew you weren't Andy Williams," she said, interrupting him mid-first verse, and curtly hung up the phone on him! I would give anything to have a picture of the look on his face. It encompassed pitifulness, amazement, and the perfect touch of delayed anger. Andy's brother, Dick, and I were rolling on the floor at this point, which only increased Andy's displeasure.

This whole scenario was absolutely mind-bogglingly funny to us at this point, but no one expected what happened next. A little background—Cary Grant had just made a series of commercials for Brut cologne (he was on the board of Faberge, Brut's parent company) and somehow through this endeavor became acquainted with George Harrison. My memory is real flimsy on the why of all this, but for some reason or other Cary Grant's name must have been on the evening guest list. Dick Williams was also an entertainer and a great imitator of famous people. (Andy and Dick began their careers as two of the four brothers in the Williams Brothers Quartet.) Dick walked over and picked up the phone, called George's hotel, and with his best Cary Grant imitation told the operator that he was Cary Grant and would she please put him through to his old pal *Gowge* Harrison. She said, "Of course, Mister Grant," and put him right through. Dick then handed me

This party had a life of its own, and we became

the phone, did a little dance in front of his distraught brother, followed by a bow and a tip of an imaginary hat, and skipped off to the bathroom singing "Moon River" out of key! I got the party info, and we almost had to be carried to the restaurant from laughing so hard.

I am not done yet. When we got to the party at Ungano's, mega-producer Phil Spector was on stage at the piano totally out of it and hogging the evening singing and boring everyone to tears. We weren't there fifteen minutes when Spector saw Andy at our table and insisted that Andy come up and sing with him. Andy kindly declined, but Spector persisted, persisted, persisted and made it so uncomfortable that Andy got up and we left after being at the party less than thirty minutes. I could tell George was very upset, but he couldn't get to Andy in time to stop our departure. Andy shared with me later that he was not an extemporaneous-type entertainer and needed a controlled and familiar environment to be comfortable. He remarked that if they were looking for a hootenanny, they should have called Pete Seeger.

The next day Andy and I were on our way to Nashville very hungover and not really talking much about the previous day's events. I know Andy was trying to shake off not only the previous evening's intake but also the sound of Dick's "Moon River" ringing in his ears accompanied by my uncontrollable laughter.

Nashville

This was the continuation of what had become a basic lost five days somewhere between Tinseltown and Looneyville. The trip to Nashville had a legitimate purpose: the only problem was with Andy and me. This party had a life of its own, and we became the dedicated medics that kept it breathing. We both had a lot of friends there, so this business trip became more of a social affair than anything else.

We stayed a couple of days, and the night before heading home from Nashville, we were sitting in Andy's hotel suite when there was an unexpected knock on the door. When Andy answered it, he pulled out his official police badge, one that he had earned by doing charity benefits for the Los Angeles Motorcycle Police Officers' Association, and announced to our

the dedicated medics that kept it breathing.

visitor that he was with the DEA and had this case covered. It turned out that our visitor was record producer Jimmy Bowen who said he could smell the acrid scent of our room from down the hall and decided that he wanted to join whoever was in there for a toke. It was ironic that both Andy and I were friends of the legendary record mogul, so everyone felt right at home. This addition in personnel also added some depth and length to our party time.

We returned the next day to LA much the worse for wear. Andy had extravagantly funded this whole excursion with first-class plane tickets, luxurious hotel suites, limos, and meals at upscale restaurants. I remembered rule one (not to pick up any tabs), which I would have put on my expense account anyway. I have a feeling that was the reason for the rule given to me by Alan Bernard in the beginning. If Andy was going to end up paying for it in the long run, then he might as well get the visual credit for picking up the check.

Beverly Hills

The day following our return to LA, I was in my office catching up on little matters that included trying to run the company that I was in charge of when Andy appeared in the doorway of my office. He wanted to know who was using the vacant office just down the hall from mine. I answered that no one was using it and why was he asking. Without answering he walked over to the doorway. Reaching inside while holding eye-to-eye contact with my curious stare, he dramatically flicked off the light switch that was flooding the unused space with wasted electricity.

I always thought he was extravagant, but I guess the three cents he saved that day on the Barnaby Building light bill helped pay for our trip.

•••••◦•◉•◦•••••

Later on in Hollywood, an interesting follow-up to this whole excursion was the quiet time with the "Quiet One" sitting in A&M recording studios, just George and me and the engineer as George carefully replaced some of his guitar parts and vocals for the live album and movie soundtrack. I don't know if it is known that some of the parts on the live *Bangla Desh* album were overdubbed, but these sweetening sessions had to do less with deception and more with giving the record buyer a more acceptable product. There are bound to be glitches in a live undertaking of this magnitude, especially in a concert that was put together as hastily as this incredible event was. It was a private time because I don't think George felt it was anybody else's business when it came to preparing a product with his name on it. Although Phil Spector was supposedly helping George on this project, I never saw him there when I was hanging about. That could be one of the reasons for the calm in the studio and a "non-holding of court" when I was there.

Track 27

DeKlein of the Roamin' Allen Empire

» *Los Angeles, California, Autumn 1973*

It was the summer of 1973. I had just returned to LA from a muggy month in Nashville, Tennessee, after completing production on songwriter Rick Cunha's *Cunha Songs*. This was his first album for Atlanta-based GRC Records, and we were fortunate in his debut to generate a semicrossover pop/country hit entitled "Yo Yo Man." I drove there and back in my new Mercedes 350 SL, deciding it was time I found out for myself about the ribbon of highway that formed the asphalt and cement foundation beneath the tour-bus homes of the country artists I had been producing. I also wanted to get my "kicks on Route 66" before Interstate 40 totally obliterated its memory.

It was good to be back in LA. I always felt more comfortable in the Hollywood Hills than I did in the rolling hills of Tennessee, regardless of how much the country songs that I produced and recorded romanticized about it. (I have never quite determined if this was my way of denying my rural roots or whether it was because a backwoods country boy was trying to go "up town," and "down home" was refusing dual citizenship). I truly liked the sunshine, the food, the people, and the fast life in this rock-and-roll paradise. Ironically, I was able to pay my way *here* in Hollywood by producing hit country records *there* in Nashville. I guess I was putting to use what I was trying to put aside. As my New York Jewish friends would say, "So, go figure!"

It was a clear, dry, hot, Santa Ana weather day, and George Harrison and I were alone at a house I had rented for him in the hills of Beverly Hills. It was a good time for George because not only had he had the No. 1 album, *Living in the Material World,* on the *Billboard* charts for five weeks this summer, but on this particular day he was also sitting with the No. 1 single, "Give Me Love (Give Me Peace on Earth)." Not bad for the Beatle in the shadows for so many years. (I personally found it interesting that he knocked Paul's "My Love" out of the No. 1 spot to get there.) My wife and

Pattie Harrison were shopping, and we were in the kitchen—he was cutting up veggies and cooking lunch, intent on the task at hand and being cautious with the carrots. He seemed abnormally absorbed, head down and talking as he was working. He had called me into the kitchen to tell me something. Even though it had been almost four years since I had left Apple Records, our personal relationship was still ongoing. Because I had been there at the beginning of this unfolding episode, he wanted me to be one of the first to know that the Beatles (or solo Beatles by this time) were leaving Allen Klein. It was ironic that I was there at the house that day when he got the telephone call that it was over.

The four of us had been outside by the pool when the call came in from London. The conversation became very extended, so the girls got bored and decided to go shopping, leaving me to tell George that we had been deserted by our women. Their departing message was that George's bad manners were going to cost us money on Rodeo Drive and that we were to fend for ourselves as far as lunch was concerned.

The final decision had just been made to dump Klein as the Beatles' and Apple's business manager. It was particularly appropriate that I should hear it straight from George. He was very aware of and sensitive to my feelings of allegiance toward Ron Kass, the man Klein had forced out of the presidency at Apple. He knew that this friendship and loyalty were reasons I left Apple Records and followed Kass to MGM records.

I'll never forget the atmosphere of graciousness that surrounded us in the kitchen that day. George had a way of making a setting very serene when he wanted to talk about personal things. It was his unique way of keeping everything in a gentle and kind perspective. I leaned against the cabinets as he stirred the upcoming meal in the frying pan. We began talking quietly about Allen Klein: our personal impressions of him, about our friend Ron Kass, and about the meal we would soon be eating. I remember that George was barefooted and had on a shapeless long-sleeve shirt and English jeans that day. (I always called them English jeans because they never looked like our pants; and besides, it seemed like English rock-and-roll stars, especially the guitar players, always had these tiny butts and little skinny legs. This always seemed to make their

Opposite page: George and me sitting by a stream on a 7,000-acre ranch in the Malibu mountains. George left a recording session in Hollywood, about an hour's drive away, to attend an affair of mine.

pants look different regardless of the cut.) So, during our conversation, this gentle, barefoot Beatle with no butt and skinny legs proceeded to elaborate on why I should become a vegetarian like he was. He told me one reason was that animals experience fear when they sense that they are going to be killed. This fear is released into their system just prior to death, and this fear is what we eat when we eat meat. This "fact" and other bits of similar information he presented that day put a different slant on hamburgers for me and made the previously unappetizing rice and veggies concoction on the stove look a lot more approachable. There was no place to sit down in the long, narrow, railroad-style kitchen, so I stood transfixed while he softly explained other more spiritual reasons for his culinary bent.

Even though what was going down with Klein was incredibly important and disturbing at that time, George's interest and mine soon seemed to tire of deep matters in the darkened kitchen. With the bright California sun streaming in through distant windows, our energies became focused on the food preparation task at hand, and our minds wandered to the cool pool waiting outside. George typically never had harsh words to say about people,* and as traumatic as this event was, he maintained this personal propriety. There were disappointments and serious questions about Klein's handling of both financial and career matters, but the tone of George's musings always stayed inquisitive and not accusative.

Soon the phones started going crazy. It was getting late, and I was late for the studio, so I said goodbye into the ear without a phone in it and headed for the flats and an all-night recording session.

* "He's (Klein) quite nice really. But there's a part of him that's odd. He operates on the basis of: 'do unto others as they do unto you except you do it first.' Thing is, they think you are going to do them, even though it never crossed your mind" (George on Allen Klein. From his book *I Me Mine*, Simon and Schuster, 1980).

Track 28

Beats and Pieces

» *London, England—Los Angeles, California, 1965–1978*

During the period of time in the '70s when Ringo lived in LA, he and I and a few friends had established the informal tradition of spending New Year's Eve together. The general plan was for him, me, and mutual friend Alan Pariser to take turns hosting that special evening at one of our homes in the Hollywood Hills. Somehow we usually managed to end up at Ringo's place. (Gee, I wonder who had the nicest house and the biggest party budget?)

The thing I always liked about New Year's Eve and other such celebrations with Ringo is that he deeply believed in tradition. On one of my first Apple working trips to London, I was fortunate to be there during Britain's Guy Fawkes/Bonfire Night holiday in November. Ringo invited me out to his house on Cut Mill Lane in Elstead Surrey for the traditional backyard bonfire that included the time-honored potato and sausage roasting. Talk about a pad. He had purchased the estate from actor Peter Sellers, and though he didn't live there long, it was quite an imposing abode. When the driver pulled up to the front of the place, it looked like a massive hotel. I was let out of the car and found myself standing there, my jaw dropped and blinking like a frog in a hail storm, as I stared up at these incredibly wide stone stairs going up to the entrance. Giant cement lions were poised on both sides, giving the feel of entering a castle. Once you were in the door, the entryway was just like you see in the movies with the grand staircase and all. I am sure you could get lost in the place, but here was the interesting thing: I was taken to a large room off to the left, situated at the end of the house. As I remember it, it was surrounded by windows, and it appeared that this was the primary room they lived in. My impression was that this was another example of Ringo's uncomplicated nature that reflected his simple upbringing and was a very attractive aspect of his personality that I observed over the following years. It was this kind of simplicity that made it so easy to be with all the Beatles. Of course, there is the possibility that I was just a commoner and was only let into that part of the house, with the more formal areas being reserved for bigger names! Maureen, Ringo's first wife, had sewing stuff set up in one corner, Ringo had a drum kit in another corner, and son Jason was set up in his crib in another. I didn't see three-year-old Zak on this visit but figured that because it was late in the evening, he had already been put to bed. The massive fireplace contained their TV set.

There were no restrictions on outside burning during this annual event. As the limo driver was taking me from my hotel on Hyde Park to the outskirts of London, I could barely see as we made our way through the narrow streets to Ringo's because of all of the smoke from so many backyard bonfires. As we stood around the fire in Ringo's backyard, he explained to me that this is England's annual fireworks and bonfire commemoration of the foiled fifteenth-century plot to blow up Parliament and, with it, King James. Hearing about it firsthand from him made it all very special, and I realized how fortunate I was to see and experience it all in such a grand manner. He was multitasking, because as he told the story, he was taking care of the putting in and the taking out of the sausages (Ringo was still a meat-eater in those days) and potatoes from the bonfire.

In the same fashion of being faithful to traditions, Ringo always brought his New Year's British rituals to each December 31 midnight hour celebration. He would take a piece of coal outside that he had gotten from

Opposite page: New Year's Eve parties at Ringo's house were always the greatest and very relaxed. It was his idea for all of us to run outside and take a quick picture. Note the New Year's Eve British tradition of marks of coal on everyone's foreheads. I'm on the left, once again joining Ringo in velvet.

the fireplace and would then bring a piece of wood into the house and give a long explanation of the tradition and meaning of it all. I think I have repeated the ritual correctly but can't remember the explanation he gave. I think it had something to do with taking out the old (the coal) and bringing in the new (the wood). Regardless, the fun for me was really all about his presentation; you could tell how much he enjoyed honoring and sharing the things of his youth and heritage.

During the early to mid-'70s in LA there was never a shortage of parties, and musical royalty like the ex-Beatles, the Stones, or a batch of Byrds was able to move freely about the Hollywood canyons, with Alan Pariser's house being the unofficial main hub where much of Ringo's social activities occurred. Alan ended up being my brother-in-law, and so

I was drawn into even more happenings because of this. I had become oblivious to the effect it would have on people when someone like Ringo would pop in at a small party at my house. My daughter, Lisa, had this backfire on her when she invited a date to one of our parties and the fellow walked in and ran into Ringo in the bar. Instead of being impressed, he was so taken aback and unprepared to meet a Beatle that he totally lost it. I guess he felt insecure because if he had known that someone that famous was going to be there, then he would have dressed a little nicer. I also think he felt a little upstaged. I don't know for certain, but anyway, he walked out in a huff, and I think that was the end of that short-lived romance.

I'll Do It Mae Way

One of the best parties Ringo gave was at a home he and Nancy Andrews rented for several years at Haslam Terrace in the Sunset Plaza area of LA. It didn't matter what the occasion was this particular time because a party at Ringo's house was always fun, and this time he wanted everyone to "put on the dog." Ringo liked people to get dressed up, even in costume if that fit their fancy, and the theme for this particular party was "Black Tie." I'm talking tuxedo time for the rock-and-roll set. With this in mind, we all got gussied up, groomed to the max, and even though, in some cases, we lived just a few minutes' drive away or within blocks of each other, everyone did the full-on "thang" and showed up in a limo. This party consisted of between fifty and seventy-five people, and everyone had a valid reason for being there due to celebrity, wealth, notoriety, or personal relationship. In some cases, they brought nothing more than pure entertainment value to the occasion.

Ringo's parties were unquestionably three notches above the greatest. He always seemed to have new and obscure electronic gadgets to keep people busy between their trips to various peripheral areas of the property where they would achieve assorted forms of cerebral enhancement. He showed off a new toy at this party called a "Metaphaser." It was a two-sided box approximately one square foot in diameter with indented glass windows on two opposing sides. It stood on a stand that placed the box right at face level. Two people would then put their faces into the opposite sides of the box and turn it on. It would go through a series of back and forth strobe-like motions, and as you looked straight ahead into the glass, it would morph the two faces into one face in continuously changing phases. I had a beard at the time, and the young lady on the other side appeared to my vision to have her highly made-up face with my beard, and then my beard would dissolve, and soon it would present my face without a beard and with her eyes, makeup, and red hair. This kept everyone mesmerized, and there was a constant line to check it out. Of course, as the evening progressed, a turn at the box became very surreal as moods were becoming more altered. The music wasn't live but was great and loud—well presented over a state-of-the-art sound system—and the room just dazzled with the eclectic mix of the current "A" list of movers and shakers.

© Nancy Andrews

This is my favorite picture of Ringo. When I think back on the crazy days in the canyons, this is how I remember him. Very handsome, don't you think?

This particular year (1978), one of Ringo's personal invitees was none other than Hollywood legend Mae West. He had recently signed on to film a cameo role for *Sextette*, which would turn out to be Mae's final film. Here is what was mind-boggling: no one even gave Alice Cooper, the Band's Robbie Robertson, Richard Manuel, or Levon Helm, Jimmy Webb, Jim Keltner, Harry Nilsson, Joan Baez, Stephen Stills, or any other famous celebrities a second look. Virtually everyone lined up, as if waiting to buy theater tickets, in front of Mae, who was seated like a queen on a throne. She was wearing what looked like one of her fabulous outfits from one of her old movies. A big burly bodyguard, Mr. America 1966, stood immediately to her left and never changed expressions the whole time. You got the sense that he was wound pretty tight, cocked and ready to unload on anyone who even suggested an inappropriate move in her presence or direction. It was so funny because the famous, the infamous, and the little known alike reverted into little kids as they paid homage to this fascinating lady. As each of us came before her, she would extend her hand for a barely touching handshake, and to each and every person she would make some cute little comment akin to her "is that a pencil in your pocket or are you just glad to see me?" line just for their edification. As each of us walked away from our brief introduction, everyone else was waiting to ask, "What did she say to you?"

The famous, the infamous, and the little known alike reverted into little kids as they paid homage to this fascinating lady.

Something unexpected happened that night that turned out to be one of the highlights of the evening. Glen Campbell decided to show up but chose to ignore the dress code. He arrived wearing something more in the Rhinestone Cowboy motif and subsequently was not permitted past the iron gate that guarded the property. No matter how much he pleaded, Ringo held the line in regard to his strict dress code and would not let Glen inside the fence. It was interesting to see Glen, one the day's most popular entertainers, with his hands on the black iron bars outside the property looking as if he were in reverse jail begging in his highest and most distraught voice to be let into the party.

Nancy Andrews is now a successful and acclaimed photographer. When I contacted her to inquire if there were any pictures from that evening to include along with this story, she told me that there were none because Mae would only attend if no cameras were there and no pictures were taken.

Bucking the System

I think one reason that Ringo and I hit it off from the beginning was our mutual love for country music. As I mentioned before, it was barely fifteen minutes into our first meeting during the 1965 *Help!* press conference in Capitol Records Studio A that he wanted to know if I could fix it up for him to meet Buck Owens. Buck was a Capitol artist also, and we used to joke that when it came to hit records, he was our one-man Beatles of country music. Out of this initial discovery of mutual interests between the two of us came the process of me sending, on a monthly basis, large packages of current American country album releases to Ringo's home in the UK. I received great joy in doing this, knowing how much he liked the music, and I was sure it was a cool thing for him to know that he was totally on top of the American country music scene by receiving these albums in advance. Some of these records would never be released in the UK, so his collection was very unique. To my surprise, I got a call from him one day asking me to stop the shipments. It seems that not only did he have to personally go pick them up from customs, but also the duty tax he was paying on them was ridiculous. This dilemma was magnified by the fact that in some cases, because I was sending him everything I could get my hands on, a lot of the records he received he couldn't have cared less about. Although that little countrified era ended in our relationship, it resurfaced in a big way when I started producing Waylon Jennings and the bad boys of country music because Ringo was really into the '70s Outlaw movement. By that time, he was living primarily here in California, and it was this part of our relationship that led up to the Roxy scenario (see Track 31) as well as the day. I was invited to play the advance tapes of Waylon's *Are You Ready for the Country* album (see Track 16), the same day John Lennon showed up unannounced at Ringo's Hollywood Hills house.

My Favorite Martin

Getting to meet and become friends with George Martin was another perk that resulted from working with the "lads." I had the privilege of attending some of his sessions in London, either when he was producing Ringo's *Sentimental Journey* album or, before that, when he was producing the Fab Four. Of course, George Martin was the king of contemporary producers worldwide, a position royally earned not only because of his abilities but also in part because of his impeccable manners and gracious attitude. You can imagine how honored I felt when he called me one day in LA and said he was flying in from London for other matters, and because he had some free time, would I mind if he stopped by to observe one of my recording sessions? He had taken note of my success as the producer of the Outlaw movement and really wanted to learn more about this contemporary form of country music.

I was working on a Tompall Glaser album at the time for ABC Paramount, and we were really stretching out on this one in LA. We had put together a real "two tone" rhythm section for the album. When George walked into the booth, he looked out into the studio and saw four very different kinds of pickers laying down basic tracks: two hard-core "duded out" cowboys from Tompall's hard-partying road band and two very cool black dudes. I have forgotten who the cowboys were, but I will never forget working with Mel Brown on guitar and drummer Charles Polk, the two men who were the heart and soul of Bobby Blue Bland's band. The track we were laying down was pure soul funk with a cowboy twang to it, and it was hot. The more we all got into it, the more the groove just dug in and got real down-and-dirty funky. George in his aforementioned impeccable and gracious manner sat quietly for about an hour observing a bizarre musical dialogue between this incredible mix of musicians and the booth while listening to music he had never imagined existed. Finally he got up from his chair against the wall when we had just finished a take and quietly bent down to ask me softly and discreetly, in his finest upscale British accent, "So this is country?"

Track 29

Mamas, Don't Let Your Cowboys Grow Up to Be Babies

» *The Land of the Free, Early/Mid–1970s*

In the old days, getting off the plane in Nashville was always a stunning experience. As a dyed-in-the-wool music person, before I hit the curb with my bags, I would start wanting to write a song, produce a record, or begin working with a band. If you were from LA, one thing was for sure: you certainly were not in Music City for the food (except for the "meat and threes"*).

* "Meat and Threes" were a wonderful food phenomenon to us California dudes. It is down-home Southern cooking at its flavorful best. For around $2.69, you could go through a chow line at one of these funky little restaurants and pick out one meat and three side dishes—creamed corn, fried green tomatoes, macaroni and cheese, stewed tomatoes, black-eyed peas, whipped potatoes, over-cooked string beans, lima beans, collard greens, fried okra, homemade biscuits, or cornbread. In the old days, Mac's Diner was on the edge of "the Row" and was famous for having a generous heart. Many of the starving musicians and songwriters were living off one meal a day, and the servers would clue into that after a while and would load up their plates with extra large helpings. My personal favorite "meat and threes" were Hap Townes, Sylvan Park, the Elliston Place Soda Shop, the White Cottage, and Mac's Diner. When things had fallen apart for me the second time around in Nashville, I noticed that after a while, it seemed like the helpings on my daily plate at Mac's kept getting bigger, too.

There was a vibrancy that came up off the streets that said, "Let's make music." In those days, the "boys who made the noise" brought their music and songs to the small houses on Music Row's 16th and 17th Avenues. Here's where the record companies, publishing houses, management offices, talent agencies, and recording studios were located. On any given day, you would find a young kid from Kerrville, Texas, walking up and down those two streets with a guitar over his shoulder, songs in his hand, and hope in his heart as he stopped one by one at the houses on the "Row," trying to get a listen from one of the "good ole boys" who ran things in this, the very center of Music City, USA.

At first the doors were wide open for me in the early '70s when I started making my way into the Nashville system, and I got to skip the "hat in my hand" street-walking part. In fact, I came roaring into town with a head full of self-importance and a reputation that arrived on the flight just ahead of me. I first entered as a vice president of MGM and then reentered as president of Barnaby, a CBS label owned by Andy Williams. This, coupled with my Beatles rep and that of being a rock-and-roll renegade who knew how to produce country records, created an

Taken at the Hangover House at a Capitol Records party celebrating Jessi's recording of "I'm Not Lisa" making it to the top of the charts. **Left to right:** Waylon, me, Jessi and Capitol's Al Coury.

attractive calling card to the lonely rebels of country music. The music industry in general is a very small conclave, and so my LA-to-London escapades had not totally gone unnoticed in Music City, and quite naturally Waylon, Willie, and the boys and I migrated into each other's trembling arms in short order.

Hillbilly Central for us was on 19th Avenue: Tompall Glaser's studio and office complex. Someone in the Outlaw gang was always recording there, and it was usually a spur of the moment happening. We were far enough away from Music Row to be different and just close enough to drive the establishment crazy. Musically it was a wonderful exchange: I brought technical/pop production values and the LA recording attitude to the table, and they taught me how to do the "feel" thing. In those days, the first thing anyone coming to Nashville to make music had to learn was that it all started with the song. The late Harlan Howard, one of Nashville's most famous songwriters, was asked to describe what made a hit country song. He simply replied, "Three chords and the truth!"

Of course, the major record companies in Nashville did not like my entrance into the starched fabric of their industry. In Nashville, in those days, it was more a master-slave relationship when it came to the record label and the artists. Major country stars were told when, where, and what to record. Artists were in and out of the studio in two or three days with the formula recording method, producing an entire album in that time. Lots of great and even some legendary records were produced during this era, but there was not much room for out-of-the-box creativity. The same producers, the same session musicians, and even the same settings on the knobs of the recording equipment were how it was done. It was the "Nashville Sound," but some people wanted the freshness that only artists who had the creative freedom to do things a new way could provide. Naturally, RCA Nashville turned down Waylon when he asked for an LA producer (me) and also said no when he asked to record somewhere besides RCA's Nashville studio complex. (After all, it was good enough for Elvis—who do you think you are?)

So we simply put Waylon's band, the Waylors, in his tour bus and headed out to LA where we could be left alone to do things our way. I financed the album and booked one of the studios at the Sound Labs in Hollywood for a month solid. The sense of freedom and recording all day and all night if we wanted to—really spending time on individual nuances and overdubs—was very invigorating to everyone in the band. The whole studio complex hummed, too, because they weren't used to seeing this ragged bunch of Outlaw cowboys in the halls. Soon the Waylors, Olivia Newton-John, Hall and Oates, Carole King, and the likes melded into this new temporary family as we shared playbacks, ideas, and even musicians. I brought in Ike and Tina Turner's horn section for overdubs, guitar players from Cher's band to share leads with Waylon, Graham Nash for vocal harmonies, and other LA pickers who loved working with this fresh sound.

When we finished mixing the album, Waylon and I flew back to Nashville, Waylon with the master tape for "Side One" in his hand and me with "Side Two" in mine. We were pretty stoked to say the least—we knew we had nailed it. The very next day Waylon walked into Chet Atkins's office unannounced and laid the master tapes on the famous guitarist and record executive's desk. "This is my next album," Waylon told him. He then turned and walked out the door. He emphasized and lingered on the word "next," and the meaning was clear to Chet that if they didn't release that album, there was no other album to release "next." That was the only "next" one there was. With frustration, they did release the album that we had entitled *Are You Ready for the Country?*. The album title was based on a Neil Young song—Neil had given us permission to change some of the lyrics in order to fit our Outlaw message.

The album went to No. 1 three times that year, topped *Billboard's* country charts for ten weeks, and was named the No. 1 country album of the year for 1976 by *Record World Magazine*. It took only a few months to be certified "Gold" by the RIAA. At the same time I had produced a No. 1 pop, country, and middle of the road hit ("I'm Not Lisa") with Waylon's wife, Jessi Colter. I had signed Jessi to my LA production company Hometown Productions, Inc., recorded her tracks in Nashville with a combination of LA and Nashville pickers, and then brought the tapes to LA to mix with a pop engineer in Hollywood's famous Sound Factory Studios. I then took Jessi and the finished mixes of her songs to the Capitol Records Tower, where I signed her to the pop division. Of course, this made the Nashville labels a little nervous, RCA in particular, because

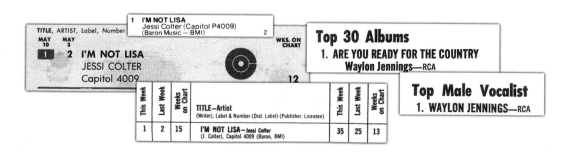

the wife of one of their major artists had broken the Nashville tradition and was having incredible success. What really rubbed more salt in the wound was when Capitol's pop division dictated her initial release back through the country division using them as the launch pad for the eventual pop hit. Not only was the Outlaw thing off and running and out of Nashville's control, but because we were making the big sellers, other country artists began flocking to LA to record. Country music really came alive and became popular with everyone from Waco to Williamsburg. We went from playing in cowboy bars for two hundred or three hundred people to sold out, rock concert–sized auditoriums with ten thousand people—and Waylon was the headliner! It was so amazing to look out at the audience and see the first few rows filled with hip teenagers who were now yelling out requests for songs from Waylon's *older* albums.

Things were getting hotter, and we thought we owned the world; we had stood up to the giant and cast the vanquishing stone. Our slingshot was lined with our misguided integrity and honest dedication to our

Excess became the norm, and worried mothers had to lock up their daughters when this band of Outlaws started partying. People expected us to be wild, and we were happy to oblige.

cause—we loved the music more than money. We didn't care if we were accepted by anyone except those who felt the same way. I categorize our integrity as "misguided" in that it was so narrow in form that it excluded too many value factors relevant to normal life. Excess became the norm, and worried mothers had to lock up their daughters when this band of Outlaws started partying. People expected us to be wild, and we were happy to oblige. It was like having a handwritten invitation to be as bad as we could ever want to be. Ironically, the worse we got, the more money we made. We used to leave rolled up hundred dollar bills lying on coffee tables when a group of people was around just to see who would pick them up when no one was looking. We never retrieved them; it was just our way of finding out who we could trust and who could ride with us. I remember

Waylon, the band, and me showing up on time for a concert at Guthrie Theater in Minneapolis. The promoter came out to the bus and asked us what we were doing there. Waylon's road manager, Johnna Yurcic, explained that we were there at the time prescribed in the performance contract to set up for our sound check. "Aren't you going to show up late and be out of it like we expected?" They wanted us to be messed up, so in time we were more than happy to oblige way beyond their wildest expectations.

Waylon and I could never totally agree who was a bad influence on whom, but that was the beginning of five lost years that ironically did beget a lot of real cutting-edge music. It also had a lot to do with changing the way some things were done in Nashville, especially in terms of the artists' control over their own creativity. No. 1 records and the resultant big bucks made our notoriety and behavior all seem acceptable not only to others but also even to ourselves. It saved us the trouble of having to rationalize our strange, crazy conduct. I am proud of the historical impact our music had on the industry but shudder when I think back on the life I led.

Nashville is different now. The small houses on "the Row" are no longer there, having been replaced by giant corporate structures, and there is no longer any place to park. If you want a real guffaw from the locals, just try walking into any of these buildings with your songs, dreams, and a guitar draped over your shoulder without an appointment or a top-notch manager, agent, and producer in tow.

These days it all has to do with lawyers, accountants, and corporate executives, sometimes in far away cities, that don't know the difference between lariats and lasagna when it comes to country music. It is all bottom lines now, and in most cases, the way business is done and the way naive and innocent people's hearts and souls are considered, bottom *is* the operative word. I think the saddest thing, though, is that the "good ole boys" in the framework of the big companies have wrested back control, and the music once again sounds automated. I must add, in all fairness, that within these city limits there still dwell super people with incredible talent and warm hearts who are there because of the music, their visions, and the cheeseburgers at Brown's Diner. They flourish and color the landscape like flowers in a vast desert. For them it is still fun, still romantic, and still the only place they want to be, and to these dedicated few, it is still about the song. I got to see it both ways, and I like their way better.

Fortunately for some of us old timers, we can still think "Cash" refers to a certain country singer.

Track 30

Mal

» *Los Angeles, California—London, England— and Beyond, 1968–1976*

I knew I would have to write about Mal Evans in this book because it couldn't be about the Beatles without being about Mal. I truly loved Mal. I had never met anyone like him. We developed a friendship and a deep loyalty that I never expect to experience again with another person. We met and that was it—pals. I believe that Mal guided me safely down the narrow corridors and tight chambers of that proverbial yellow submarine and guaranteed me smooth sailing with his four captains. His verbalized acceptance, approval, and trust of me was passionately imparted to the Beatles, and this, I believe, helped give me immediate and confident acceptance on their part. Many times I would test the waters with Mal before approaching one of them on a business matter.

He was the first person I met in the Beatles empire—I was possibly the last friend to talk to him before he was killed.

Mal was a big, lovable, soft-spoken, gentle giant of a man. I'll never forget a time in October 1968 when he and I took Jackie Lomax on a tour of the United States to promote the album and a single that George Harrison had produced. (At that time, only the single "Sour Milk Sea" was released.) As it was one of our first Apple releases and one of George's

Mal and me by the pool at my
Hollywood Hills home.

first productions, we knew it was important to do a good job. Mal was the consummate road manager and treated Jackie with the same respect and care that he afforded the Beatles. The three of us had hung out, partied, and shared a casual relationship until we took Jackie on the road. Then things changed. Jackie was now elevated to star status in Mal's mind, and that was the way he was to be treated while we were on the road. Jackie's every wish and desire was taken care of—no different than if he were John Lennon or George Harrison. Mal expected me to act in the same manner. I set up the promotional itinerary, and Mal set up all the incidentals and preceded Jackie's every move, whether it was walking in front of him down the hall or going curbside at the hotel to make sure the limo was indeed waiting. Jackie was always able to go straight from his room into the waiting car without having to suffer the inconvenience of being a star left waiting in a hotel lobby. As with the Beatles, when Mal was in attendance, he was everywhere at once taking care of everything.

I remember one night in Cleveland when we spent the evening at a local rock club with the music director, disc jockey, and station manager of the main Top 40 station there. We were sitting at a table along a railing that bordered the walkway through the middle of the club. Our table was in a section that was elevated about a foot-and-a-half higher than the floor of the walkway. Mal had his back to Jackie and was engaged in deep conversation with the disc jockey about Jackie's record when a strange thing happened. Jackie and I were sitting in our seats, hanging over the railing and watching the activity in the club while the next act was setting up. Suddenly, a scruffy young guy appeared right in Jackie's face and started picking a fight with what he figured was this skinny little wimp with long black hair and a sissy-type proper accent and all. Like radar, Mal sensed something was awry with his artist in this very noisy club and in one motion rose up out of his chair, turned around, and with the added advantage of the foot-and-a-half riser was suddenly hovering over this obnoxious little twit. I only knew Mal's loving and kind side, and until this night, I had never seen a scarier look on a man's face or a man who looked any bigger than Mal did when he unfolded that big body out of his chair and, like a raging blowfish, doubled in size. Simultaneously with his repositioning, Mal let out the loudest roar three inches away from and directly into the twit's face. There was no conversation or male posturing or even face saving. I am sure the twit made a record-breaking situation evaluation because either he disappeared magically or immediately made a faster-than-the-speed-of-light exit out of the immediate area. Mal stood transfixed for a few long moments just to make sure no more trouble would enter our space and then quietly sat down and returned to his conversation. What I remember most happened a few seconds later. Mal turned back around to Jackie, softly patted him on the arm, gave him a warm look as if to say, "Everything's OK—Mal's here," and then resumed his conversation once again. When I think of Mal, that is the look I see on his face. Of all the times we shared, I think I have chosen to remember him that way.

The promo tour was a success. The record and Jackie Lomax were not.

Of course, George was concerned about the record and wanted to know if our tour was doing any good. He therefore kept in touch with us all during the trip. He surprised us by picking us up at LAX when we flew in after the tour was over. It was so ordinary. He met us at the gate, and

Mal and me in a private car on a Philadelphia to New York City train.

the four of us fell in step talking nonstop all the way out to the car. Nobody noticed us. We were all very tired but went to George's rented house that evening and listened to music until late into the night.

During the Apple meetings in the summer of '68, Mal rented a room in the hotel next to the suite where we would gather each day. During a break, Mal had motioned me next door and handed me a big cigarette. It was popular in England those days to carefully roll the tobacco out of a filter cigarette, leaving the paper and filter intact, and then chop up some hash, mix it with the tobacco, and then repack it into the paper and filter. I was fairly naive in these matters, but I did take a couple puffs knowing that it was not a totally ordinary cigarette. I also wanted to be cool with my new mates. (Will high school ever let out?) I walked back into the most important meeting of my life, and possibly Capitol's history, and immediately started having trouble concentrating and became incredibly paranoid. You can imagine how I felt with not only the Beatles and Apple executive staff but with Stanley Gortikov, the president of Capitol Industries, looking on. To make matters worse, this is when John Lennon started showing me the nude pictures of him and Yoko. Fortunately, Paul knew what Mal had done, and it was kind of an initiation trick on the new guy, and that is why Paul came to my rescue when he did. If Gortikov had known the condition I was in and had disapproved, it would have been of

no matter because the Apple corps would have bailed me out since I was now their guy *and* I was so obviously cool!

I knew Mal outside of Apple. I knew Lil, his wife. She and Mal and their kids came to LA and stayed at my house after the Beatles broke up. The youngsters were thrilled to be there. I lived alone in a large, secluded house in the Hollywood Hills with a giant swimming pool, and everything was so California, just like they had seen in the movies. The weather was sunny and incredible all the time, and they looked like prunes at the end of each day from spending so much time in the pool.

Mal and Lil eventually separated, and Mal came to live in LA. By now I was in the Outlaw mode with Waylon et al., and so Mal and I became the Englishman and the cowboy riding hard herd on the Sunset Strip until the sun came up many mornings. Mal had a rough time in LA, and things were not going well for quite a long time. I was sitting home late one afternoon working on my tape deck editing a sequence for an album I had just produced. I had a tomorrow deadline, and tonight was the *Billboard* Award Show. Jessi Colter was up for "New Country Artist of the Year" based on her hit record I had produced entitled "I'm Not Lisa." As Jessi's producer, I had been asked to accept for her in the event she won because she was on the road and couldn't attend.

Final sequences are often hard for producers, and I was deep into my work when suddenly my phone rang. I answered, and it was Mal. I asked him how he was doing, and he started rambling on about how well everything was going. Something seemed peculiar even though he was professing optimism, and in the middle of his good news, I asked him what was wrong. "Nothing is wrong," he said. "Paul and I just worked out some problems, and he is going to give me credit for some of the things I wrote with him—" I interrupted again, asking him what was wrong. "Nothing," he continued, "and besides that, I am signing a production deal with Atlantic Records and my book is going great and because you were left out of all the other books, I am making sure you are all over it and—" I had known Mal too well and for too long, and somewhere beneath all this good news I sensed something I had never felt with Mal before.

Something was horribly wrong. "Mal . . . Mal," I said. "Stop and listen to me for a second. Something's wrong, isn't it?" There was silence on his end. "We need to talk, don't we?" I asked. Momentary silence.

"Yes," he said softly.

"Mal, I can't meet you now because I have to leave for the awards show in a little while, but can we get together later tonight or first thing tomorrow for lunch?"

"Not tonight," he replied.

"How about I'll meet you tomorrow for lunch at Musso & Franks, OK? OK. Mal—I'll see you then."

"And the new female country artist of the year is—Jessi Colter. Accepting for Jessi is her producer, Ken Mansfield." Those were the words I was hearing, but they were way off in the distance and deep in an echo chamber.

I could see the words coming out of comedian Flip Wilson's mouth as if in slow motion, and the trophy in his hand was diffused and without shape. Just prior to the announcement, Diane Bennett, a friend and social columnist for the *Hollywood Reporter,* had come up to me and, putting her arm around my shoulder, said, "I am sorry about Mal, Ken."

I turned quickly—"What do you mean—about Mal?"

"I thought you knew," she said uncomfortably. "He's been shot."

Flip was extending the award in my direction, and I was ushered on stage walking in a half-turned position facing Diane. "Mumble mumble" and I was back into the audience and at Diane's side. "Is he OK?" I asked her, and she told me what had happened.

Harry Nilsson filled me in a few days later. He told me that it seemed Mal had become increasingly despondent that night and began taking large amounts of drugs that only made matters worse. He was staying with his girlfriend, Fran Hughes, and had taken a gun upstairs and locked himself in the bedroom. She was afraid he was going to do something crazy and so she called the police to protect him from himself. I am told that, for whatever reason, they shot six warning shots into his head that night to keep him from hurting himself.

There is that part in all of us that always wants to make us feel guilty or responsible for the death of someone we are close to. For some reason I can't pin that dragon on myself even though I was strategically positioned in this event. I think it is because I loved him too much to knowingly do anything to harm him or to not be there if I thought he needed me. I also know in my heart that Mal would never blame me. These were crazy times, and we were all pretty much missing a couple of bottles each out of our six-packs in those days. Time and events seemed to drift in and out of reality at their own given pace. Sometimes we would hop aboard our wild horses and ride like blazing daredevils on the frighteningly fast track we had inherited with the fame of it all. Sometimes our ride would stumble, and we would fall off. It was funny at first because we were young and invincible. We would jump up laughing, dust ourselves off, and leap back into the fray full force, unabashed and unblinking. The problem is that the ride kept getting faster, and the destination became more and more obscure.

Sometimes we would fall off and not even know it.

Mal fell when I wasn't looking.

She's a Little Bit Country, He's a Little Bit Rock and Roll

» *Los Angeles—Sausalito, California, 1977–1987*

The LA years were exceptionally heady times during and following my stint as a director at Capitol Records, a U.S. manager of Apple Records, the VP of MGM Records, the president of CBS/Barnaby Records, and eventually the head of my own company: a thriving Hometown Productions, Inc. where I was not only producing several name artists but also movie soundtracks and TV theme music. Our circle of friends in those days included the Beatles coterie as well as other English rock-and-roll stars, the current hot rockers of the LA music scene, and many of the rich and famous of the movie crowd, as well as the hip country Outlaw artists of which I was the reigning producer at the time. The swinging doors of our Hollywood estate hideaway, affectionately known as the Hangover House, swung wide, long, and often with the ins and outs of probably the most eclectic gathering of the creative and the crazies of that era.

You know you are in Hollywood when your dinner guests have names like Dolly and Ringo. I have experienced many exciting nights with some pretty incredible people during my thirty-plus active years in the

Dolly signing the wall at the Hangover House. Yes, that is a wine glass in her right hand—no, that is not a cigar in her left hand. It was the brown magic marker she was using to sign the wall.

© Nancy Andrews

entertainment business, but there are a few, and they are usually the most common of events, that really bring a smile to my heart when I think back on them. Such was the night that I had Dolly Parton and Ringo Starr over for dinner—each one unaware that the other was going to be there.

Dolly and I became friends over the years, and she had migrated to the West Coast along with Waylon Jennings and the other Nashville artists I was bringing to LA to produce in an attempt to break the good ole boy chokehold on country artist careers in Nashville. Ringo and I had a decade-old relationship at that point, not only through our business associations, but we had also developed a close friendship as

The swinging doors of our Hollywood as the Hangover House, swung wide, probably the most eclectic gathering of

part of a small group of insulated and isolated pals during the years he lived in LA. These were particularly exhilarating times on the Sunset Strip night scene as artists such as Waylon and Dolly were beginning to play in clubs like the hot spot on the strip, the Roxy, which heretofore was basically reserved for contemporary rock stars, many of whom were from the British Isles (Dire Straits and others). Not only were some of the country stars appearing in places like these, but they were also packing the places. One night, around the time I was producing Waylon's *Are You*

Ready for the Country album, Ringo and a gang of his UK mates showed up en masse for Waylon's first booking at the Roxy. Situated above the Roxy showroom was a private club called On the Rox, and only the elite of the elite pop scene got to hang there. Ringo had called me to let me know he was bringing his entourage to see Waylon's show and had reserved the Rox for a private party afterward. He wanted to invite Waylon and his gang up as his guests.

You have to visualize this: after the show, when Waylon, the Waylors (his band), the Outlaw gang that rode herd with us, and Ringo's British crew had situated themselves in the room, it was a bizarre scene. Here was this bunch of cowboys with their beards, cowboy hats and boots, and suspicious looks all sitting at the tables on one side of the room, separated from Ringo's rock-and-roll pals by an almost perfect dividing line of tables down the center of the room. The English rock crew, with more of a glam look, was similarly ensconced on the other side of the room. Both sides were looking across this great cultural divide at each other in semi-bewilderment. At this point, I crossed into the little no man's land as Ringo did the same. We hugged and called forth each other's comrades and introduced them, and in a short time, we managed to merge the two contingencies. Once the ice was broken and the hard drinks and longneck beers flowed, it turned into one fabulous party. Ringo

estate hideaway, affectionately known long, and often with the ins and outs of the creative and the crazies of that era.

and I decided that night that we might have missed our true calling as diplomats for foreign cultures.

As I mentioned earlier, Ringo was a giant country music fan, and starting from the first day we met in August of 1965, it had been a point of communication between us. He was very intrigued by Dolly's career and had once stated to me that he would love to meet her. Coincidentally, Dolly was a giant Beatles fan and, knowing that I had worked with them, had jokingly mentioned that someday she would like to meet them, Ringo in particular. So, one evening when Dolly was spending a few days in LA on business, I invited her over to have dinner at the house. I also invited Ringo over for dinner the same evening, not letting either one know the other would be there.

The evening came. Both invitees were thrilled at the surprise, and the intimacy of the evening really made the whole thing very special. Dolly arrived first and alone by cab, followed by Ringo and his lady, Nancy Andrews, and then our mutual friend Alan Pariser and his wife, Lezlee. Besides the wonderful meal and great conversation, an incredibly funny thing happened later in the evening. Another member of our select group that rallied around Ringo's "star" was a successful producer named Stewart Levine (producer to Simply Red, the Crusaders, Hugh Masakela,

Top:
I always found it amusing that a Beatle, who was constantly hounded to have his picture taken with people, was always pulling friends together and snapping a picture with his other hand. These snapshots were typically out of focus and perspective—this was one of those from that night. That's Alan Pariser in the middle.

Bottom:
A before-dinner chat at the Hangover House with Ringo, Dolly, and me.

BB King, Lionel Richie, Boy George, Jamie Cullum, Aaron Neville, Sly Stone, Joe Cocker, Patti LaBelle, and many others). Stewart was a giant Dolly Parton fan and had found out from Alan about the dinner party and the surprise we had cooked up for the evening. Stewart insisted on being invited as part of the evening affair, but I kept explaining that I really wanted to hold the guest list down and keep the focus on just Ringo and Dolly spending time together, and refused his request. He wouldn't back off and finally coerced me into accepting a little plan he came up with. He asked if I would just let him come up to the house after dinner and knock on the door and pretend he was delivering me a tape as a fellow producer. He said he wouldn't come in the house, but would I please just call Dolly over to the door and introduce him to her. He promised that once I made the introduction, he would politely leave. He couldn't have cared less about seeing Ringo because the three of us saw each other all the time.

As planned, the doorbell rang after dinner, I answered it to greet Stewart, and per our contrived scheme, he was holding a cassette tape in his hands. I said hello to him as designed, but he threw away the script; he didn't even respond or look at me. Instead of placing the cassette in my hand, he pushed right past me and headed straight into a barroom that was often the activity center of the house when us guys were hanging out. He knew the layout of the house and assumed that was where everyone would be, including Dolly.

Ringo, Alan, and I had been standing in front of the fireplace in the barroom chatting when Stewart arrived. Meanwhile, Dolly and the ladies were in the living room doing girl talk. While I was telling Stewart that he was not sticking to the plan (or our agreement), Dolly suddenly appeared in the doorway and began to ask me to freshen up her club soda. In mid-sentence she stopped and got this wide-eyed and most incredulous stare on her face—it was very obvious that she was looking directly at Stewart about six feet away. Stewart (who was used to being around famous people) also froze like a drooling fan, and there was this momentary silence as the two locked gazes.

After a very pregnant pause, Dolly began to speak and in a stuttering, shaky voice asked Stewart if he was Stewart Levine, the famous producer. Stewart mumbled a quivering yes while becoming even more dazed and schoolboyish as Dolly proceeded to gush over seeing him in person. She continued to explain that in her lifetime she never expected that she would ever get the chance to be in the same room with Stewart Levine, let alone have the privilege of meeting him. She went on further saying that she was a giant fan of his and had absolutely adored him from afar for quite a long time. Now, by this time, not only was Stewart about ready to faint, but Ringo, Alan, and I had joined him in the dropped-jaw position of amazement. We turned to each other and quizzically asked ourselves, "Stewart? Is she serious?"

She then delivered the fatal blow by announcing that she was going to have to leave the room for fear that she would no longer be able to contain herself and might jump his bones right in front of everyone. She made an abrupt about-face, as if fearful of being unable to control her emotions, and returned to the living room. At this point, there were four stunned men standing in complete silence, frozen like mimes. After an appropriate lapse of time in which all four of us found ourselves trying to

This is me and Stewart Levine still cracking up at the joke Dolly pulled on us that night at the Hangover House.

cope with an extreme sense of disbelief, we turned and stared at Stewart. The identical look was on everyone's face: "Wha?"

No one had yet uttered a word in the silence of the moment when we heard muffled laughter coming from the living room. After a four-man rush for the barroom door, we all paraded into the living room where Dolly and the others were. Upon seeing us, they all broke out in hysterical laughter. They were laughing so hard that they couldn't explain what had just happened, but it was obvious what they had done, and we all fell out on the floor. In a nutshell, when Stewart crashed our party, Dolly could see that I had let someone into the house and asked who it was. My wife explained the whole ruse that Stewart and I came up with, and Dolly decided to spice up the evening a bit with her little act. I think Stewart was so stunned by what had gone down that he wasn't even the least bit disappointed that Dolly didn't really have the hots for him. He thought it was a very funny bit, totally got behind the whole ploy as a real "gotcha," and just enjoyed the fact that he had accomplished more than just meeting her; he got to share an experience of a lifetime. It was also the perfect note to end the evening, and everyone left at the same time. Dolly had caught a cab to get there, but I believe Stewart drove her back to her Hollywood hotel that night.

Track 32

Save a Partridge, Ride a Cowboy

» *Hollywood, California, Summer 1978*

When asked who my favorite artists to work with as a producer were, I have two that come immediately to mind: Don Ho and David Cassidy. Both were surprisingly incredible talents and highly underestimated by the public. It is amazing what a producer can learn about artists' abilities when you get them under the microscope of the studio where the equipment and technology lay everything open and bare. I could learn even more during the time I would spend with them in preproduction: learning how they think, how much they know, what their shortcomings and strengths are, and how I was going to assemble this knowledge into a game plan with the goal of getting the best possible performance out of them during the recording process. The initial information gathering is an important time because, during this phase, I would not only get an understanding of their artistry and talents, but I also found it very important to crawl inside their nature to find out how malleable they were in terms of being open to new ideas as well as how willing they were to occasionally step out of their regular groove if needed. As a producer, it was just as important for me to ascertain the areas that I needed to stay away from, the buttons I must never push, and the areas that were sacred ground in their artistic makeup.

As a total package, I found David Cassidy to be the most intriguing, the most complex, and absolutely the most delightful performer I ever worked with. David was a superstar; "was" being the operative word as far as his public persona went. This perception by the public was one of the pitfalls of having been a giant superstar and then suffering by comparison in the aftermath when one's career accomplishments never seem to live up to the previous extreme heights of success. In time I found out that David had it all on all the levels needed to qualify as a superstar.

Here's how it all came about.

I got a call from my attorney, longtime friend, and manager-by-default, Dick Whitehouse, saying he wanted to meet me for lunch to discuss something. I asked, "What's up?" and he replied that we would cover that over lunch. When your attorney calls you while you are living in the heat and throes of the recording business, it is either really good news or really bad news. In-between news is reserved for less wobbly occupations. I responded that I had a pretty full plate coming up that day and that it would help if I knew what we were going to spend a couple of hours discussing over lunch just in case it was something that could be handled over the phone. Once again, he told me we would discuss it over lunch.

I kept pressing him until he gave me a snippet of what the subject matter was. He told me that he had been approached by a manager about producing a particular artist, but that being said, he still refused to disclose

David Cassidy and me in session at Larabee Studios in Hollywood. David would not allow cameras in the studio, but my oldest son, Kevin, who was assisting on the sessions, took these shots on the sly. Because the studio was kept dim and he couldn't use a flash or be obvious, the pics are quite loose.

who it was. I kept pressing the point and finally was able to establish that it wasn't a new artist but an established artist who had had a giant hit record or two in the past. I then wanted to know if by "established" he meant just "established," or were we talking "famous" here? He made it clear that the proper classification was "famous." That was all the information I was going to get out of him. Lunch or nothing, take my pick. I told him OK, but it would have to be a late lunch because I had to wrap up a couple of things first. We agreed to meet at Martonis, which was a popular music biz hangout in a semi-seedy part of Hollywood. Martonis was legendary for all the deals that went down all hours of the day and night in its darkened interior. It was ideally located a few blocks from Hollywood and Vine amidst a plethora of recording studios and record companies.

I actually got there first and was halfway finished with a scotch mist when Whitehouse walked in. In perfect timing with his seat hitting the chair, I said, "OK, we're here—who is it?"

"David Cassidy," he replied, putting his chewing gum in my drink for effect and to match my rudeness up to this point. I was a very hip producer by my own account at the time; by mistaken general music industry consensus, David Cassidy had fallen into the has-been category. As far as I was concerned, he was a teenybopper artist, and I was the Outlaw dude who used to be with the Beatles. Not a good career move, as far as I could tell. But to be honest, my career was on the verge of tanking if I didn't come up

with a hit soon, and also, in reality, David was a legitimate artist with a strong record-company commitment and a lot of good ideas for a new album. I guess you could say that we were fairly equally matched at that time—two creatively desperate song-laden souls looking for a home back on the charts.

Anyway, my immediate response was a definite no, and my body language let Whitehouse know that I was not happy with the lunch topic or the state of my Juicy Fruit-infused Chevas Regal. I just wasn't interested in the project—period. Lawyers are used to verbal abuse and illogical responses, so without a change in the sideways, lean-back position he had taken in his chair, he simply said he anticipated my response and had gone ahead and made dinner reservations for David and me for 7 p.m. that night at the Imperial Gardens Japanese Restaurant and Sushi Bar on the Hollywood end of the Sunset Strip—regardless of what I wanted to do. "Now hear me out," he said. "I think this is a good project for you, and all I am asking is that you meet with David before you make up your mind. He has already agreed to you producing his album, if he feels good about it after having dinner with you. All I'm asking is that you meet with him at the Imperial Gardens, do the meal deal, and then tomorrow give me a call. I am picking up the tab, so you have nothing to lose. If you still say no, I will accept your decision and make the appropriate phone calls to his management."

The Imperial Gardens was a real hot spot, popular with the music people, and in those days was enjoying the popularity of the sushi craze that had recently hit the Hollywood set. The sushi bar was downstairs facing out to the glitzy street, and in the upstairs dining room of the restaurant there was a separate area set aside for private dining. These were little mini-rooms enclosed by shoji screens, with pillows and low tables where you could sit on the floor Japanese-style in total privacy yet still have a sense of the ambiance. It was a place where the rich and famous could dine without fans disturbing their meal. I showed up right on the dot at 7 p.m., and when the shoji screen was opened, I found David Cassidy already sitting there. We introduced ourselves and then immediately started talking—nonstop for over three hours. We closed the place down. We were best friends five minutes into our dinner meeting. The ritual of the sushi meal and the plush little environs created the perfect setting for us to really get to know each other, and that night the cowboy and the partridge joined forces.

I called Whitehouse the next day and said it was a definite go and that I was truly excited. I also sincerely thanked him for hanging in there with me.

I told him that David had great ideas and we were actually getting to work on things that afternoon. It's pretty amazing how things unfolded because we became virtually inseparable for about two months with our relationship morphing in and out of creative synergy and just being good friends having a good time. David turned out to be a super talent and possessed the most incredible laugh I had ever heard. It came from deep down inside and was genuine and warm. It made you want him to be happy just so you could hear it. The project went well on all levels except one: upon completion, the ever-looming record company/artist management/attorney politics entered the picture with the net result being that the album to my knowledge never got released in America, although as a publisher I have been notified of licensing requests pertaining to international release.

We were very disappointed by this outcome, but David went on to star in a TV show called *David Cassidy—Man Undercover*. The legendary David Gerber produced the show, and I was hired as the music producer and arranger for the title song, so our little team of two managed to stay together a little longer. The NBC TV series lasted only one season with its opening segment airing on November 2, 1978, and the final episode airing on January 11, 1979.

Because we didn't know the separation was going to be permanent, we never said goodbye.

As is the way in the entertainment business, over time we drifted out of each other's lives. Because we didn't know the separation was going to be permanent, we never said goodbye. We were almost brought together by a mutual friend in the early '90s and came within less than an hour of hooking up with each other in London. Unfortunately, his flight was late getting in and mine took off on time.

It has been very pleasing to me to see his talent prove out in the long run. Not only did he once again become reestablished as a big star overseas, but he then continued on as an incredible stage success in the United States.

David and I had spent an intense six months together, and I don't believe I ever enjoyed my chosen vocation more than I did when I was working with him.

I miss things like that.

"I think I loved it!"

Across the Universe

» *High Above the Sunset Strip,*
  December 8, 1980

They say everyone remembers where they were on the days John Kennedy and John Lennon died. As clichéd as this statement may be, it definitely works for me.

I had sold the old Lash Larue estate up in Laurel Canyon that was my home, hideout, and entertainment center for almost ten years. My career as a record producer had lost its focus *and* impetus all at the same time. It is interesting how fast it all falls apart when the downward slide begins. It is definitely a momentum thing that in my case became an irresistible force that I couldn't stop. It was like I was frozen in my tracks as the problems heated up and my abilities to deal with it all cooled down. Some of it had to do with too many drugs, some to do with bad choices of pals and business associates, and a lot to do with my head-in-the-sand naïveté that had me believing that the good times were going to rock and roll forever. The simple explanation: it took a lot of money to maintain my people and accustomed lifestyle. No one was more surprised than I was by my lost invincibility when the out-go was not being fed by an equal amount of in-come. A missed project here, a bad business deal there, a couple of wrong career choices along the way all blended into a cocksure attitude that it would all turn around eventually—so let's keep the party going in the meantime. Soon my energies were being diverted from the creativity that had made the good life possible and were now being focused on just trying to hang on to things as they were going away. Also in the true Hollywood manner of the way it is in Tinseltown, I didn't seem to have as many people on my team on the way down as I did on the way up. *Gee, surprise, surprise!*

As I drove away from that house for the last time as a resident, it felt like everything was crashing down behind me. I, thusly equipped and thusly stripped, came rip roaring out of the canyon of laurels and out onto the edge of the cliffs that hovered high above the Sunset Strip. Dumping my antiques, beard, and the cowboy crazies that I clowned around with in the desperate dirt of that ridiculous rodeo that I once called my life, I deposited myself dazed and demi-defeated into a rented modern glass castle with white and steel furnishings. The view ranged all the way from Catalina Island to the San Gabriel Mountains and all of the LA enclaves in between. From this perch I could see everywhere and everything— especially now that career-wise I was nearing nowhere with nothing. I didn't know whether to expect the phone to ring with some big new production offer or whether any minute I was going to hear a big flushing sound as it all went down the toilet.

The house belonged to Donald Byrd, the famous jazz musician and lecturer. One of the great features for me, as a producer, was that he had built an office directly off a control booth that looked out into a big home studio. This meant I could run my Hometown Productions, Inc. from my desk while observing the happenings in the studio through the open control room door. This was going to be especially helpful when I had bands rehearsing for an upcoming project. I could listen and watch out of one ear and eye while doing business on the phone without interfering with the creative process that is so sacred in our business. As the studio wasn't occupied as much as I would have liked to it to have been, it also doubled as a great hangout place for my teenage son, Mark, and his friends, who, of course, were all famous recording artists in waiting. One of Mark's closest friends was a young guitar player named Saul Hudson. Saul virtually lived in that room when it wasn't in use, and almost anytime of day or night I could look out through the studio window and there he would be sitting on an amp with his head down playing the guitar long after the rest of the gang had gone outside to shoot baskets or head out for the Sunset Strip. I remember walking out into the studio one day and interrupting him—I wanted him to know that I had worked with some of the greatest guitarists of our time and that I was hearing something evolving; there was something very special in the way he played. I made an honest prediction to him that someday he would be equally as famous. A band did start forming in that studio over time, and you could see things starting to come together. I am not sure when they started calling him "Slash," and I was not sure when the band took on the name "Guns 'N Roses." I am sure it was bound to happen, and it did.

In this adjoining office to the studio were floor-to-ceiling wall cabinets across two complete walls that were designed for the storage of tapes and session supplies. When I'd moved in, I had simply piled all my tapes, files, memorabilia, and personal junk behind the doors of these cabinets.

'NO COMMENT' — GEORGE MARTIN
UNFINISHED MUSIC NO. 2: LIFE WITH THE LIONS
JOHN LENNON/YOKO ONO   APPLE RECORDS
MADE IN MERRIE ENGLAND. NOV. '68

I was thereby able to avoid organizing things by simply not opening the doors and conveniently ignoring the contents therein. For whatever reason, one day I decided to attack this area. I wanted to start pulling out gold records, pictures, and awards to hang on the remaining office walls.

Ironically, the first boxes I pulled off of the shelves were filled with things from my Apple days, things that I had never even bothered to unpack at the Laurel Canyon house. It wasn't long before I was sitting on the floor totally surrounded with John Lennon pictures, letters, and signed recordings. I remember I became softly overwhelmed by some enormity that I couldn't understand as I looked at his face and slipped into a contemplative mixture of awe and dreamlike remembrances of the occasions I was in the same room with him. Memories began cascading and merging until I soon became stoned in a moment of recollected confusion. Something was happening inside me, and I was soon lost in trying to put John Lennon, the Beatles, Apple, Capitol, MGM, Andy Williams, the Outlaws, Guru Raj Ananda, Idaho, Hollywood, and the deep meaning of disco into some addled perspective of my current digs and dilemma. From far away, an echoing ringing started in my ears, and it finally came rushing full bore into my consciousness. I reached up, grabbed the phone from my desk, and pulled it down to the floor beside me. I said hello, but all I got in return was a series of sobbings and mottled verbiage that I couldn't make heads or tails of. About the only thing I could understand was a sniffling, wavering—"I-I-I'll c-c-call you back."

The sound of the phone being rocked into its cradle brought me out of my dream, and I started sorting out my John Lennon stuff from the rest of the Beatles days' leftovers. Once again the phone rang. By this time, I was basically back in the real world, and Nick Gilder's second attempt to call me was less emotional. I had just finished producing the "Hot Child in the City" glam rocker's *RockAmerica* album for Casablanca Records. Nick was a total John Lennon fan, which was one of the mutual respect glues that held our producer/artist relationship together. His belief in my abilities as

Opposite page: John sent me this "one of the first" copies of the *Life with the Lions* album, but I didn't notice that John had signed it. Overrun with thousands of LPs, in later years, I began unloading most of them at a used record shop in San Francisco. As the buyer for the store was restacking the piles of records, *Life with the Lions* ended this side up on top of one of the stacks where I noticed John's handwritten note for the first time. It was immediately retrieved, and I returned the 25 cents they had paid me for the album.

a producer could be my ticket out of Nashville music. My respect for his brilliant talent and uncanny understanding of universal rock themes made us close friends and creative compatriots. He was one of the few artists with whom I wanted to maintain an ongoing, continuing, personal relationship. Critically acclaimed in the United States, *RockAmerica* was severely attacked in his homeland, Canada. By calling it *RockAmerica*, they accused Nick of turning his back on his heritage, and he was hurt and confused by his unintended political statement. (The irony of all this is that Nick was born in London, England, and moved to Vancouver BC where he was raised.)

Upon his death, I suddenly felt removed from any sense of anything personal. At that point I took my proper place in the general public as a shocked mourner. My sense of loss and pain was not that of someone who had known him but that of a minuscule thread in the infinite fabric of mankind.

By his second phone call, Nick had gathered himself together enough to tell me that John Lennon had just been shot. I was holding a letter from John in my hand. I looked at the pile scattered around me, and John was looking at me from everywhere. Telling Nick I would call *him* back, I laid down the phone and cried.

The news of John Lennon's death had a strange, unexpected effect on me. I had met John Lennon and had worked for him and his company. I also had been yelled at, criticized, and challenged by him. I had actually been a small part of his existence, especially with the Zapple thing, which he personalized by including me in his quest. Upon his death, I suddenly felt removed from any sense of anything personal. At that point,

I took my proper place in the general public as a shocked mourner. My sense of loss and pain was not that of someone who had known him but that of a minuscule thread in the infinite fabric of mankind. I was simply a member of society deeply moved by a tragic loss that was shared and felt by us all. It was no longer personal but universal pain that I suffered. I may have met him when he was alive, but like everyone else I was never going to hear from him again. Shortly afterward I listened to *John Lennon/Plastic Ono Band*, his first solo album, and I began to understand him for the first time. From that point on I could hardly listen to the music he had made after the Beatles broke up. It was so personal that I would get embarrassed listening to it. I almost had to look away as if I were ashamed for eavesdropping or peeping into his most private feelings. Listen back sometime, and see if you have ever known a man who laid himself out so raw and naked before all who would listen, learn, care, or understand. I know now that the reason I couldn't understand John when he was alive is because what he was laying out was so incredibly simple. His fame was obliterating his message. The end product many times was his frustration.

Two things were taken away from all of us when John Lennon died. The first was the dream and the warm hope that lived in the possibility of something we all wanted to see reunited and returned to us intact—the Beatles.

Something else happened when John Lennon died, and like the Beatles, the second thing was bigger than we could ever imagine. What happened was we ended up with a hero that we didn't want. We didn't want John Lennon to be our hero. We didn't want him to be a martyr for our cause. We just wanted John Lennon to talk to us through his art and music about what was going on around us.

"Across the universe—something changed our world—images of broken light danced before us like a million eyes—they called us on and on—across the universe. . . ."

Now we are left alone in his silence.

What Would Dinner Be Without Olive Oyl?

This is probably my favorite story about Ringo Starr, an episode that really goes beyond any one of us, and one that as far as I know has never been told. It has to do with the coolest time I ever spent with him, and is probably the most revealing of his character. It also took place right after John Lennon was killed. The lead-in to this evening will give you insight into how relationships form and have a peculiar way of becoming special. It is almost like a bunch of odd balls were gathered together in ones and twos over the years from the discordant pool halls of the music business absurd and then magically ended up being racked together for the long run on the snooker table of ordained existence.

I began in the music business as an entertainer, and over the course of time of being out on the road, it was natural for my band, the Town Criers, to end up on the same bill with other groups more than once. Because of the repeated backstage gatherings with one particular group, I formed a lifetime relationship with a less-than-blazing guitar player like myself named Denny Bond. Denny was in a band called the Californians in the early '60s, and we were close enough friends for me to describe his guitar playing as, shall we say, "pedestrian." I can say this because he played like I did, except maybe better. Also, just like me, as middling as his guitar playing was, he was a better guitar player than a singer. Maybe that was the reason for the Bond bond. Denny came from a wealthy upper-class San Diego family and had been schooled in the finest traditions at the nation's finest schools with the family intent that he would become one of the nation's finest lawyers. I think it was our divergent backgrounds that brought us together—a communal curiosity that changed both our lives.

Eventually I tired of the artist fantasy and left the road to set up a nightclub in La Mesa, a suburb of San Diego. I converted the old abandoned city hall into a "folk theatre" where established acts like Bud and Travis, Joe and Eddie, and Nina Simone performed, and the new wave folk era artists such as Pat Paulson, Mason Williams, original members of the Byrds, and the Association were at various stages in making their formational "bones" in the business. Like most ventures in the entertainment business, the folk club was soon struggling and at a point of near financial collapse when Denny decided to use some of his family wealth to bail me out and become a partner in the club—strictly as a sideline to his preordained career as an attorney. His parents did not like our association—it was too common law: I was common and Denny was groomed for law! The nightclub did eventually fold, but by that time Denny's heart had really developed a leaning toward the music business.

While he was marrying the daughter of the senior vice president of a major airliner, I was in the process of making my move to Capitol Records. When this golden opportunity came (via an invitation from the manager of Capitol artists the Four Freshmen) at Hollywood's most prestigious label, I really didn't have the proper clothes to wear to the job interview. This chance of a lifetime fortunately occurred while Denny's wealthy parents were off on a cruise or away on some exotic vacation. Denny invited me over to his house and into the dream world of his father's closet full of expensive furnishings. I think Denny really enjoyed this gentle defiance on his part, and we spent hours enjoying being the male version of two girls who had snuck into Princess Diana's dressing room. Before it was all over, I was outfitted in the finest imported fabrics, a silk tie, matching gold studs, and a classic Rolex. His dad was a little shorter and a bit heavier than I was, so I had to wear the pants low and take a big tuck in the back to make things look right. Anyway, I kept my jacket buttoned, and with my butt extended, my interview was successful and I pulled it off big-time. I find it ironic that not only did I get the job in someone else's clothes, but it was the senior Mr. Bond's suit that helped make it happen.

It wasn't long before Denny joined me in Hollywood, and we began teaming up on the side with our own company, BondMan Productions. Even though I was skyrocketing through the ranks at Capitol, we were also going gangbusters. As we expanded our services, we eventually changed BondMan to "Artists Counseling Talent Services," an awkwardly created acronym for "ACTS." When the legendary show biz columnist Hedda Hopper passed away in 1966, Denny and I rented out her second-floor suite of offices on Hollywood Boulevard just off Vine Street, which was conveniently just around the corner from Capitol. About that same time, Jerry Lewis decided to renovate his offices in Beverly Hills, and we were able to purchase his slightly used carpet for our space. This was our start—Hedda Hopper's office with Jerry Lewis's carpet! Not only did Denny and I feel we had the right stuff to make it in the biz, we had the right stuff from the biz to furnish our efforts.

I would spend my days at the Capitol Tower on Vine Street just off of Hollywood Boulevard and in the evening go around the corner, snagging an Orange Julius and a hot dog along the way, and join Denny for the heart of a glitter night in this fascinating place. When I looked down from our windows onto the boulevard, I couldn't help but notice that there were no potato fields out there. I was a long way from Idaho—I guess I had just clicked the heels of my cowboy boots together and there I was on Hollywood Boulevard. Eventually, much to the Bond family's chagrin, Denny became a full-time entertainment manager, producer, and music and film industry entrepreneur—possibly all because of his dad's suit. Over time he managed to mold his law degree into a very successful industry practice. Our formal business ties morphed away as I continued to move rapidly up through the ranks of the record labels, and Denny became involved in developing some extraordinary entertainment careers in their formative years. I could no longer ride two horses at the same time and had to make a choice. I figured Denny and I would be friends forever and Capitol was the momentary prize, so I put my full-time energies into the record company, while Denny built his organization. Over the years, his clients and my companies would "come together."

Ironically, one of Denny's law school roommates and eventual law firm partner was Bruce Grakal and therefore—"any friend of yours is a friend of mine." Bruce and I unknowingly planted the seeds of our personal and business relationship at this time. (I told you this chapter is about Ringo, so hang in there and you will see what I mean as we watch all the odd-numbered balls start falling into the same pocket!) At this point in the story, Denny was molding the career of this incredible new talent on the LA scene: Harry Nilsson. Another automatic friendship was formed, and as I had already started producing records for a couple of major labels, it was only natural for me to help Denny and his young client by including one of Harry's compositions on one of my projects. I will never forget the look on Harry's face when he came into my office to hear a playback on one of his earliest recordings as a songwriter. My recording and production, although considered cutting edge at the time, were basically inelegant at that young stage, and I can't even remember the artist or which Nilsson song I chose. Harry, on the other hand, was an out-and-out genius from day one, and his contributions to the fabric of the music industry were nothing short of magical. Still, in those early days, he was childlike and thrilled. I am sure he had no idea that he would evolve into one of the industry's legends.

To know Harry Nilsson was to love him. He always had a smile on his face, and the familiar arm/hand position usually held something that had to do with that.

It was about this time that I became involved with the Beatles. If there is one sentence I have heard a thousand times more than any other sentence that I have heard in my life (other than "Are you sure you want to do that?") it would be, upon finding out I used to work with the Beatles, "Oh, I am the world's biggest Beatles fan." Well, I am here to tell you now that I can put that contest to rest. Harry Nilsson was the Beatles biggest fan in this or any other world—period! (What was lovely about that is that, in time the Beatles ultimately became equally enamored of Harry's talent.) In the beginning of all this, there was no question in Harry's mind that he was going to meet the Beatles, that he was going to get to know the Beatles, that he was going to become best friends with at least half of the Beatles, and that he was going to end up being part of their history. You can imagine how, in the early days, Harry could see me as the door opener to all this. We were young men, but we already had a little history going with each other, and outside of me he probably had very little chance of pulling this dream off, or at least as I underestimated and thought at the time. In looking back, I honestly can't remember if I did have anything to do with the deep friendships that developed between him and Ringo and John Lennon, but that is of little import, because I believe now that there was no stopping it. I heard recently that my friend the late Derek Taylor discovered Harry's music while living in California and reported back to the boys about this great artist.

As time evolved, Harry was not only friends with the Beatles themselves but had become a part of the Apple corps' fabric and everything else that had to do with all the players' lives that were involved in this phenomenal time. Sharing the same best friend, (Beatle's road manager) Mal Evans, also drew Harry and me even closer. (The rack was beginning to fill up with a lot of 8 balls who didn't have a cue!) Harry was one of the lead cowboys on our Sunset Strip rodeo ride, and the three of us saw more than one sunrise bursting forth from the dew-dampened asphalt of the Sunset Strip. I remember one night in the '70s when I was on a tight deadline to finish producing the *Byron Berline and Sundance* album for Warner Brothers Records. Shortly before I had left for the studio, Harry had called me about the three of us (Mal being the third) partying that night. It was a spur of the moment thing on Harry's part—a casting of types who were perfect for an excursion into his own off-beat time signature. I told him that I might be in a session all night because I had to deliver the final mixes to the record company by noon the next day. Mal also couldn't accept Harry's invitation for whatever reason, which cut the proposed party down considerably.

Harry being Harry with a mission, and not real good at "a table for one, please," kept checking with me during the session to see when I was going to get done. I am sure Mal was receiving the same affable attention. Eventually, though, it seems like he would have given up when I told him around 3:30 a.m. that I still had an hour or two to go. I got quite a surprise when I walked out of the back of the studio to get in my car at a little after 5 a.m. The sun was just coming up over the parking lot and there was Harry, angelically illuminated by the morning back glow, sitting on the front fender of my new Mercedes—legs dangling down over the darkened passenger-side headlight with a giant Martini in one hand held up in "Salud" position and a second Martini perfectly chilled and poised on the hood of the car. He didn't say a word but motioned to the other front fender in a refined invitation to my reserved seat to join him. All he said while holding his glass in the waiting "clink" position for my glass and with that helplessly sweet childlike gaze was: "Now I believe the party will begin?"

It seemed that particular party would go on forever, but Harry and I reluctantly put the chairs on the table and turned off the lights when Mal was finally called away, officially disbanding our threesome. It was, in a way, like it was with the Beatles—there are times when you can't replace a member of a team. We were no longer a trio. Harry and I continued our friendship, but it was almost like we had been in the same band that was no longer together. It just never seemed the same without the big guy.

The LA police department brought Mal down in a haze of bullets, alcohol, and confusion in January of 1976.

Four years later, John Lennon also died from gunshot wounds.

Upon learning about John's tragic death, Ringo flew from his holiday in the Bahamas to New York City to pay respects to Yoko. After doing so, he called Harry, Alan Pariser, and me to tell us he was flying to LA the next day and asked that we get together with him that night when he got back. He just wanted to get away from the gravity of the whole situation and lighten things up for a moment. Then, on top of all that was going on surrounding this tragic event, a very bizarre thing happened. Some nut called the airlines or a radio station to let them know that he was going to assassinate Ringo when Ringo got off the plane at LAX. I believe the caller even gave his name. I was never made privy to what eventually happened that day with the law enforcement assemblage, but I believe the aspiring gunman actually showed up at the airport. One thing is for sure, and that is that he did not get within a mile of Ringo's arrival gate.

Anyway, our night on the town was already in full motion, and undeterred, we decided it would be fun if we hired a limo for the evening. Logistics dictated that Ringo would be the last one on the pickup route. Harry, Alan, and I had just learned about the assassination threat shortly before we were picked up, and on the way to Ringo's we were concerned that this last little bit of madness and unwanted melodrama may have put a damper on things for Ringo, especially since the perfect evening out had been arranged to put a little levity into the life of our emotionally battered friend. We soon learned how determined he was to put it all aside for a while. His home in Beverly Hills had a long sidewalk that went straight from the street to the entrance. As soon as we pulled up in front of his house, the massive entry door quickly opened ever so slightly, and we could see someone peering out to the street from the darkened interior behind the door. Then, like a dashing Inspector Clouseau, Ringo, in his best imitation of Peter Sellers, darted out the front door to hide behind the nearest tree. A furtive brow peeked slyly from behind that tree, and then he made another furtive dash on tiptoe, with hands raised in praying mantis format, to the next tree, which was slightly closer to the limo. It took about five trees to get him to the waiting chauffeur who was patiently standing to the rear of the limo and holding the door open. Ringo popped into the seat and then slowly crossed his legs in complete calm and asked how things were going, as if he had just sat down on his living room couch.

It was the perfect night to accomplish Ringo's purpose. First of all, we had all known each other for many years, and I believe Ringo needed to be with old friends. Second and typically, any encounter longer than ten minutes with Harry without everything going bonkers would be a world's record. When Harry was on the scene, all other scenes seemed to melt into the distance. Third, we were going to begin the evening in a private room at Ringo's favorite Beverly Hills restaurant, the very "in" Mr. Chou's. Of course, the best was saved for last as Harry was personally presenting the centerpiece of the evening—he had

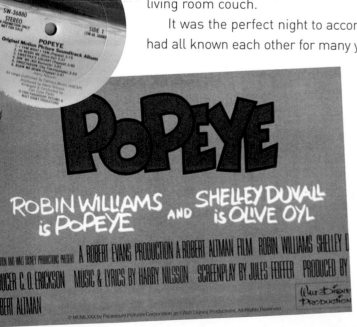

just finished his work scoring Robert Altman's new *Popeye* movie, and we were going to enjoy a private advance screening at a plush executive screening room on the movie lot. Whether the movie was good or bad was entirely beside the point. We all loved whatever Harry did, and everything had a special ring to it that night—nothing on earth was going to spoil this soft, easy, and gently joyful evening.

Fine friends, a funny film, and fabulous food. No one spoke much afterward on the way back to Ringo's; it had that feel of leaning back after a fine repast and just savoring the evening. Ringo never brought up the events that had just transpired on the East Coast, and I found myself admiring the manner in which he handled the whole situation. There is no doubt how deeply he felt about John at that time. It is difficult to keep it simple when times are hard. He nailed it that night.

So in summary, let's check out the rack at the pool hall: Denny Bond and I were partners as we entered La La Land. I did my turn with the corporate thing, and then a decade later when I set up my own company, Hometown Productions, Inc., we came back together, and he became my first show biz attorney both for business and personal matters. Denny and Bruce Grakal were law school roommates, which was the reason I met Bruce in the early '60s, well before he began his trek into the *Star Wars* arena. Denny represented Harry Nilsson in the beginning years, and that is how I met Harry. Denny and Bruce circled around in the industry for a while and then became law partners later on. Harry and Denny had terminated their relationship, and some time after, he and Bruce had gone their separate ways. Bruce subsequently became Harry's attorney. Harry became friends with the Beatles when I was working with them, which reignited and deepened our relationship on a separate level from Denny. Time passed and Harry, I believe, was ultimately responsible for bringing Ringo to Bruce. The irony in this is that I had nothing to do with bringing Ringo and Bruce together. When Ringo, Bruce, and I sat down to a business dinner in 1990, we realized that we all had decades-long relationships but had nothing to do with establishing each other's personal and business relationships.

This all began in the early '60s, over forty years ago. To this day, Bruce continues to represent Ringo and over these later years has for the first time acted as my attorney.

I think we just ran the table, and in looking back at it all I think I can chalk it up to good fortune.

Track 35

I Am
My Father's Son

» *Nashville, Tennessee, July 1986*

It was the spring of 1986. Even though I had been living full time in Nashville for almost two years, my accomplishments and confidence were at an all-time low. I couldn't get arrested career-wise, even though I had had so much success in the past as a producer in Nashville, with Waylon and the Outlaw movement in particular. My career was at a standstill, yet I still had better production and industry executive credentials than most of the reigning powers-that-be on Music Row. The doors to success were not shut in my face—they were closed so tightly I couldn't open them with a crowbar. Low-level "custom" producing gigs often paid the bills, but I could not get on board with any of the legitimate labels either as a producer or as an executive.

I got so desperate at one time that I applied for jobs outside the music business just to pay the bills. When I got turned down as a UPS driver, I started feeling something was definitely wrong. When I got rejected after applying for a used car salesman job down on Broadway, the street that ran from just below Music Row into downtown Nashville, I knew I was in real trouble.

I finally got a job as a "down rigger" and general stagehand flunky at Nashville's newly opened Starwood Amphitheater. Starwood was like many of the country's outdoor amphitheaters built in the 1980s to attract major acts during the spring, summer, and fall. Technically, I was still in the entertainment business, but the view was a little different from what I was used to. (Kind of brings to mind the joke about the guy who walked behind the circus elephants and shoveled manure. When asked if he wouldn't like a better job someday, he responded, "What? And leave show business?") I was now a part of the stage crew—unloading equipment trucks as they came in, setting up the lights, sound, and staging for the evening concert, moving equipment during the actual concert, and then tearing down and loading the trucks at the end of the evening. It was a start at 6 a.m. and wrap it all up at 2 a.m. the next morning kind of thing many days. One can only imagine how grimy, dirty, and smelly a person can get by mid-afternoon in this kind of occupation. You definitely didn't dress up in your best knickers for this gig.

I was almost fifty, and most of the young bucks who did this for a living were in their twenties. I was in good shape and enjoyed outlasting, out-lifting, and out-distancing these young upstarts. If one of them was sagging while picking up the heavy end of scaffolding, the most common phrase they heard from me was: "Ya got kids, ya got nuthin!" In time they would say it before I did. I did have their respect because they knew my background. They knew I was the "old-timer" and had already seen the things that they hoped to experience someday. It was almost like being a professional athlete who had seen better years: the young dudes about to run them over have great admiration for them as they leave them by the sidelines. They know that at least the old-timer has "been there"—that unique place they hopefully will occupy someday, however brief it may be.

I am leading up to something here.

As I looked into his face, I had this eerie feeling I was looking into John's face twenty years earlier.

Julian Lennon was still riding a wave of success from his debut 1984 release, *Valotte,* and the hit singles from that album that included his 1985 Top 5 hit "Too Late for Goodbyes." On tour in the summer of '86 promoting his second album release, *The Secret Value of Daydreaming,* Julian had been booked to headline Starwood in early July. It was a hot, muggy, Midsouth kind of late summer day, and he had just finished his sound check when we passed each other on the ramp that led from backstage down to the dressing areas. Just as he passed I said, "Julian," in a soft voice. He stopped and turned. Even though I was greasy, smelly, and dragging, he sensed something and looked at me as if he was expecting to see an old friend. "Julian, I'm Ken Mansfield, and I used to work for your father," I continued. He immediately turned the rest of the way around and came back to me, obviously wanting to hear more. He didn't see, or better yet didn't even care about, my state of professional disrepair as he faced me; his eyes only took in what his ears had heard and his heart had sensed—a chance to know more about his father. We exchanged some brief pleasantries and then, leaning against the iron rails that bordered the ramp, two men in a timeless tradition had this poignant, personal, and heartfelt conversation.

I shared with him small details of the many exchanges I had had with his dad almost two decades earlier. I felt as we talked that it was important to him to gather as much information as he could, just so he could put some more pieces together of a relationship he had lost. It was actually a little

freaky for me; as I looked into his face, I had this eerie feeling I was looking into John's face twenty years earlier. The similarities in appearance, sound, and mannerisms were so striking I felt like we were leaning on the railings outside of the short set of stairs that led up to 3 Savile Row.

We hugged in parting—me leaving a little grease on him and him leaving a lot of memories and mixed feelings in me. It is hard to find a place to cry in an amphitheater with about 150 stagehands, musicians, and crewmembers in every nook and cranny of the facility. I had to wait until I was able to sink into the dark shadows of the stage curtains as I watched him perform later that night. I never could have imagined this scene twenty years ago today.

Fire and Rain
(I Never Thought
I'd See You Again)

» *Nashville, Tennessee, July 1986*

The encounter with Julian Lennon was not the only lingering taste of the apple that fell from the fading tree of a time gone by that landed back into my life during my brief stint at the Starwood. The other one was possibly not as touching but definitely more profound. If you remember, James Taylor was one of our first artists on Apple Records and absolutely one of our finest. The pairing of James and producer Peter Asher (who was also the head of Apple A&R at the time, as well as the Peter of "Peter and Gordon") was magnificent. As I have related in other crevices of this tome, Peter and I were very good friends and shared for many years our own little long and winding road that was delightfully strewn with fortunes, flowers, scintillating success, and raucous roadside attractions, as almost hand in hand we rode in different limos together down its length and breadth of possibilities. There was a fork in this "high" way, and as James and Peter sailed off into the entertainment biz stratosphere, my ship lost momentum and eventually became grounded on unfamiliar shores.

So here I was, operating in this space in time where I was "humping" amps and "pulling" cable backstage at the Starwood Amphitheater, and on this particular night we were preparing for James Taylor, who was headlining the show. Of course, somewhat to my ego-centered dismay, this was one of the events that Peter decided to fly to from LA to spend some time with his artist. When I found out he was going to be at the concert, I knew I was going to have to reach down deep inside for a handful of "tough" to get me through what was coming. I had been proud of all I had accomplished over the years, so I had "pride" down cold. That night I received, as I did in my encounter with Julian Lennon, an advanced course in humility.

James Taylor had first met me as the head of Apple Records U.S. and had known me through the years as a close friend of Peter's. The last time James and I saw each other, I was a vice president of MGM Records and had spent the evening in the studio with him and Peter,

listening to their latest playbacks of tracks from the soon-to-be-released Warner Brothers LP *Sweet Baby James*. Our last real conversation had to do with me trying to talk them into releasing "Fire and Rain" as James's first single off the album instead of the title track, "Sweet Baby James."

On this particular afternoon in Nashville, James was caught quite off guard as he looked into my sweaty and greasy face in response to me asking him where he wanted his stage monitors placed during his show.

As I bent over, I could feel his stare at my back and behind. The "Handy Man" himself was thrown off-tempo and caught mid-chord in gentle confusion as he contemplated my presence, position, and purpose in this unexpected encounter. The momentum of the activity that surrounded us overtook the awkward ambiguity of the situation, and he was pulled back into the staging preparation for the evening performance. Later on, between sound check and the actual concert, and as if in some kind of ethereal yet bawdry ballet, he and I and Peter converged in almost exactly the same place that I had met Julian Lennon—on the ramp between the theater and the dressing rooms—and had a chat. Neither asked what was going on with me, and we talked like old times, ignoring the incongruity of my current circumstances. The outer edges of the apple may have rotted away, but as many of us have learned over time, and as I just mentioned, the core remains solid. I haven't seen or talked to James since that dog-day afternoon, but Peter and I did reunite years later when I was president of the prestigious Mobile Fidelity Sound Labs. My company was the leader in audiophile re-mastered gold CDs of the major historic recordings of the music industry, and he was the key to obtaining the rights to Carole King's classic *Tapestry* album. Not only did my ego and I feel better about my position during this get-together, but I also know I smelled a lot better.

The outer edges of the apple may have rotted away, but as many of us have learned over time, and as I just mentioned, the core remains solid.

Track 37

Kass Reinventing the Apple

» *Nashville, Tennessee—London, England, 1986*

I had not talked to Ron Kass in quite some time when out of the blue and into the gray haze of winter in Nashville I received a call from him at my new main Mansfield and Associates offices in the United Artists Tower. The newly decorated and furnished suite of corner offices was located on Music Row West in the heart of Music City's "Music Row" and boasted a daily view of "the boys who make the noise." (Sixteenth and Seventeenth Avenues are the famous heart of Nashville's "Music Row," and a few years ago these two streets were honored with new names—Music Row East and Music Row West. In addition, they were made into one-way streets in order to handle the tourist traffic flow their fame was attracting.) The suite was designed and furnished in plush, art deco modern motif with the mandatory Beverly Hills peach and green colored furnishings, walls, and carpets. The walls were adorned with Beatles pictures interspersed with signed Leroy Neiman and Michael Young paintings. A bit different from the brown shag carpeted offices that adorned most of Music Row in those days.

It was good to hear from Ron. Even though we didn't talk to each other much in those days, we were always in touch and had established a lifetime closeness that automatically erased the sometimes long times between communications. We chatted for quite a while, catching up on what had transpired since our last conversation, and then after Ron had established what I was doing business-wise, he asked if I was open to a new proposition. I definitely replied in the affirmative because every time Ron Kass had made me a business offer in the past, my quality of life and financial statement greatly improved. I waited expectantly to hear what he had to say, bearing in mind that Ron always painted on large exotic canvases. Even though I knew all this, I wasn't prepared for what he had in mind.

"If we started up Apple Records again, would you come back as U.S. manager?"

After I picked myself up from my peach-covered floor, I managed to ask him what he was talking about. According to Kass, he had just returned from London, and it seemed that over the last few months he had held exploration conversations with some of the Beatles, Yoko, Derek Taylor, Neil Aspinall, Tony Bramwell, and Peter Asher. The concept for reconstructing Apple would be not to just start up the company as an active label again but to staff it only with the original members so it really would be Apple Records and not just some sterile corporate business venture. (Historical note—Apple never did cease being. Neil Aspinall still ran it out of offices at #48 Charles Street in London and spent most of his time in the agonizing defense of its assets and purity. It seems Neil went from listening to screaming teenyboppers to screaming at lawyers. He spent forty years with the Beatles, resigning from his position as Apple's chief executive in 2007.) As a practical matter, there were a lot of potential profits that Apple's status could generate from its catalogue through reissues, repackaging, and release of unreleased masters and projects. (At this time in the mid-'80s, it had been a decade since the label had released any product whatsoever.) There was one reality that had to be addressed and overcome and that was the "been there, done that" aspect of the financial contribution that the reemergence would require. Kass said the remaining Beatles and Yoko had no interest in that scenario. But because of the conversational interest he was having, he felt that if we were able to put together the funding for the label, he had a running chance of putting the whole thing back together.

So, what he was asking me was, if he was indeed able to reinvent the Apple, could he have my commitment to return as U.S. manager. He wanted this fact to be part of his presentation. As far as I was concerned, what he was really asking me was, "Do you want to return to the most exciting time of your life? Do you want to rejoin your favorite people in the whole world?" The whole possibility rushed over my imagination like a warm tremor, and I said yes. I jokingly added, "But one condition though—that the U.S. office be located in Nashville this time instead of LA." I was getting comfortable in Nashville and didn't really want to go back to La La Land. Without skipping a beat, he replied that he thought that would be no problem so—"Are you in?" I calmly said yes into the receiver to my longtime friend. Inside my very being, "yes" was swirling a million times around as if in neon, and I thought I was going to explode with joy. Even if Ron's request was the impossible of impossibles, just being considered as an integral and important part of this great adventure was all the payment I would ever need.

Ironically, I was in the midst of putting together some other deals with Ted Solomon, a new friend who loved the Beatles and whose expertise was locating large amounts of money for plausible business ventures. This was right up his alley and just what he and I were looking for. Whatever else we were working on ceased, and Kass, he, and I began mammoth teleconferencing. It wasn't long before Ted, Kass, and I were on a plane to London. I had an old suit in my suitcase that I had bought on Carnaby Street in the '60s. This was the same suit that I wore during other Apple meetings, and I was going to pull it out and wear it, symbolically, at these new ones. More importantly, *in his suitcase*, Ted had papers reflecting a $10 million commitment from investors if the Apple deal was put together. He had the Apple seed money, Johnny!

So here I was—back on a plane to London for Apple meetings—twenty years later.

Kass being Kass, he had ensconced us in the private St. James Club just off Bond Street, and like Peter Brown many years before, he had prepared our "shejule" well in advance. The first day we took it easy, walked familiar streets, and stood outside 3 Savile Row on the sidewalk talking for about an hour while looking up at the past and imagining ourselves back inside those windows once again. Kass and I wanted Ted to get an inside feeling of the Apple experience before meeting with Neil. We spent the day retracing steps and events for his education and entertainment.

Kass was acting strangely on this trip. He was constantly excusing himself from our activities and also leaving the table at restaurants for long periods during the whole time we were in London. His demeanor was different than I remembered, and there was a moodiness that I had never witnessed. I could not remember him spending that much time in the "john" before. He also was moving funny. When we were walking about, we would tease him that he was walking around so stiffly that it looked like the laundry had put too much starch in his shorts. He would shrug us off with comments about bad airplane food, jet lag, and his personal apprehension about accomplishing the task at hand. We accepted his explanations but in no way let up chiding him about the starched shorts bit. I knew Ron didn't do drugs, and his long disappearances into the various bathrooms puzzled me.

These musings were swept aside as soon as Tony Bramwell joined us and we began meeting with Neil Aspinall. Tony was the promotion manager for Apple and had committed to the new plan. This was a welcomed job opportunity for him, and as I had a sense that possibly his career, like mine, wasn't exactly at its sparkling greatest at this particular time. Tony made fun of my old suit and didn't seem to be as overcome by nostalgia as I had imagined. Ted wanted to buy one just like it, while Kass wouldn't be caught dead in it, and as expected, Neil didn't even notice. (I eventually passed this suit on to my youngest son, Mark, when he was living in Italy, and he left it there. I guess some people aren't as big a history buff as I am!)

In his suitcase, Ted had papers reflecting a $10 million commitment from investors if the Apple deal was put together. He had the Apple seed money, Johnny!

As Neil, Ron, Tony, and I were sitting in local pubs and in essence reconducting a modern version of the original Apple meetings, I would sometimes fade out because this was quite a trip for me. It was almost like I could close my eyes, block out a couple of erratic decades, and it was as if I had never left. Neil was now mellowed out and actually rather worn out with all the un-fun aspects of his current responsibilities in looking after the Apple enterprises. He looked great after recovering from a serious heart attack, and I believe that traumatic event gave Neil the blessed freedom to reevaluate his life's work. He explained how he had established a better job description with the lads, and this enabled him to spend more quality time with his wife, Suzie, and the kids. I always liked him a lot, although to this day I have never been quite sure how he viewed me beyond a warmth and courtesy he always extended, although somewhat guardedly. Tony, regardless of what was going on with his life, still portrayed that aloof cocky attitude from when he was on top of the promo world in the old days. Kass was still the consummate class act, and I am sure if form is to remain true, I probably still came off as the expectant puppy dog looking at the world and all it had to offer as a red rubber ball. I actually like being naive and positively expectant, but sometimes it is so inappropriate. All the while, Ted Solomon was in Piccadilly Circus heaven as he listened and watched history being reviewed and revisited. Most of all, though, I think he was most excited about the possibility of it being recreated. Neil liked Ted, and this was good. The financing was an absolute cornerstone of this whole discussion.

Ron Kass and me outside Kass's Beverly Hills hotel sometime in the late '60s.

The meetings went well although details were still vague, which was necessary at this point. This was merely a fact-finding mission, and everyone left with things to think about and assignments to fulfill before we could proceed further. As Neil always appeared to me to play his cards very close to the vest, I was not sure where he would land on this issue once it edged closer to reality. The one thing that was for sure was that all the duckies had to be in a proper row before any further meaningful discussions could be had with any of the Beatles or Yoko, who represented John's holdings. It was also mandatory that Neil had to be 100 percent convinced that it was a good idea.

Ron's strangeness was evolving into preoccupied remoteness as we began summarizing our duties. We tried to create follow-up schedules before we each made our way "back to the U.S. of A." We agreed on a plan, and Ron returned to California. After a long flight homeward, I said goodbye to Ted at Washington DC's National Airport and carried on to "Music City USA" with an armload of assignments to accomplish as my part of the impending proposal. We had established a timetable and would all regroup in about two months in order to continue to the next step—assuming everything was in order.

I couldn't reach Kass after we returned. He wasn't answering or returning phone calls. Even his partner at his movie company couldn't find him. I had his sister's phone number and had conversed with her over the years, and she couldn't help me either. Time was running out on the assignment due dates that each of us had committed to as our individual parts of the preparation needed for the next meeting. Kass had dropped out of sight. As Kass was the starting point of our efforts, this made zero sense until one day his sister called me and gave me the phone number where he was staying in Arizona with his fiancée, Anne. I called the number, and Ron answered the phone.

He spoke in a soft, level tone as he quietly explained what had transpired since we hugged goodbye in London. Upon returning to LA, Ron went to see a doctor because he hadn't felt well during the London trip and was quite honestly uncomfortable the whole time. They discovered a cancerous tumor in his gut the size of a grapefruit. Ron was given six months to a year to live.

Without Ron there would never be the Apple we had envisioned. For some of us, he was the core, the sweetness, and the heart. It was around him we would all rally. When we all learned the news of his fate, I can't remember even one conversation about continuing on with the whole idea. Ron and I must have imparted the "feel" of the whole thing pretty successfully to Ted when we were "educating" him in London as to the essence of Apple, because Ted never mentioned it either. The three of us became closer friends during this time. Both Ted and I visited Ron in LA before he died. Kass looked great and held court in dying as he did in living—in a suite at L'Ermitage Beverly Hills. As always, there were little finger things to eat on porcelain plates and unpronounceable champagne on ice if one preferred.

He died October 17, 1986—eight months after London. I didn't go to the funeral. I couldn't think of him that way.

I didn't ask God why on this one. I really didn't want to know.

'50s Rock and Roll

» *Beverly Hills, California, 1990*

"Sooo . . . when are you writing *your* book?" I looked across the table into the face of a very familiar but much different Ringo Starr than the Ringo I first met over twenty-five years earlier. His features had deepened, yet seemed to have softened with the passing years. We had last seen each other about four years earlier. It was here in Los Angeles, but under much different circumstances.

At that time Ringo and his wife, Barbara Bach, had decided to leave LA, so Ringo invited a few old friends over for a goodbye get-together. As the evening eased to an end, Ringo, Harry Nilsson, Alan Pariser, Timothy Leary, and I were standing in a semi circle in front of the fireplace in his den. Our ladies, including Barbara, were in the other room. We were winding down our recollections of how we had all met when suddenly Ringo and I realized that we were staring at each other. We both knew what was happening. We were searching familiar faces looking for the two young fellows we had met a quarter of a century earlier. I love the hardy Englishman loyalty to old friendships that prompted him to warmly say for my benefit before the small gathering, "But I've known you the longest, Ken."

For a transcendent portion of the last few decades, we had both done about as much to our bodies, minds, spirits, and lives as we could with the plethora of drugs and "fast lane" living that was at our disposal for so long. Eventually things began unraveling for both of us, on different levels, as the '80s wound down.

So we each bailed out of Hollyweird: Ringo via the Sierra Tucson Rehabilitation Clinic in Arizona on the way to his "Rocca Bella" digs in Monte Carlo while I flew upwind in that wintertime period of my life and took the northern route along California's rugged Mendocino coast. After an ill-fated layover there, I made a sharp "right" turn, eventually crash-landing in Nashville. Like a sorry gutted goose I migrated southward back into the "night-life" weakened arms of my old Outlaw cowboy friends for a much needed soft landing into familiar territory.

Shortly before Ringo and I made our non-encore exits to our respective houses of rehabilitation, I hit total financial bottom and was not only forced to sell my Laurel Canyon estate but basically the entirety of the antiques and goodies housed therein. I had collected these treasures over the years from the various journeys I had been on, and it was hard to let go of the things that had become a part of my personal history. Because of the extent and value of many of the items, I had hired a company that specialized in matters such as these and would bring in their experts and organize the items of the estate. They not only assessed the value of each item, but upon completion of that phase would gave advance notice to preferred collectors and then notified a limited general clientele later about the antiques and collectibles becoming available. In the process of cataloging our collection, they ascertained that some items had limited value and therefore created a bargain-basement category. These were set aside in a designated corner of the giant main room: the "great room" as my Nashville compatriots would call it. In essence, this gathering of stuff was relegated to the dollar bin portion of the estate sale. In their upscale minds these were items of little value beyond the appeal to garage sale-type buyers—actually the upper class of garage sale enthusiasts, I must add.

I let Ringo know what was coming down and the date and time of the advance viewing. What is interesting is that I would never approach him for help by requesting some charitable involvement in a public aspect of his career (management, production, etc.), which would not only bring in some income but would boost my status in the industry. Also, I would have never considered approaching him on a more down-to-earth level—

like asking him flat out for some financial aid to help me through this rough period. I would never ask because of my pride, and he would never offer out of respect and fear that I would be insulted. I will never know if I should have approached him; there is a great likelihood that he would have been happy to help out. It was just too dangerous a proposition to interject into a relationship that I treasured as a lifetime thing. My guess is he felt restricted from offering assistance for somewhat the same reasons.

The day of the private sale arrived, and he and Barbara were two of the first customers to show up at my door. Here is where we drop back into the essence of the Beatles and the thing that permeates their very persona and the main constant that has always made them special to me. I have had special times and incredible relationships with many very famous people, but there has always been a missing personal depth that relegated these things to mere memories that are somehow forgotten over time. In the case of the Fab Four, though, there is this almost indescribable everlasting element that prevails because of the genuineness of their personal character. While Barbara roamed the premises looking at the more intriguing items, such as the 1840 antique plantation piano that we had shipped in from Tennessee, Ringo went straight to the bargain buckets and picked out some scrappy pieces and made his helpful purchases. There wasn't anything he really wanted or needed. I had been to his house, and he was definitely not lacking for things.

We knew "we could work it out." The deal is done and everyone is happy. It is now time for *Time Takes Time,* Ringo's first studio album since 1983's *Old Wave.*
Left to right: Me, Ron, Peter, and Ringo

What surfaced that day was a combination of contradictions: he wanted so much to help in some way, but his thrifty upbringing led him to the bargain buckets and the purchase of items as modest as obligatory candlestick holders.

By 1990, Ringo's All Starr Band concept (the inaugural edition of which had hit the road the previous year) had helped energize his live performance reputation, but his recording career was somewhat below the flush handle level. He had, in the late '80s, suffered a horrendous experience with legendary country producer Chips Moman, which resulted in a very poorly produced record that not only turned off the recording industry executives but created a situation that ended very badly between Ringo and Chips and fostered a lot of legal hang-ups. At this point in his career, Ringo had beat a bad path into a corner of the industry that left him less than in demand as a recording artist. Jimmy Webb wrote a song entitled "The Moon's a Harsh Mistress"; the entertainment industry can put that lunar lady to shame when it comes to the way someone is treated once they stumble even ever so slightly from high perches.

I started thinking about all this, and because I had been blessed to have been in a position to observe firsthand and up close what a true talent Ringo was and what he had to offer, I came up with a recording concept that I thought might be a way to work his way back into the current mix. It was strategically important to come up with a concept that was sound on all levels creatively and commercially. It was also important that it would be one that would allow him to hold his head high and not appear that he was coming from behind. He was a Beatle, which always looked pretty good on a resume, but I did think there was quite a bit of resistance to overcome and that there was a proper way to go about it. I no longer had any phone numbers for him,

Peter and me sorting out details.

so I called Neil Aspinall in London at the Apple office. Neil rightly being Neil would not give me any private phone numbers, but he did agree to pass on the message to Ringo. At this point in my life, I still wasn't talking or writing about my time with the Beatles. A few of us from those days had taken an unspoken oath to keep it all to ourselves. All my wife, Connie, knew about the Beatles and me was that I had once worked with them. In a way I think it was a bit of an abstract matter for her—not a real flesh and blood kind of thing until she walked into our office the next morning and turned on the answering machine to pick up messages. Ringo, as only Ringo can do, left a wild message on the machine, and there was no doubt who was talking. I wish we had kept that tape. Anyway, he left a number, and before the day was over, we were catching up on the last few years. He didn't really care for my creative concept but agreed that we should meet and talk about me representing him for a record deal structured conceptually more to his liking. I was extremely well connected at most of the major record companies during this period, as well as having great relationships with some of the hip and well-established boutique labels that were distributed by the majors at the time.

He was going to be in Los Angeles for a few days in about two weeks. He asked if I would consider flying in from Nashville and meeting him there. Fortunately and coincidentally, I was producing a new record on the legendary Flying Burrito Brothers at that time and had wanted to do the mixes in Los Angeles anyway. To our delight, we would be able to meet and have a long overdue dinner without the customary aid of agents and managers.

We met a few weeks later for dinner at Portifino, a restaurant in the Beverly Hillcrest Hotel where I was staying. Joining us was our mutual, longtime friend and attorney, Bruce Grakal.

When Ringo and I first saw each other in the lobby, it was obvious that we were both curious as to how the other would look. Comparatively speaking, we each looked and felt great. The last time we had seen each other we had had a lot of room for improvement: Ringo was 5' 8" and had weighed only ninety-seven pounds (six stone) at that time. I was 5' 9" and so skinny and drawn that I could sit on a dime and you could still read "In God We Trust" around the edges. Ringo joked over dinner about his new lifestyle. "These days I exercise and play golf. I'm finally free of drugs and alcohol, and I'm learning to eat right. I even attend classes, if you can believe that. I've finally become everyone I used to hate!"

Back to Ringo's question to me at dinner that opened this chapter. "*My* book? Well—I have had a lot of offers," I replied, "but my memories aren't quite sleazy enough and that is all everybody is looking for!"

"Why don't you just make things up?" he offered. "That's what the rest of them have done!" The wry look on his face was one of both helpless consternation and gentle acceptance of so-called "insiders" and their literary distortion of the Beatles, both as a group and as individuals. He framed all this with a suggested shrug of the shoulders and an implied "What the hey, I'm used to it" toss of the head.

"Oddly enough," I told him, "my memories of the Apple days and my times with the Beatles are more like scenes from *A Hard Days Night* or *Help!* That is really how I see the period of time I spent with you guys. I always had the feeling that you projected a certain 'proper' and upbeat side to me so that I would be impressed with the great business sense you had in the way you ran Apple. I felt you were putting on this contrivance so I could see how 'together' you all were. I had it all figured out that after a few days at 3 Savile Row, you wanted to send me back to the States pumped, hustled, and primed—totally ready to really go to work for you."

Ringo cocked his head as he shot a sideways glance to Bruce. I had learned over the years that this particular version of Ringo's many animated looks meant that somewhere soon in this conversion I was going to be the recipient of a Beatles-style barb, the type he and the other three made famous over the years during interviews and press conferences.

Ringo joked over dinner about his new lifestyle. "These days I exercise and play golf. I'm finally free of drugs and alcohol, and I'm learning to eat right. I even attend classes, if you can believe that. I've finally become everyone I used to hate!"

"Oh yes, Ken, the Beatles really didn't have that much to do in those days. We would just sit around and think of ways that we could act to impress you—sort of an all-out effort by the four of us to convince you that we were important enough to warrant your incredible music industry talents! You know to this day we still consider your visits as the times of our finest performances!" He followed the last line with his warm and hearty laugh that I love so much. His delivery of this zinger embarrassed me into the realization of how wrapped up in my own world I had been in the early days. I actually believed that, just like everything else, even the *Beatles'* world revolved around me.

We continued to eat, talk, reminisce, and laugh like old school chums. It was simple fun with good, simple people. In the '60s, I looked forward to the time when the Beatles "thing" would be over so Ringo and I could just be friends. Because of the fleeting nature of fame, I figured it would all be over someday and then we could just hang out and brag about our "fifteen minutes" and what big deals we all were in the "old days." Back then I had no idea (I don't think Ringo did, either) that the Beatles would be an eternal force in rock and roll and the entertainment industry. Even today, more than forty years later, there is a class difference between a superstar of Beatles proportions and everyone else in this exclusive rock-and-roll galaxy. To his credit, superstar Ringo has a way of ignoring all that—most of the time.

That night over my Cabernet wine and his cranberry juice, he told me that for the first time in years he was totally free of all contracts. Mr. Starkey was open to something new and officially able to do anything he wanted. We agreed that I would represent him to the record companies for his first new album of studio rock and roll in almost a decade. The album became the 1992 Private Music/BMG release *Time Takes Time*.

Also that night, and of equal importance to me, I felt that my silence had been noted and honored and that Ringo had just released me to write about my feelings and memories of my time with the Beatles and Apple Records.

My subsequent negotiations on Ringo's behalf with Private Music's president Ron Goldstein and label owner Peter Baumann were greatly enhanced by the fact that Ringo had a unique marketing appeal to their

Having a Beatle as your calling card into the rock-and-roll part of this (ad)venture was stepping forward briskly with a pretty heavy opening act: prestige with a capital *B*.

company. Private Music had earned a reputation as a successful "new age" label largely due to the success of Yanni and Suzanne Ciani, but Baumann wanted more and decided to open up his vision into becoming a full spectrum pop and contemporary music label. Having a Beatle as your calling card into the rock-and-roll part of this (ad)venture was stepping forward briskly with a pretty heavy opening act: prestige with a capital *B*. Peter was also smart enough to know that in time a Ringo Starr product would have incredible historic value, so he was able to approach this investment musically, strategically, and corporately. Because he was a Beatles fan, he also found the whole idea pleasantly personal.

The whole Private Music relationship began the next day after my dinner with Ringo and Bruce. I flew home to Nashville in the morning and started making calls from my office that afternoon. My first call was right back to LA to Private Music A&R chief Jamie Cohen. Jamie had recently told me about the internal musical desires at the label, and I felt this was just what they were looking for. For me it had all the elements that I felt

Ringo needed in a new recording situation. He needed personal attention and expected proper respect for someone of his stature. He was pretty fed up with bad experiences and a lot of the attitudes of the major label syndrome, but at the same time he needed the power of a major distribution system. Private Music by concept was probably the only totally perfect place for him at that time. They were distributed by powerhouse BMG/RCA, whose president, Joe Galante, was a friend of mine. Private Music was an extremely well-funded, personal, high-class label with great vision and the heart of artist understanding at its very core.

Peter Baumann was a member of the internationally acclaimed Tangerine Dream, one of rock's most avant garde and visionary groups. He was an artist *and* a European and completely dedicated to professionalism in a label that was his own personal and preferential—private music. He had wisely selected previous Island Records label topper Ron Goldstein as his president. Goldstein had that same kind of knowledge and class reminiscent of Ron Kass, which made Ringo comfortable. Jamie Cohen had a street edge and rock-and-roll remembrance that Ringo needed from an A&R executive.

After a brief conversation, Jamie became very excited about the opportunity and wanted to talk to Ron and Peter about Ringo. He made me promise not to talk to another record label for twenty-four hours.

I agreed.

The next morning I walked into my office to an unexpected conference call with the three of them. Baumann was very officious and concise as he graciously informed me that he would like to meet Ringo. I countered in form that, of course, everyone wants to meet Ringo—after all he was a Beatle. I did say, though, that if he wanted to talk about a record deal, I would meet with him first, and if I believed he was serious, then I would set up a meeting with Ringo and Bruce. I added that a sure way for me to know if he was serious was if my travel agent notified me within the next hour that a prepaid first-class round trip plane ticket was waiting for me at the Nashville airport for an early flight back to LA the next morning.

There was.

I went.

He was serious.

I was picked up at LAX, elegantly delivered to a Beverly Hills hotel, and then taken to the Private Music Melrose Avenue executive offices. We spent the entire day in meetings, and then Peter, Ron, Jamie, and I capped the day's discussions with a wonderful dinner at Chaya Beverly Hills. Peter was flying out the next day at about the same time I was returning to Nashville, so we agreed I would meet him at his Bel Air home for breakfast. We would then finish up our conversation and negotiations in his limo on the way to the airport.

As planned I went to Peter's home early the next day, and by morning's end most of the major deal points had been worked out, subject, of course, to Bruce Grakal's and Ringo's approval. Suddenly I realized we were experiencing a "pregnant pause" and that I was the focal point of a very intent stare. As it was Peter's silent moment, he finally broke it by asking, "OK, Ken, what's Ringo going to cost me?" I was well aware that at this point we had discussed just about everything except the actual dollars for Ringo and the recording budget. I took a deep breath because I knew that this was the time to play my ace. I also knew I had to bring a "winning hand" home to Ringo and Bruce. "Peter," I said as coolly as I possibly could, "the five most popular and famous names ever in the history of the music entertainment industry are Elvis Presley and the four Beatles. Only three of these five gentlemen [this, of course, was before George's death] are still with us. I'm offering Private Music one third of the most famous entertainers of all time!" He sank slowly back in his leather chair, stroked his chin, and said with a warm sarcastic grin, "This is going to cost me, isn't it?"

I can't disclose the particulars of the financial arrangement we made that day, but I will admit that it was consistent with the "bigger than life" aspect of the world's greatest band. I do know that I will never forget the look on his face as he attempted to maintain a characteristically unfazed sense of propriety as he pondered the deal.

He agreed to my offer.

He *was* serious.

Back one last time to dinner with Ringo and Bruce. While Bruce and I focused on the business and legal structures of the deal, Ringo

If we had said to ourselves when we were in our next rock-and-roll album when we were in our reminisced. "The Beatles were a really great little *rock-and-roll* band! *That's* why we made it! Just like the old days, I want to make an album with that basic hard-driving essence." He was almost entertaining himself as he began to envision upcoming recording sessions while Bruce and I discussed the parameters of a potential deal. Ringo became more animated as he talked, suggesting potential band members and producers. He glanced periodically at his watch and mumbled something about meeting up later with his wife, Barbara. As he spoke, his words moved back and away in my consciousness as if in a warm echo chamber. Time and this moment went into slow motion, and I thought to myself that although he looked different now, a full quarter of a century had passed since we had first met, and yet he really hadn't changed at all. I remember sitting on the floor of the basement Apple recording studio during the *Let It Be* sessions—Ringo would periodically stare at his watch as the day drew on into evening and the others were arguing (creatively for the most part) about whatever song they were working on. He was ready to play, and play passionately, or go home. As soon the session was over, he was off the drum stool, out of the door, and into the car. In the beginning, middle, and to the very end I believe that Ringo will always want nothing more than just to play music and then go home to be with those he loves.

Suddenly, all three of us stopped in the middle of the moment. We looked around the table at each other and began laughing. If we had said to ourselves when we were in our twenties that we would be planning Ringo's next rock-and-roll album when we were in our fifties, not one of us would have ever believed it.

Fifties rock and roll! The beat of rock and roll had entered, shaped, and shaken our lives in the '50s. Now we were in our fifties, and there was still that something shaking and beating inside that made us feel like we could rock and roll on forever.

I needed this project; things had been pretty bleak career-wise for a long time. Ringo knew that. It was nice to get a little help from a friend.

twenties that we would be planning Ringo's fifties, not one of us would have ever believed it.

Track 39

After-Dinner Brink

» *Beverly Hills, California, 1990*

The *Time Takes Time* album project was born that evening at dinner with Bruce and Ringo, and it soon began to take shape. A few weeks passed (time was taking very little time), and things rapidly progressed from a fledgling business concept being discussed between two old friends to a concept with real business and musical muscle. As the recording process began to gear up, there was a lot to do on many levels; putting the new recording deal together required me to fly in to LA from Nashville on more than one occasion. There were extensive contractual matters to iron out. Even though I had negotiated the overall points, it was up to Bruce Grakal to get into the nitty-gritty, finer points and to nail down what we fondly call the boilerplate of the contract. That was one side of the coin, but then there were the creative, social, merchandising, promotional, scheduling, and musical direction type things to take care of.

In the middle of all this, Ringo decided that it was time to stop smoking cigarettes, which for a while took the edge off his normally laid-back demeanor—or should I say put an edge on!

After a hectic day's work in LA executing some of the myriad tasks necessary to complete the upcoming release of this, his first new album in quite some time, Ringo invited me to join him, Barbara, Bruce, and Hillary Gerrard for a late dinner at Le Dome, Elton John's eatery on the Sunset Strip. I originally turned down the invitation because I was tired from the day's activities, but after I got back to my hotel and proceeded to inspect the room-service menu, I rethought his offer and decided it would be nice to just relax together like old times even though sitting down for dinner at 10 p.m. meant we would probably not actually eat until after 11 p.m. I called him from the hotel and added myself back onto the guest list. As I had flown into LA only a day or two earlier, this was equivalent to having dinner at 1 a.m. Nashville time. I was used to adjusting to time-zone changes after decades of long distance travel, but I grew up country, and we eat supper at 5:30 p.m.; it was a little late for the visiting cowboy to be strapping on the feedbag.

After an incredible dinner that night (I had the bouillabaisse) and a whole lot of great retro reminiscent dialogue, Ringo and I walked out to the parking lot and handed our respective ducats to the valet. As we waited for our cars to be pulled up, I began rattling off a bunch of things for him to do because I was leaving the next day and was anxious to make sure all the bases were covered from our end of the arrangement concerning the things that I had told the label I would have him take care of.

I think the combination of Ringo having no ciggies for two days, a late dinner just settling in, and a lack of being in the mood to discuss business, all combined with his deep desire to not have a manager, piled up and pushed a button inside him—we got into a yelling match outside the restaurant in front of some surprised onlookers (including a stunned wife, Barbara) and parking attendants. I can imagine how it looked. Ringo and I ended up about twenty feet apart yelling at each other. I guess I had gone from relaying, in my mind, things that needed to be done to appearing, in his mind, to be telling him what to do. Maybe in the process I got a little too much into scheduling his moves, and that to him was overstepping my position. I thought I was just taking care of business and had never dreamed of becoming his manager. I was trying to manage a situation, and he took it that I was trying to manage him. "I don't need no manager," he yelled to me specifically and to the surrounding crowd in general.

"Well, who asked you anyway?" I replied with even more gusto. "It certainly wasn't me!" This exchange was accompanied by various British and American versions of gestures that included hands on hips, fingers waving in the air, heads thrust back and forth in dynamic punctuation, and loud dialogue with numerous vitriolic inflections.

My car was brought up between us at that point, and I just looked him off, if that is possible because he had already turned his back to me in defiance. I got in the car and drove off without paying my tab with the valet. (I think I actually unwittingly stuck Ringo with it unless he and Barbara drove off the same way and Bruce had to clean up after us.)

Before I got to La Cienega Boulevard, which was just a short distance down Sunset Boulevard from the restaurant, I was startled at the realization of what had just happened. I was so surprised at his unexpected outburst that joining in an out-of-character exchange for both of us was pretty amazing to contemplate. We had never talked to each other like that before over all these years—and this was especially incongruous since we were involved together in such a cool project that I had put together. This was possibly the best thing I had ever done for him, including all the things at Apple. I really started freaking out inside. Was a longtime friendship over? How did this affect my position in the record deal? How would this affect other mutual relationships? If it was going to be like it happens in a divorce where you have to divide up the friends, I knew I was definitely going to come out on the short end of that deal.

I really started freaking out inside. Was a longtime friendship over? How did this affect my position in the record deal? How would this affect other mutual relationships?

Needless to say, I got very little sleep that night because in some ways I was hurt, but mostly I really treasured the relationship and had a hard time entertaining the fact that it could be on the brink of being over after all these years—especially over nothing.

Even before the sun came up I gave up trying to sleep, so I got up, packed my bags, and booked an earlier flight back to Nashville—I just wanted to get away from it all. I felt sick inside. I was confused and very depressed. I needed a soft place to land, and I just wanted to go home and wait to see how it was all going to come out. I certainly didn't want to sit around in a hotel room with nothing to do but hope for a phone call or a way to sort it all out. It was all so incredibly important to me on so many levels.

I arrived in Nashville early the next afternoon and went straight home instead of to the office, which would be my typical routine. That night I got a phone call from Bruce Grakal. He nonchalantly asked how I was doing, and knowing that Bruce had never called before just to find out how I was doing, I surmised that he was calling on Ringo's behalf and that the proverbial axe was about to fall, cutting off what, at that time, was a twenty-five-year relationship. Bruce is not big on just chatting, and after what could be considered an abundance of small talk on his part, he said, "Hey, about last night. Forget about it. Ringo wanted me to let you know that he was a little edgy with giving up smoking and all and didn't mean anything about anything last night. He's OK if you're OK."

Feeling inside that the weight of the world had just been lifted, I kept my composure and mustered up the casual reply, "Heck yeah, tell him not to worry; I knew everything was cool! I didn't think anything about it! Just buy him a pack of ciggies before I come back next week and put it on my tab!"

The Starr dinner party

Ringo/me   Hillary/me   Bruce/me   Barbara/Ringo

"I had the bouillabaisse."

Track 40

Hollywood "High"

(My neighbor's cousin used to go to the same high school as Frank Sinatra's chauffeur's kid did.)

» *Newport Beach, California, Early-1960s*

It's late, and the floor is covered with water in places and—to top it off—four medium-sized people were given one narrow athletic locker to store stage clothes and personal belongings. The wooden benches will serve as a dry place to stand while we dress. The benches also double as the only place we can set our acoustic instruments while we prepare to go on stage at the Newport Dunes outdoor concert theatre. It is the early '60s, and we are the Town Criers, and we're riding the wave of folk music hysteria that was launched by the Kingston Trio via an unlikely song sensation entitled "Tom Dooley."

The money we would end up sharing would barely pay for the expenses involved in bringing us to this stage, but the applause and limited adulation were like savings deposits into our ego banks—the interest on this investment was always just enough to keep us going. The main thing was—we were the headliners that night! Like so many of us that ended up "in the circuit," we were college fraternity brothers who used to play at campus beer busts for free drinks and pizza. Then, through one of those oft-romanticized magical sequences of show biz events, we came to the attention of a Beverly Hills talent agent. The mad

Your comrades were either crazier than you or approximately as crazy as you were, and even less dependable.

dash for the hearts and charts of music lovers of the world officially began in befuddled earnest after this magic moment. Whoever these people may have been, once they showed us their embossed card with a catchy talent agency name and a Hollywood business address, we were hooked; they could have been retired axe murderers for all we knew. What we did know was that we were one step away from headlining the Palladium and ordering take-out food from the Brown Derby.

It was different then. The way you went about making it in the music industry was clearly defined, and there were very few shortcuts. Aside from the very rare exceptions to every rule, you knew you had to prepare yourself for years of hard work, horrendous disappointments, multitudinous rejections, third-world diets, evaporative living locations, questionable family lives, and a back full of emblematic scars from the emotional knife wounds along the way. Five people sleeping in a van filled with band equipment and dirty clothes became more than an occasional thing.

It was meant to be like this: the quixotic hard times and hard knocks were what it took to build the cynical muscle and armadillo-esque shield needed to become a successful entertainer. It was a dastardly design, painstakingly fueled by an impracticable mix of desire, musical madness, and occasional talent. All this was wrapped up in the knowledge that we

Here we are with Mitzi Gaynor at our first major event appearing with her and Steve Allen at a charity benefit in Beverly Hills. The original Town Criers were, from the right, Dan Hale, Tom Scali, (Mitzi), Me, and Steve Isaacson.

This was the second Town Criers—Bing Drastrup replacing Dan Hale. Here we are performing at our first major auditorium gig as the opening act for Dick Gregory. As exciting as it was for us, it did feel a little odd being four white folk singers playing to an audience who came to see one of the leading black activists of that time. Steve always stood on our left—then one day he left.

The second Town Crlers reunited for the first time in Phoenix, Arizona, in 1993, 40 years since we had been together. It blew us away because it took about 10 minutes to fall back into our old relational patterns, and when we started singing the old songs, we couldn't believe we still remembered our parts. I find it interesting that we posed for this picture in the same performance lineup as above. Tom, me, Bing, and Steve on our left.

had embarked on a 99-percent-failure-rate kind of occupation. The potential reward of beating the odds usually left people incapable of handling what they had accomplished—and usually even less sure that they had the right to be there in the first place. Your comrades were either crazier than you or approximately as crazy as you were, and even less dependable.

The amazing thing is the incredible bond between brothers in arms that comes out of this whole dizzying mess. Because the dictated process of earning your dues takes what seems like an eternity, you become the absolute kings of making the most of every moment. You develop this unique talent for forming deep friendships that last a lifetime—just from sharing a dressing room or an airport lounge with a fellow loony who, just like you, knows how to make three chords and a Fender amp howl in such a way that changes people's lives.

There is not a lot of wiggle room left over after years of this unrequited non-reality when the band bus drops you off for the last time. The applause has faded, and sometimes a few of the wounds have failed to heal. For most members of this unique fraternity, life becomes another long road trip, this time one of just trying to catch up and to understand. The fact that no one has better stories or has had a more exciting life is a severance package of sorts, but unfortunately none of it fits into the slot at the ATM machine. A peek at your scrapbook and fifty cents still won't buy a cup of coffee at Starbucks.

But hey—this is not what this book is all about. We are talking here about that other one percent.

Did I ever tell you I used to work with the Beatles?

This was the third and final incarnation of the Town Criers performing on Regis Philbin's local TV show (KGTV) in San Diego, California, circa 1963. Gary Long (bass) replaced Steve when he left. Bands do have disagreements and when we would have a falling out, Tom had an unusual way of handling his frustration. He did it the Italian way—instead of punching one of us out he would go home, cook a whole box of spaghetti, and eat it until he got sick. Then he wouldn't be mad anymore.

Fading out
of White

It was early 2006, and more than a decade since I had seen or talked to a Beatle. Just for old times sake, I decided to call Ringo and was surprised that the fifteen-year-old phone number I had in my address book was still good. It had been a private home number back then but is now a business number with an answering machine. I left a wacky message like we used to do and hung up wondering if he would return the call. He didn't. I know chances are that an assistant picked it up and never gave him the message, and I prefer to think of it that way. This is not totally pride and delusion on my part because there have been times in the past when I have tried to get past some nineteen-year-old intern, some kid who probably lived at home and had Leif Garrett posters on her wall. They were so imbued with their personal importance that they wouldn't take a simple message for Paul even after I politely explained that Mr. McCartney had specifically given me that certain private phone number and asked me to call at that particular time. But that's life in the slow lane I guess.

Speaking of Paul, a friend of mine met him recently and mentioned that she's a friend of mine. They said Paul lit up, asked about me, and sent his best. I admit that made me feel good because it has been a long time. Anyway, I thought that was going to be just about it with the lads and me these days. Au contraire—Ringo and I did finally hook up that summer for a brief get-together in Santa Rosa. For me that was the coda in my rock-and-roll rhapsody. It was strange to look into his eyes—we were babies when we first met over forty years ago—and although it was a warm and personal encounter, it had a certain awkwardness about it. There was a tender realization that a truckload of past ramblings isn't always enough to keep old friends on track. For old times' sake, two slightly worn veterans of pop history took a spurious ride down memory lane one last time. After an almost traditional exchange of niceties, we struggled to find things to talk about and keep a real chat going.

For old times' sake, two slightly worn veterans of pop history took a spurious ride down memory lane one last time.

It is all so different now. I left the entertainment business over a decade ago, and as anyone who has been in the business knows, it only takes about ten minutes to fall off the fast track and be totally out of touch. Fortunately for me, my exit from show biz was a mutual decision— we mutually grew tired of each other right around the same time, so it worked out perfectly. It was another time and another place, and I am not foolish enough to try to recapture it other than in intrusive reflections—in fact, I rather find a fresh freedom in just letting it go. What's also fortunate for me is the fact that all my incredible relationships didn't come to an end; they just more or less gently faded away, off into the distance of another time—warped and otherwise. This slow fade-away of old friends lends a kind softness to the ending of it all.

I have always said that my greatest talent was an incurable naiveté that kept me from thinking that anything was impossible or that everyone I came in contact with wasn't just as excited to see me as I was them—Beatles or otherwise. I think that is why it worked with them and me—the assumption on my part that they were as impressed with me as I was impressed with them. I guess I could sum it up with the comment that Capitol president Stanley Gortikov made to me once on a plane ride from London to LA after a series of meetings with the Beatles. I was the young upstart in the company, and not only had I been climbing pell-mell over the other executives on my way to the top, I was now sitting in first class with the man himself. I took this opportunity to ask him for an evaluation of my progress, obviously expecting a glowing report. I admired Mr. Gortikov more than anyone I had ever met, and I knew he had his eye on me and that he liked me. He thought for a minute and then simply said, "Well, Ken, you have a certain lack of humility." I guess he was saying to me that that was exactly what it took to make it in show biz! At the same time, in his wisdom he was pointing out what could become my Achilles' heel somewhere down the long and winding road that lay ahead.

OK. I know that all this is real fluffy and nice, and there are those who may ask, "What does all this blather have to do with the Beatles?" I must respond in a kindly and slightly road-worn manner, "More than you may think." If you want to know the totality of the Beatles' story, you have to accept that there was a beginning and an aftermath, both of which were made up of diverse people drawn together from all over the world. Somewhat off-centered and a little out of focus at times, these were the people who added the delicious mixture of their hard sweat, tangled dreams, and sweet hapless hearts. If the Beatles' music and legend last forever, then also the people who were there are eternally ensconced in the echoes of the events that transpired. No one, be he a Beatle or a buddy, came away from those times unscathed or untouched. Many of us now feel free to write about it because it is far enough in the past that there is no betrayal in telling our stories.

Over the years, a few of us from those days have once again established contact with each other either in person, in extended phone calls, or in e-mails—they always end with unspoken and unwritten promises that because we had been uniquely touched we would always keep in touch. I guess it is in a soft way something akin to the feelings veterans from our foreign wars have for each other. At one time or another, Peter (Asher) and Gordon (Waller), Ringo Starr, George and Pattie Harrison, Hillary Gerrard, Paul and Linda McCartney, Mal Evans, Ron Kass, John Lennon, Jack Oliver, Tony Bramwell, Neil Aspinall, Chris O'Dell, Jackie Lomax, Larry Delaney, Stanley Gortikov, Donovan Leitch, and others from those days spent in the trenches and/or "on the roof" have one by one crossed the threshold of time back into my life for brief periods of ageless connection and reflection. Sadly, many of these comrades are no longer with us.

There have also been interesting people whom I didn't know from that time who have come into my life and added even a little more spice to the whole enchilada—such as a recent dialogue with Andrew Loog Oldham (original manager/producer of the Rolling Stones and owner/founder of Immediate Records). Our communication began out of this very sort of thing I am referring to, after stumbling onto each other's writings about our reminiscences of those remarkable years and events as seen from perspectives coming from two sides of the ocean. Andrew and I have been drawn together especially because of our personal experiences with Allen Klein and our deep friendships and mutual admiration of Ron Kass, as well as a certain commonality having to do with the two hot bands we worked with.

Still living on separate continents (he now lives in Bogotá, Colombia, instead of London), we are drawn to review our lives today as we try to understand our survival and eventual outcome from those events. We find now that we are more concerned with our eternities than the one-nighters of old. Another example of this is that, not too long ago, I found myself chatting with producer/engineer Alan Parsons (Pink Floyd and the Alan Parsons Project) backstage at one of his concerts. I was invited by his current bass player, John Montagna, and learned to my surprise that Alan was also on the roof that magical day in January of 1969. As far as he and I knew, we had never met before, even though there could have been times that we were in the same place at the same time. We were quite surprised when we found out during our discussion that we were veterans of a very special engagement and feel to this day a certain camaraderie because of that. A small irony in this meeting was that, as a

If the Beatles' music and legend last there are eternally ensconced in the producer. I always looked up to Alan as my point of personal production aspirations. I found his studio work to be the most creative and encompassing of any producer/engineer of our day. Over the years, I had always mentioned that I wish we could have met—and yet we were together five or six stories up on the same roof on the same day on Savile Row over a third of a century ago.

Yes, this is about the Beatles, because they were real and the business they were in was real and the people were real and the broken records and the broken hearts really are all a part of it. When you read the remembrances of others who worked with and for them, those special, secret sauce characters who experienced the heat and heart of this phenomenon, you often come across the little moments and happenings that inspired some of the Beatles' greatest creations. Everything from "Ob-La-Di, Ob-La-Da" to "Get Back" (hi Chris O'Dell) to "Strawberry Fields Forever" came out of the simple people, obscure events, and small places of their lives. The Fabs, friends, and fans alike shared these expressions and became like fused ripples in the wildly wondrous waters that seem to flow on forever once that rare and beautiful rock was rolled into their stream of international consciousness.

What is really special is to have been there, standing on the banks of it all, and to hear the splash it made when it filled the airwaves and souls of the waiting world.

It's all over now, so treat us kindly. I can see her in the distance, the proverbial fat lady as she comes running out of the fog of mixed realities and onto the empty stages of our memories, singing loudly, and kicking dusty discarded press clippings into the air while clutching a torn and stained backstage pass to her abundant and heaving chest. A little applause and a few vague promises will keep her and the rest of us dancing until the final curtain.

Help!

forever, then also the people who were echoes of the events that transpired.

Here, There, and Everywhere

Once, in an e-mail exchange having to do with our transcendent travels, Andrew Loog Oldham stated that "the road always tells me who I am." I think of that comment now as I look back on the long and winding road that led to this book. The *here of where I am* is indeed all about where I have been, and the *there of it all* has already been staked out by the ones who have gone before me. I have always said that we are made up of three things—our past, our present, and our future, and that if one of these is missing, then so are we. All my dedications and appreciations are sent in these directions and to those who have filled timeless spaces in my life. The living and nonliving are always alive somewhere inside my being, bouncing around and coming to mind as if in rescue when I need the strength of their memory. It is to these and those I dedicate my knees and prose.

HERE (the Now)

Brent Stoker once again joins me in the hard tack roll as contributing editor. Not only has every word and detail he labored over made this a better tome but also with each syllable and timeline our friendship has expanded. When it came to detail and accuracy, "steady as a rock" and "straight as an arrow" are the time-worn clichés I am bent to ascribe to the perfect compadre—a pal o' pen who has faithfully shared this long journey of many years. He has become the literary Tonto to this lone stranger by always keeping the direction true and the intentions pure. Like hapless conquerors, it is the pages of a finished manuscript that now fill our hearts in the space saved for rewards and spoils. To you, Brent, I softly and with genuine respect say once again—thank you.

Bucky Rosenbaum is the fresh breath of air that oxygenates my creative core. When one person can enter a man's life like a mixed bag of M&Ms that contains every color of sweet things in life, you know you've got something. Bucky is the consummate executive who willingly takes charge of my ramblings; he is the man of supreme moral fiber who gives me the compass that aims at who I would like to be. He is also the young mentor that once told this old child that I could be a man of letters someday. Most of all I see him as a gentle man who knows what he believes in, and that trait makes him easy to find because I always know exactly where his heart is. To you, Bucky, I am thrilled to share my adventure, am blessed by your friendship, and thank you for being my literary agent.

THERE (the Then)

I can still see your faces, hear your voices, remember your words, feel your goodness, and dance to the music left in the echoes from your hearts. To me, you will never be gone—you just went away.

John Lennon
George Harrison
Mal Evans
Ron Kass
Derek Taylor
Brian Epstein
Linda McCartney
Maureen (Starkey) Tigrett
Stanley Gortikov
Harry Nilsson
Billy Preston

Gene Clark

Roy Orbison

Waylon Jennings

Frankie Laine

Johnny Cash

Buck Owens

Don Ho

Rick Danko

"Sneaky Pete" Kleinow

Rocco Catena

Alan Pariser

EVERYWHERE (the Always)

Big green eyes and a soft voice came into my being one hot, Tennessee, August day out of nowhere and became the depths, the heavens, the wind, the sun, and a beauty that filled my life with the sweet smell of eternal matters. It is to her love that I bow down, and it is because of her love I am lifted up. To you, Connie, I give what you have given to me—unconditional love. I thank you for being my everything. Baby, I'm amazed.

AND BEYOND

To the blood of my blood I leave these ramblings as a legacy of eventual understanding that you may have about the oddity of my years and the slant of my being. I am your brother, Dale, and I bless you who grew up with me in the dust and rivers of our northwestern Idaho homeland. I am your father, Kevin, Lisa, and Mark, and I love you—we have history, memories, and through you I will live on into the sweetness of our heritage. I am your grandpapa, Stuart and Max, and within your young hearts I am given a glimpse into the length of my days.

God bless us all.

Afterwords:
Let There Be White

» *Nashville, Tennessee*

I've known Ken for twenty years. Being an enthusiastic rock-and-roll fan in general and a Beatles fan in particular, I was excited to meet him and hear his firsthand stories of the Beatles, Capitol, Apple, the ex-Beatles, and many other artists, producers, and the like.

Shortly after we met, I told him that over the years I'd read lots of (make that, *most of*) the many books and articles written about the Beatles. Through those sources I was familiar with most of the participating players' names and their stories. I wondered why certain associates were rarely mentioned. When I began working with him, the pictures, letters, and other communications between them were clear evidence of his involvement.

Ken said he kept silent all those years because he never wanted to betray the inherent trust that his professional relationships and resulting friendships with the Beatles and so many other artists deserved. That was a pretty admirable attitude. Only in 1990, when Ringo offhandedly gave him the green light for a book, did he consider letting the Apple out of the box, so to speak.

With *The White Book*, Ken is still not betraying the trust that his relationships with these players (not just the Beatles and their pals, but Andy Williams, Harry Nilsson, Waylon Jennings, Brian Wilson, Dolly Parton, Roy Orbison, David Cassidy, and others) deserve. His intent is to shed a little light on their true character as he saw it, show how the times affected everyone (including him), and maybe tell a few fun or revealing stories along the way.

It's obvious Ken loved the players and treasures the time he spent with them.

Many successful performers believe in their talent but also secretly question the mind-boggling success that might accompany it. Ken is like that too. He believed in his talent as a music industry executive and producer, but he never got too far from his Idaho roots. He still has an attitude that says, "Who? Me? How did I get swept into such incredible times?" That's one of the many reasons I enjoyed working with him on *The White Book*.

Thanks for inviting me along, Ken, and giving me a taste of the Apple.

—Brent Stoker, 2007
Rock and Roll Historian and Contributing Editor

Liner Notes

Last Glance

A special gathering of Beatles historians and authorities watched over me in my portrayal of the various vignettes contained in *The White Book*. Their very nature requires that they could rest in assurance that they have kept a keen eye on the facts. In addition to contributing editor Brent Stoker's attention to detail, Bruce Spizer and Marshall Terrill, accomplished authors as well as longtime students of the phenomenon called the Beatles, double-checked the double checking for accuracy. I must thank Marshall especially for the long, tedious hours he spent going over the final manuscript page by page, paragraph by paragraph, sentence by sentence, and word by word, correcting, questioning, commenting, and encouraging our efforts—just because he wanted to—kind of the cowboy way of doing things. Bruce and I have shared years of exchanging insights and information on many levels concerning the Fab Four era with the results being scattered about in fair exchange in our literary works. Then once *The White Book* was in a somewhat final order, Elisa Stanford stepped in and burned the midnight overheads molding and summarizing the content into intelligible proposal form.

Of course all this would have been for naught without a publisher. As the Beatles were the best in the entertainment industry, it seems only appropriate that I would be blessed with the best in the publishing business. Special thanks to David Dunham and Joel Miller who believed in *The White Book* and brought me into the Thomas Nelson family where I have had the great honor of meeting up with the finest Marketing and Sales team this side of Fargo, North Dakota, in the persons of Brian Mitchell, Dave Schroeder, and Gabe Wicks *and* the most creative design team this side of Delight, Arkansas—Lori Lynch and Kristen Vasgaard. I would also like to acknowledge the editorial team for *The White Book*—Kristen Parrish and Alice Sullivan—as well as giving rave reviews to all the members of the Thomas Nelson Publishing group who worked so hard on this project. In the final phase, two friends from the British Isles, Jack Oliver and Pete Dicks, jumped into the "pond" with Nashville's Country Music Hall of Fame and Museum Audio and Video Curator, Alan Stoker, to lend a much needed hand in pulling the last bits together. To them I say—good show mates and thanks y'all.

I have been additionally blessed by learned friend, author, and publishing executive Wayne Hastings, who has been an encouragement and inspiration from the early days of my journey as an author. Through our mutual stirrings in writing words, Wayne became a mentor by enabling me to see things more clearly along the way.

Special thanks to Ringo Starr and Bruce Grakal, Paul McCartney and John Eastman, Yoko Ono, Olivia Harrison, and Neil Aspinall for permission to include Beatles photos and personal correspondence—and to Nancy Andrews who graciously offered choice photos from her collected works. All other photos and reproductions are from my personal collection or unknown contributors.

As in all my writings, a tithe goes to Mercy Ministries because I believe so deeply in its founder Nancy Alcorn's incredible vision and efforts in the healing and restoration of young girls' lives. Nancy is the deepest and dearest kind of friend who has stood beside Connie and me making sure we always kept our eyes and spirits looking up.

Once again I must admit that I was privileged to find myself in the midst of magical times and magnificent people. I openly accept the happenstance and good fortune of it all. My only regret in all this is that I wish I could have just told the stories as stories without having to be so concerned about the scrutiny and attention to detail required when it comes to the Beatles. I like the blurring that happens as we grow older and look back. It is almost like having an ethereal airbrush that smoothes out all the rough spots and makes it all look so good.

I have never heard anyone say anything bad about an apple, so now that it looks like a wrap, I can't help but notice that I am left with a real good taste in my mouth.

Then was then . . .
and then there's now.

. . . with Alan Parsons

. . . with Robin Leach

. . . with Ringo Starr

. . . with Jack Oliver

. . . with Gordon Waller and Peter Asher (Peter & Gordon)

Published in Nashville, Tennessee, by Thomas Nelson. Thomas Nelson is a trademark of Thomas Nelson, Inc.

Thomas Nelson, Inc., titles may be purchased in bulk for educational, business, fund-raising, or sales promotional use. For information, please e-mail SpecialMarkets@thomasnelson.com.

Mansfield, Ken.
  The white book / Ken Mansfield.
    p. cm.
  ISBN 1-59555-101-8 (alk. paper)
  1. Mansfield, Ken. 2. Sound recording executives and producers—United States—Biography.
3. Apple Records. 4. Beatles. I. Title.
ML429.M26A3 2006
782.42166092—dc22
[B]
2007013171

ISBN 13: 978-1-59555-101-6

Printed in the United States of America
07 08 09 10 RRD 5 4 3 2 1

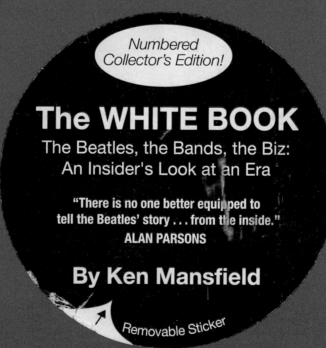

Numbered
Collector's Edition!

The WHITE BOOK
The Beatles, the Bands, the Biz:
An Insider's Look at an Era

"There is no one better equipped to
tell the Beatles' story . . . from the inside."
ALAN PARSONS

By Ken Mansfield

Removable Sticker